Praise for Diana J. Ensign's HEA...

"In this book Diana Ensign gently .... ries of life, death, grief and love. She a ...., and displays each story as simultaneously ....niversal. HEART GUIDE proves to be an excellent ⸳ ⸱ journey companion." — Kelly Garry, LCSW, Counselor in grief, loss, change & transition

"Those whose lives have been shaped by the deaths of loved ones share the limits of loss that may isolate us from relief. Diana Ensign has listened carefully to people who are intimate with grief and encouraged them to share with others their process for recovery. If you are wrestling with grief, read this book for insightful lessons on returning to hope, joy, and laughter." —Elsa F. Kramer, editor, *Branches Magazine*

"My heart is in joyful gratitude and wonder! This is a gift to all who grieve, all who suffer a yet unattended grief, and all whose grief has been silently, secretly festering for years. I celebrate each personal story shared." —Louise Dunn, author, *Beyond Your Past*, www.HeartlandMiracles.com

"Diana Ensign's reverent approach to asking deep and stimulating questions about death opens a safe space to explore grief. In our positivistic culture, we are expected to carry our suffering alone, not burden others with it. These stories make clear that grief is a universal and profoundly human experience. It is in sharing our grief that we develop the capacity to be open to our suffering and to the suffering of others and to the reality of death as a human experience that needs community support." —Ingrid Sato M.S., LMFT, LCSW, Co-founder of *Friends of Awakening Sangha*

"In this fine collection of personal interviews, Diana Ensign gently and skillfully 'listens into speech' a variety of honest, heartfelt, and healing stories. Her compassionate, non-judgmental and attentive ear enables each grieving soul to find its voice and to give expression to both pain and resiliency. The result is a gift to us all, as we come to understand that the most deeply personal insight turns out also to be the most universal truth: love bears all things." —Rev. Dr. Bruce Johnson, Unitarian Universalist Minister

"Few losses are as painful as the death of someone close. In this beautifully written book, compassionate guide Diana Ensign shines a light on the road through grief. For those who have experienced the loss of a loved one, here are strength and genuine words to inspire and comfort."
—Richard Brendan, M.A., Speaker, Counselor, Radio Host

Also by Diana J. Ensign, JD

Traveling Spirit: *Daily Tools for Your Life's Journey*

Spirituality for Daily Living blog

Website: **www.dianaensign.com**

HEART GUIDE

True Stories of Grief and Healing

Diana J. Ensign, JD

Published by SpiritHawk Life Publications.
Indianapolis, IN, USA

Library of Congress Control Number: 2017908973
Ensign, Diana
Heart guide: true stories of grief and healing/Diana Ensign.—1st edition
p. cm.
ISBN: 0988332000
ISBN 9780988332003 (pbk.)
1. Grief —Miscellanea. 2. Death—Miscellanea. 3. Loss (psychology)—Miscellanea. 4. Spiritualism.

Printed in the United States of America

In Loving Memory

(Alphabetical Order)
Anonymous (son)
Michael Dwayne Beasley Jr.
Fred and Phyllis Brown
Margaret (Libens) Brown and Willis Brown
Edith Harris Camp
James (Jim) Carey
Elizabeth Catharine Childs and Orlo Eckersley Childs
Florence (Edna) and Floyd Douglas
John Duren
Thomas Jay Eastwood
Doris Ettinger
Donald (Don) Bruce Fisher
Carl Marshall Grey
Gina Maria (Belissimo) Guerin
W. Edward (Ed) Harris
Terry Hudson
Rodman (Rod) Curtis Hughes
William and Dorothy Humphries
Moses Jenkins
Richard Steven Lane
Ellen Lovberg and Ralph Harvey Lovberg
Adam Maletta
Annette Marie (Bittner) Meier
Braden Miller
Jerry and Ruby Miller
Mary Monahan
Samuel (Sam) Xavier Motsay
Stephen Oberreich
Bruce Lennes Osborn
Gordon Robertson

Carol Ann Robinson
Aaron Kent Sims
George Siskind
Clifford (Cliff) Stockamp
Joan Veder and Dara Gail Veder
Dennis Walker
Lorna and Robert (Bob) Walter
Thomas (Tommy) Allen Weaver
Laura Kate Winterbottom

"It is only with the heart that one can see rightly; what is essential is invisible to the eye."

— ANTOINE DE SAINT-EXUPERY

CONTENTS

Introduction   xv
Prologue   xxi
   May I be at peace ~   xxi
   Vanessa Kathryn Hughes (brother, cancer)   xxii

Chapter 1   An Unexpected Jolt   1
      May my heart remain open ~   1
      Medical Mishap   2
      Michelle Qureshi (parents, AIDS)   2
      Sudden Crashes   7
      Rev. Carla Golden (boyfriend, plane crash)   7
      Kindra L. Renninger
      (grandparents, car accident)   12
      Dangerous Addictions   17
      Anonymous Mother (son, suicide)   17
      Justin Phillips (son, overdose)   26
Chapter 2   Navigating Grief's Currents   32
      May I be healed ~   32
      Unraveling the Layers   34
      Cheri Stephens (parents, car
      accident & cancer)   34
      Karen Peck (sister, suicide)   40

Lori Robinson (sister, suicide) 47

Dona M. Robinson (daughter, suicide) 55

Chapter 3   Caretaking 60

May you be a source of healing in the world ~ 60

A Heavy Load to Carry 62

Joseph Mooradian (mother, cancer) 62

Janet S. Brown (parents, Alzheimer's
& dementia) 70

Thomas Robertson (father, lymphoma) 77

Summer Hudson (non-biological
father, cancer) 85

Barry E. Childs-Helton (parents,
Alzheimer's & cancer) 94

Chapter 4   The Precious Gift of Time 103

May we be at peace ~ 103

Letting Go 105

Lia M. Guerin (mother, leukemia) 105

Debra L. Lambert (father, stroke) 109

John & Bonnie Bittner (daughter, leukemia) 117

Nicholas J. Bittner (sister, leukemia) 125

Life Lived Well 127

Franklin D. Oliver (grandfather, stroke) 127

Ralph H. Lovberg (wife, leukemia) 132

David Traylor (life partner, rapid onset MS) 139

Sandra G. Harris (husband, brain tumor) 147

Chapter 5   Balm for the Soul 155

May we know the beauty of our own true nature ~ 155

Creative Expression 156

Katharine J. Oberreich (father, heart attack) 156

Ellie M. Siskind (husband, heart attack) 162

Meredith A. Eastwood (husband,
cerebral hemorrhage & father, suicide) 166

A Meaningful Vocation 171

Sophia Stockamp (father, brain tumor) 171
Amy M. Walker (father, cancer) 177
Rexene L. Lane (brother, car accident) 183
Paul J. Brown (parents, heart disease) 188
Bonnie L. Bomer (baby, birth defects) 196
Chapter 6 A Deeper Faith 204
May we be healed ~ 204
Seeking Solace 205
Rev. Vanessa A. Robinson (son, car accident) 205
David W. Douglas (parents, cancer
& heart failure) 210
Hayley McGinley (boyfriend, car accident) 214
Delynn Curtis (son, cancer) 223
Chapter 7 Creating A Living Legacy 229
May we be a source of healing in the world ~ 229
Making a Difference 231
Jeanine Motsay (son, overdose) 231
Edmund (Ned) & JoAnn Winterbottom
(daughter, violent sexual assault) 239
Cathy A. Burton (husband, car accident) 247
Roberta (Bert) & Donald (Don) Miller
(son, suicide) 254

Epilogue 263
May our hearts remain open ~ 263
Justin Phillips (a year later) 264
Acknowledgments 269
About the Author 271

HEART GUIDE

INTRODUCTION

*"Those who have suffered understand suffering
and therefore extend their hand."*

— *PATTI SMITH (singer/songwriter)*

A famous story in Buddhism, *The Parable of the Mustard Seed,* tells of a woman named Kisa Gotami whose only son has died. Carrying the child's lifeless body from house to house, Kisa pleads with her neighbors for medicine to cure her son. The neighbors think she is crazy. Eventually, someone suggests that she visit the Buddha for help. Arriving at the Buddha's home, she again asks for medicine to bring her child back to life. The Buddha instructs Kisa to go back to her village and gather for him a collection of mustard seeds obtained from each neighbor. However, she can only collect mustard seeds from those homes where no one has lost a child, spouse, relative, or friend to death. After seeking day and night for a home untouched by death, Kisa realizes that she is not alone in her suffering. Returning to the Buddha empty handed, she becomes his first female disciple.

The stories here also arise from travels to many households. They are the true accounts of people whose lives have been touched by death. In reading these narratives, we bear witness to the torrent of raw emotions that accompany the loss of a loved one, and we learn how individuals and couples manage to go forth in the world after loss. With each person's story, we discover universal life experiences that make us human: our pain and sorrow, our heartfelt compassion, our capacity to care for one another, and our love.

For this book, I interviewed close to 50 people from across the United States. Their ages range from 19 to 89 years old. The amount of time since their loved one's passing varies — from four months to four decades. I asked each person: *What helped with your grief? Do you have any suggestions for someone facing a similar loss?* I also inquired if they had any spiritual or religious practices that were helpful. My main objective, however, was simply to listen mindfully and give each person an opportunity to discuss what he or she felt was important for the reader to know about grief and healing. I spoke with people who are religious (Christian, Buddhist, Islamic, Jewish, Unitarian Universalist, Lucumi/Santeria, Pagan), people who are spiritual but not religious, and people who have no faith practices or religious beliefs. While the people interviewed differ in age, race, religion, gender, nationality, and geographic location, the common thread woven throughout their tales is an incredible resiliency in the face of anguish and a love that surpasses impermanence of the human condition.

My background for this project includes the death of my biological father in my 30s. He died in a drunk driving accident after leaving the bar with a friend. He and his friend were both killed. Similar to the people interviewed, my intense awareness of suffering has led me along a life path I never could have imagined. I explored numerous spiritual teachings in my own healing process. Yet, this book is not written from the perspective (or advice) of an "expert." The insights here arise from the individuals and couples *living* with loss. They share wisdom from the heart.

Those facing the death of a loved one remind us again and again, everyone grieves but often in different ways. As Justin (who lost her son) states, *"There's absolutely no right or wrong way to grieve. Sometimes we say to ourselves, 'Oh, am I allowed to be feeling this way? Should I not be feeling this way?' No one else should tell you how to grieve. You get to grieve however you want!"* John (a farmer who lost his daughter) says, *"How do you cope with anything? You sit down and figure out what you can do. But this ole world, we're not in charge of it. You just do the best you can."*

Sadly, some individuals mentioned that their grief could not be discussed with friends (or in some cases with family members) because of the stigma associated with certain types of loss, such as deaths by suicide or drug overdose. The anguish felt at losing a loved one in a horribly violent way is not sugarcoated here. As a caring community, we need to learn how to listen with compassion — even when the stories are extraordinarily painful and raw. Our willingness to listen with an open heart is how we begin a true practice of loving kindness toward all who are suffering.

Barry (who lost both parents) notes, *"Human beings organize experience by telling stories. Speaking as one who studied folklore for years, I'm aware that it's a prominent factor in orchestrating our relationships and also moving us on from one stage of life to the next. It seems to matter the kind of care you put into the story, trying to get it right and trying to honor those who figure in the story."*

A few people also declined to be interviewed — not wanting to reopen old scabs over sensitive wounds. I want to thank these individuals, as well, for reminding us that sharing intimate details about the death of a loved one is not easy. As Michelle states in her interview, *"It's a hard story to tell."*

As you begin your own journey through these pages, please keep in mind that you are not just reading a book. You are gathering heart knowledge from the lives of real people. Pause as necessary, and be gentle with yourself. As a well-known quote reminds us, "It's okay if the only thing you did today was breathe."

Janet (who lost both parents) points out, *"You can read all the Buddhism in the world and all the gurus in the world, but there is something about walking through the journey and just experiencing it. You come out the other side so much more whole than when you went in. That's the gift. It sounds hokey, but it's true. It was also important for me to hear other people's journeys while I was going through mine. ... I might find someone going through something worse or going through something similar and hear how that person handled it — not advice but just telling their stories. That's valuable."*

When we courageously speak our truth or quietly listen with compassion, we are no longer strangers. We are friends. Perhaps, that is the greatest gift of all: learning to connect and care for one another in an authentic manner that transcends ordinary daily interactions. Sandra (who lost her daughter and her husband) says, *"When we gather as a family, we tell stories. We tell stories about Edith and Ed and anyone else who has passed. We think that telling their stories is a good thing to do, and it speaks to the fact that the people we love are still with us. It helps us to know that we're not alone in missing them."*

With tremendous gratitude, I offer this heart guide for grief and healing. May we *always* know the abundant love that surrounds us.

Diana J. Ensign, JD

Loving Kindness Meditation

Tibetan Buddhist Prayer

May I be at peace
May my heart remain open
May I know the beauty of my own true nature
May I be healed
May I be a source of healing in the world

May you be at peace
May your heart remain open
May you know the beauty of your own true nature
May you be healed
May you be a source of healing in the world

May we be at peace
May our hearts remain open
May we know the beauty of our own true nature
May we be healed
May we be a source of healing in the world

PROLOGUE

"Guess now who holds thee?" —
"Death," I said. But, there, The silver answer rang, —
"Not Death, but Love."

— ELIZABETH BARRETT BROWNING

May I be at peace ~

Kintsugi is the Japanese art of repairing broken pottery with gold. This repair makes the item more precious than before it was cracked. It is believed that when something (or someone) has suffered damage in this way, an exquisite beauty remains.

The art of healing also begins with the recognition that we are broken — often in ways we cannot easily articulate. We know our pieces will never fit together again in precisely the same way. Unlike pottery, we also recognize that our grief isn't something to be "fixed."

Healing the heart is a deeply personal process. Only WE know what brings peace to our soul. While undergoing this difficult work of healing grief, seek the support of others as needed. Stay open for guidance as you proceed. Place your hand over your heart, close your eyes, and slowly breathe.

It is deep within the heart that we find our gold: the love we hold for those who have traveled with us on this earth journey.

⊷⊱ ⊰⊷

Vanessa Kathryn Hughes (brother, cancer)

"There's no one magical key" — Vanessa is in her 30s. She has gorgeous, long red hair and works as an actress. She lost her brother Rodman (Rod) Hughes. He was 26 years old. (Her mother, Delynn Curtis, shares her reflections in Chapter Six).

We all came home for Thanksgiving: Rod, Jerry, and me. I'm the oldest, Rod is the middle child, and Jerry is my youngest brother. At that time, our mom was living in a rural area of Indiana, and I was living in Chicago. The day before Thanksgiving, Rod went into the emergency room. His stomach was hurting so bad he thought he had appendicitis or food poisoning. He was having these sharp pains. The hospital did all the scans, and the results came back that he had a huge tumor in his stomach.

The cancer itself is called Leiomyosarcoma (LMS). It's a rare form of cancer, and the doctors don't know much about it or what causes it. The medical profession sometimes just doesn't know why things happen the way they do. This cancer type was one of the worst kinds. Rod passed away six months from when we found out. It was quick. Obviously, by the time he found out the cancer was in Stage 4. I don't know how long he was sick. Rod was the type of person, ever since he was a baby, where it would be an emergency before he would even speak up or say anything about it. He was always that way.

The doctors did crazy doses of chemo and radiation. Something insane like 20 treatments over a two-week period, but I don't remember exactly. It was incredibly rough, and he didn't make it through all that. It was too much on his body. I was traveling back and forth from Chicago because I still had to work and take care of things there.

The whole thing with the hospital was frustrating. I'm not a doctor; so I can't point to specific medical reasons for my concerns. But I watched how Rod reacted to the treatment and how the cancer itself reacted. I firmly believe that different cancers react to things differently. I am not sure regular chemo and radiation were the way to go. When you're in a situation like that, you try everything you can. That's all we — collectively as a community — know right now. We know this treatment has worked sometimes on some cancers. So, we try that. When you're faced with something very heavy and frightening, such as a cancer diagnoses, you do what you think is best. Sometimes, you try what you don't think is best but whatever will work.

The hospital was not a kind or nurturing environment. Hospitals, especially in rural areas, are not well-equipped to deal with family members of the person with the disease. We were in and out a lot and told one thing or another. It wasn't easy for anyone involved.

As Rod progressed through the cancer, I reached out to a friend who had become an oncologist and worked at a hospital in the city that does educational and experimental treatments with cancer. When the other hospital said there was nothing more they could do, we took Rod there. The doctors were making some progress before things turned for the worse. Even with all the research we did, it's difficult to know what to do.

I'm a little fuzzy on what all happened because it was such a blur. My understanding is that Rod started to react better to a particular medication. He was eating a little bit more. But it was like he was burned from the inside out from all the cancer treatments. Not that he actually was burned, but that's the way he felt inside. So, he was eating a lot of ice. Some of the liquids he was trying to digest got into his lungs, and it caused pneumonia. The doctors think he asphyxiated. That is what ultimately killed him. With terminal diseases, it's usually something else that actually causes someone to die.

Before that point, Rod had said he wanted to die at home. He didn't want to die in a hospital. When we knew it was just a matter of time, we made the trip back home with Rod in the ambulance. The doctors were pretty convinced that he wasn't going to make the trip. We wanted to try anyway. He did make it home, and he was with us for just a couple of short days and then he passed.

What, if anything, helped you cope with your grief?

I don't know if I can honestly say I've gotten through all of that. (Crying.) I apologize if I get a little emotional over this. I made a promise to Rod before he passed and to myself since he passed. I know he wanted us to be happy. That was his biggest desire for us, especially toward the end. He said that he wanted us to be happy, love each other, and forgive each other. I took that very much to heart. In honor of Rod, I try to make decisions so those things happen.

I did go to counseling afterward to deal with the trauma of everything and the quickness of it. I don't know that I'll ever be over it, but I know that things get easier with time. A year and a half ago, I wouldn't even have been able to have this conversation. (She pauses to take a deep breath.) I can talk about it now. But it's still hard.

I'm not someone who necessarily turns to prayer, inner reflection, and faith like my mom does. For me, action is more healing. That is something I try to do on a daily basis. It might be something like making one decision to react in a different way. For example, when something upsets me with my boyfriend or a close friend, the choice I make is to take a moment and breathe. I'll ask myself: "What's the choice that is forgiveness? What's the choice that is love? What's the choice that is going to bring more calm to the situation?" I'm human, so it's not perfect. (Laughs.) However, it is in the forefront of my mind now when I react to people.

I try to act so that I'm making someone's life easier, better, or happier. To me, that is the best way to honor Rod.

Do you have a favorite memory of Rod?

I have lots of good memories of Rod. Some are memories of him being this incredibly chunky, little toddler — with rolls upon rolls of bright red hair — and him running around everywhere. Once for Halloween I did his makeup; he wanted to be one of the Batman characters. So, we did that together.

He threw up on me a lot when we were kids. (Laughing.) As a kid, he would get motion sickness really easily. One of my memories — he must have been around two years old — was when my mom and dad were taking us up to a White Sox game. Rod had eaten, of all things, hot dogs! And he just unleashed it all over the sweater I was wearing as we were pulling into the parking lot. My parents didn't have the money to buy me anything there to wear, and so, they were trying to clean me up. I sat in this vomit sweater the entire game. (Laughs again.)

Also, Rod always had this amazing, energetic smile. The week before he passed, we had a good conversation about what he needed to do in his life if he got through this and how he would go about it. I guess it's just the sense of peace, calm, and happiness we had with each other before he left.

Do you have any religious or faith practices that helped with your healing?

I have some good memories of going to church with my family. As I grew older, though, church wasn't necessarily the right thing for me.

I resonate a little more with the Buddhist philosophy of meditation or just being quiet. But I don't have any particular thing I follow or practice. My one consistent belief is: "Doing, not saying."

There is a lot of rhetoric in religion. Some people don't follow through with actions, or they argue about everything. I always think: *Don't just talk about it; do it in small ways.* I've incorporated that belief into my life.

If you can show someone you care, that's more healing than words. If you can spread love somehow, then that's what you should do.

Is there anything you learned from Rod's passing that you want to share?

It's completely okay to not know how to deal with any of this. It's okay to do whatever you need to do to help you. There's no one right way for any person to react. There's no one magical key that will help you get through it. There's not. It's rough, and it's going hurt. But you can always make those choices to be as positive as you can, and you can talk about the things that are amazing about the person. Definitely reach out for support outside the circle of everything going on. Connect with people who are not immediately involved because sometimes your job is to be the strong person, even though you're falling apart inside.

It would not honor Rod to *not* get through this. I've had many successes of just doing normal things again. Allowing myself to laugh. Allowing myself to have joy is very healing for me. I've not healed an incredible amount, but the healing starts small, and it continues to happen.

It helped me to get back in the swing of things as soon as I could. If I couldn't get through a day, I honored that and took a day to stay home with my grief. I allowed myself to feel it, but I put a sort of limit on myself. Even though you're feeling the pain, you can't let it overtake you.

I try to focus on things I know will bring me joy. I didn't focus on the feeling of darkness that falls over you when all of this happens. You redirect yourself to remember: *What are the things that bring me happiness? What are the things that bring me joy?* Try to continue to do those and not pull away from normal life, as much as you possibly can

Cherish people. You don't know when they'll go. That's something on my mind now. You just never know. Don't wait to tell people you love them. Don't wait to live your own life and to do the things that are fulfilling and will make you happy.

✦

CHAPTER 1

AN UNEXPECTED JOLT

"What we have once enjoyed we can never lose.
All that we love deeply becomes a part of us."

—*HELEN KELLER*

May my heart remain open ~

When our heart is struck by sudden grief, an aching gap remains — not unlike a tree scorched by lighting. The death of a loved one can be excruciating under any circumstance. But when such loss comes without advance warning, it can be particularly unnerving. In addition to the grief of losing the person, there may be unresolved issues: things left unsaid, missed opportunities, or longstanding conflicts. There may be confusion as the mind struggles to grasp — without prior preparation — news of a loved one who is gone forever (at least physically). Additionally, our sorrow may be further compounded when we think the death could have been prevented (such as in instances of medical mistakes, drug overdoses, or suicides).

The stories in this section touch on the shock aspects of grief. As the mother whose son committed suicide readily admits, *"The shock wasn't just a week or a month. It carried with me for probably almost a year. Somebody might say that sounds weird, but that numb shock feeling is just now wearing off. I don't know how to explain it to somebody who hasn't been down that path. I'm still just trying to get by."*

During such intense heartache, small rays of healing often arrive gradually and in unforeseen ways. For Michelle (who lost both parents to AIDS), quietly watching the sunset every evening is the heart medicine she applies to sooth her profound sorrow. For others in this section, beloved pets, dreams, music, prayers, nature, or meditation bring solace.

With stories of loss, our heart wounds become holy ground — needing tender care and deep reverence for all that resides there. As a famous Rumi quote states, "The wound is the place where the Light enters you."

＊＊＊

Medical Mishap

Michelle Qureshi (parents, AIDS)

"Only the love remains." — Michelle is a musician and composer. She has dark, wavy hair and is in her mid-50s. Married to her husband, Anwar, she has a 12-year-old daughter, Layla. Michelle lost her parents, Jerry and Ruby Miller, to AIDS. Reserved and soft-spoken, Michelle invited me to her home for this interview in March (the anniversary month of both parents' passing).

We lived in several cities while I was growing up. The moves essentially mirrored the economic growth of my dad's work. We'd be in one type of home when he was in the steel mills, another home when he became a foreman, and then, with his own business as a steel broker, we shifted to a custom-built, suburban home. My mom was a homemaker. She loved to fix things up in the homes, not just decorating, but also changing flooring and tearing down walls! I have five siblings: four girls and a boy. I'm in the middle. When all of us were out of the house and in college, my mom began creating oil paintings on canvas. It was a new outlet for all her creative energy.

My father had heart surgery, and his recovery from the surgery overlapped the time of him shifting from work to retirement. During this period, my parents moved to Florida. They sought medical help in Florida because he wasn't getting better. Everyone we knew who had that surgery had a new lease on life.

In the process of trying to get medical help, my parents encountered either really incompetent doctors or an ignorant system. The doctor in Florida never even requested my father's medical records. It was not suggested that the blood transfusion could have been an extension of the problem. This was in 1985, and the blood transfusion should have raised a red flag in the medical community. At that time, hospitals were not legally bound to test blood for the HIV virus. So, they didn't.

On Valentine's Day in 1990, my father went into the hospital, and the doctors finally ran the AIDS test. That was indeed the problem. His blood transfusion had been tainted with HIV-infected blood, and AIDS had developed. He never got out of the hospital in Florida once he went in. He died a month later on March 19.

I had finished college and had just started my music career in New York City. With my father ill, I moved down to Florida thinking I would help take care of him. But everything happened so fast. Once I was in Florida, I remained there with my mom after my dad passed.

We realized then that our mother needed to be tested as well. My mom got tested, and she was positive. We sought some alternative medical help for my mother. However, her condition was not changeable by that time.

Eventually, the AIDs virus developed. The lesson my siblings and I learned from never getting my dad out of the hospital was that we all quickly congregated with my mother when she became ill. We had hospice come. A couple of different nurses checked on her and kept the pain at bay. She died March 28, 1993, three years after my dad.

I was 29 when my dad died and 32 when my mom passed.

Suing the hospital wouldn't change the outcome. So, my siblings and I didn't go that route. But my parents' deaths have impacted our lives tremendously; not just the loss itself but the *how* of it. Basically, with AIDS, the body is starved and there's nothing left. It's horribly dramatic.

At the time of my parents' deaths, I was not married. Consequently, my two younger siblings and I raised our children without grandparents or parents to help us figure out how to handle a family, a spouse, a child, and everything. (She sighs deeply.) Their loss has greatly affected all of us.

What is your favorite memory of your mom or dad while growing up?

It's the sweetest thing; I don't think I fully appreciated it until I was older. My sister is 15 months younger. When I was five or six, my mom helped us build these flower boxes so we could have something to put our flowers in. I have an old black and white photo of my sister and me sitting by our flower gardens. (She grows quiet and stops talking.)

What has helped heal your grief?

After my parents died, I stayed in Florida for a time. While there, I sat outside and watched the sun set every night, for months.

I'm still waiting for March to be a time where I can celebrate the life of my parents because it's always been a very tough month. As time goes on, my desire would be to get past this idea of, "Oh, this dark month of March," and quit burdening myself with what went wrong and unexpected in life. I'd prefer to embrace this entire new area of discovery I've had recently with Reiki (an alternative energy healing method) and understand what really happens with death.

I share stories of my parents with my daughter so she can at least imagine what her grandparents were like. I know, at my core, my parents aren't totally gone, as far as the energy. I've shared with my daughter many times that only the love remains. The people don't remain, but the love does.

Have you felt any connections with your parents since their passing?

I had an interesting experience that I was not ready to see at the time. After my mom died, I had gone to New York where we had a small wake with family and friends, and then I had to make that long drive back to Florida once again, alone. I wasn't planning on stopping; I would normally drive straight through, as I was wont to do in those earlier years. I was driving, and the weather was horrible. It was storming with torrential rains. I have no idea where I finally decided to briefly stop. I was in a deep state of grief, and I would preface this story with we weren't raised religiously. We were raised to know right from wrong and to be good people. But we weren't raised with any of what can be called the burdens or trappings of religion. We were a God-loving, not a God-threatening family.

Anyway, I was feeling a real loss of connection with people. I was leaving my siblings (after gathering for the wake), and I'd just said goodbye to my mother. I had no one intimately related to me to go to.

In this pouring rain, I just wanted to hear someone's voice. So I pulled over and telephoned a friend in Florida to let her know I was on my way back. I was in this telephone booth, which tells you how dated this story is. This friend answers the phone and asks, "Where are you?" I didn't even know. I had to be somewhere in the Southeast. I was looking around, trying to read anything to figure out where I was. The first sign I saw read: *Ruby's Church of Christ.* I just blurted that out without feeling the impact of what that meant. Then, I got back in my car and drove to Florida. (She pauses.) My mom's name is Ruby. I believe she was trying to reach me. The ways to connect with those who have passed feel coincidental to me, maybe because that's where I'm at right now. It's clearly up to me to remove that veil so I can see things more clearly.

After wrapping things up in Florida, I moved back to New York. It was a hard and very fragile time for me. My mother and father were both wonderful people and wonderful parents. I'm still in touch with my mom's best friend Peggy.

Do you have any religious or spiritual practices that help with the grief?

Prior to losing my parents, I had taken the Shahada, which is the formal step into the faith I had been studying. I was drawn to the mysticism of Sufism as well as to the people amidst this wide range of cultures that share the Islamic faith. I find strength in prayer and meditation.

Even though I considered myself a spiritual person before, this experience brought me even deeper into my spirituality. It has become an invitation to a more esoteric understanding of life and death. (She pauses reflectively while sipping her tea.)

Music is my healing path. I've written several pieces in memory of my parents. The writing process is healing in itself, and I find the power of music to offer healing is a gift I am able to share with others.

Do you have any suggestions for someone going through something similar?

It's a hard story to tell. There's not anything that someone needs to say. People read stories, and it's heard on its own.

⊷⊱ ⊰⊶

Sudden Crashes

Rev. Carla Golden (boyfriend, plane crash)

"Tell the people in your life that you love them; don't wait." — *Carla is an ordained Unity minister. Born in Wichita, Kansas, she is married to Reverend Bob Uhlar, who is also a minister with Unity. She lost her first love, a boyfriend in college, who died in a plane crash.*

The young man killed in the plane crash was John Duren. I was attending a retail merchandizing school for a year in Wichita, and I met John. We lived in the same athletic dorm. It had men's and women's sections, and he was attending Wichita State University. I was 19.

We met before school started in August. We went to a mixer — as they used to call them — and he asked me to dance. Then we started dating. I met him and fell in love.

John was a very spiritual person and had a deep faith. I really appreciated his values. He was President of the Fellowship of Christian Athletes on campus. We came from the same background. He was a Methodist, and so was I. He loved to dance and had a great smile. He was also on the football team. We only dated a few months, but we were together every day.

What is your favorite memory of John?

Two memories stand out. I wouldn't say they are favorite memories, but they are the memories that come back. The dorm we lived in was right across from the cemetery. We used to walk together in the cemetery because it was quiet and cool with the trees. August was really hot in Kansas. I remember walking through the cemetery, and John came upon a grave with a headstone that had a picture of a young woman who was about our age. As we stood looking down at the grave, he said, "It seems so sad that she died at such a young age." That memory came back a lot after the plane crash.

The other memory is the night before he was killed. We would meet in the cafeteria for dinner after he got off football practice. That night, we got together for dinner as usual, and he was really excited. The coach had told John that he was going to be on the first string at the next game. John had always been the second string B team. So, he was thrilled that he'd be starting in the next game in Utah. The football team flew out in two different planes. They had a black plane and a gold plane. Being on the first string, he was going to be flying on the gold plane. He was very happy. Unfortunately, I was coming down with a cold or the flu, and I wasn't feeling too good. John wanted to spend more time together to celebrate, and I said, "I'm just not feeling that well tonight. I'm going to my room and going to bed early, and when you come back, we'll celebrate. You can tell me all about it." We parted kind of quickly.

The next day, I stayed home from school. My roommates came in after they got out of class and turned on the lights. I was still asleep. They told me one of the planes had crashed. Nobody knew at that point which plane it was. We quickly turned on the radio, and we began to listen. Eventually, it was reported that the gold plane had gone down. Actually it didn't go down; it flew into a mountain. The pilot took a different route. He was trying to give the players a scenic view of the mountains. The plane didn't have the altitude to fly over one of the mountains. It just didn't have the power to go up that fast.

That was the most horrendous day of my life. They announced that there were four or five survivors, but they didn't give their names. I remember just being glued to that radio in my room and waiting to hear who they were.

Later, when we went to the cafeteria, they announced who had been recovered and was now in the hospital. At first, they didn't read the names of those who died. There was still that sense of, "Well, we don't know. Maybe they're wandering in the forest or something." At some point, I found out John was not alive.

Did you have any religious or spiritual practices that helped with your grief?

I was really struggling with what I believed. My first reaction was to get angry with God, asking, "How could you do this?" John had wanted to be a minister. It was beyond my comprehension that God could allow this to happen. My parents didn't understand how I could be so close to someone in such a short time. I don't think they realized the depth of my grief or how much I cared. Eventually, I found my faith again. But it took a while.

I took transcendental meditation classes and went to see psychics. I wanted to communicate with John and find out if he was okay, and understand what was going on, and where he was, and if there really was a heaven. I was searching. One of the psychics said John had not been able to fully transition to his next plane of existence; he felt too tied because of my grief and the sense of not having a chance to say goodbye or reassure me.

I also felt guilt. Mainly, it was because of that last night where I wasn't in the now moment with him. I didn't celebrate with him. I felt like I was very self-centered, focusing on my own illness and not being there fully for him. That took a long time to work through and release the guilt.

Later, I realized what an impact John had on my life because of his faith. I prayed. I began to feel supported, and I had this sense of not being alone.

Is there anything else that helped with your healing process?

Initially, I did a lot of distracting myself, keeping busy. Everybody goes through a certain amount of that. Let's face it, the grieving process is painful, and we want to avoid feeling that pain.

John loved to make tie-dyed shirts. He would create them. And he always said, "I'm going to give you one of my tie-dyed shirts and make a special one for you." After the plane crash, his roommate saw me in the cafeteria and said, "I don't know if you want it or not, but I found one of John's tie-dyed shirts that he made a week or two before the plane crash." I said, "Yes, I'd like to have that." It was red, and that was my favorite color. It seemed like a message: That shirt was supposed to be mine.

Afterward, I went out on dates with people who didn't mean that much to me. Here again, trying to escape the feelings. I don't remember counselors back then.

Every time we would go to the cafeteria, there was an area where the football players would all sit. And they weren't there anymore. The few who survived were in the hospital or at home recovering. Almost the whole A team or first string was wiped out. It was about 36 players, along with the coach and his wife and various other people, and the supporters of the team who were on the plane.

Eventually, the school had a memorial service for all the players. It was an incredible experience. So many people there were grieving with such sadness. It was very cathartic. The people coming together for that memorial service helped with the grieving. It was like someone took a thumb out of a dyke, and it just flowed. It was definitely a community grief.

What prompted you to go to seminary?

It's a calling. I met Bob, and we had similar spiritual beliefs. We got married and traveled around doing workshops at various Unity churches. We visited over 200 congregations around the United States and Canada and really enjoyed teaching the spiritual principles. So, we both applied to seminary.

During my chaplain training, I worked in a hospital in Kansas City. A woman there shared with me about her daughter coming back. She described her daughter and what her daughter was wearing. At first, I thought she was talking about her daughter visiting her in the hospital. Then, she shared with me that her daughter had died two years ago. Before that, we didn't really think this woman was going to die. But I contacted her brother and let him know that he needed to come soon. The next morning, she was on a ventilator and sedated.

When my father was about to die, we had a conversation about dying. I reassured him that people who were in the process of transitioning had people from the other side come to welcome them and help them transition. He said, "Well, I hope it's my mother." His mother had died when he was four years old. On the day he died, he said, "Momma." I knew his mother had been there to greet him and welcome him over.

So many people are afraid of death. I know my mother was afraid of dying because she thought she hadn't been a good enough person. It was very hard to reassure her. We brought in a Baptist minister and a Methodist minister, and that persuaded her a bit. But she still didn't want to close her eyes. She was afraid she wouldn't wake up. Because of my experiences, I no longer fear death.

Do you have any suggestions for others?

My suggestion for grief is to feel the feelings. Don't try to distract yourself. Spend time alone in meditation, and don't rush yourself through the process. It takes as long as it takes. Go through the grieving process. I always hate when someone tells someone to "Get over it. It's been over a year now. Move on." I don't think anyone can tell someone exactly how to grieve. The important thing is not to avoid it.

Another thing that helped me that I didn't mention earlier, if you have regrets or feel guilty about something, write that person a letter. Express your feelings. The other regret I had was that I never told John I loved him. In writing that letter, you can just empty yourself of all these unsaid words, thoughts, and feelings. It's an important thing to do. You feel a lot lighter afterward. Grieving helps you bring closure so you can move on to another relationship or experiences in life.

Also, appreciate the now moment. Tell the people in your life that you love them; don't wait.

⊰⊹⊱

Kindra L. Renninger (grandparents, car accident)

"Make sure you're surrounded by people who are positive influences." — Kindra and her husband Isaac have two small children. She lost her grandparents, William and Dorothy Humphries, in a car accident caused by a driver on methamphetamine. Kindra was 23 years old at the time of her grandparents' deaths.

My grandparents lived in Jasper, Alabama. I always called them Grammy and Grampy. The accident was at 9 o'clock in the morning. It was Labor Day weekend, and they were traveling back home from their lake property. A guy crossed the centerline and hit them head on.

I was babysitting for a friend that morning. My cousin telephoned me and asked for my mom's cell phone number. We never really talked on the phone; he stayed in touch via Facebook. He didn't want to tell me what happened because they wanted to let my mom know first. I had to pull it out of him. He said my grandparents had been in a bad accident, and they needed to get ahold of my mom. I said, "Okay, my mom's at work." He told me that Grampy was at the hospital, but they couldn't find Grammy. That's all I was left with.

I remember thinking, "Please Jesus, let them be okay." But all I could spit out was, "Jesus!" I thought I was going to pass out. I called the mom of the child I was babysitting and said, through tears, "Your son is okay, but I need you to come home." She sent my roommate to take over watching the child. I sat with my roommate on the couch, and she was praying for me. I was in shock and couldn't talk. We were just praying they would find Grammy, and we would know more details soon.

One of my other friends came and picked me up. Then my mom and dad met me in Anderson, Indiana, and we drove down to Kentucky. My aunt and uncle from Tennessee drove up to Kentucky as we were driving there. We dropped my mom off with my aunt and uncle. They continued on to Alabama. Then, my dad and I headed back north. It was pretty much just a waiting game.

The family didn't know where my Grammy was because the accident happened in a different county from the Birmingham hospital where they had flown Grampy. Because my Grammy had instantly passed, they had taken her to the coroner's office in the county of the wreck. The next of kin they located was my Grampy's brother, who is older than him and not in good health. So, he was very confused. He contacted my aunt. When my aunt got to the hospital, she was asking about my Grammy, and nobody knew anything. It was many hours later before we heard the news about Grammy.

Grampy never regained consciousness after the wreck. He died early Saturday morning.

After Grampy passed, my dad and my brothers came to Anderson. I have twin brothers. One brother had started at DePauw and the other was starting at Indiana Wesleyan, and it was move-in day. We all met at my house and started driving down to Alabama. We got there Saturday evening. We had the funeral on Sunday and then drove back Monday.

I had spoken to my grandparents the morning of the wreck. I was the last person to talk to them. I had called that morning to tell Grammy I had a job interview on Tuesday. She was really excited for me and said she'd be right there with me.

I went to my interview and got the job. But after I started working, I felt homesick. I told my mom I wanted to move back home. I was afraid of losing my parents. It took a while for me not to be so paranoid when I couldn't get ahold of them. You can reach people immediately by cell phone, and it would scare me when I couldn't reach them right away. But I kept working and didn't move back home. That was just part of the grieving.

Is there anything that has helped with your grieving process?

I'm a big fan of Jeremy Camp's music. He's a Christian artist. I went to the concert with friends and started attending a church where I got plugged into a Bible study with college kids my age. The first night I went, I opened up and shared the story about my grandparents. They were very supportive. I knew they were praying for me. I could call them up, and we could go hang out. I spent a lot of time with my church friends. It's important to surround yourself with Christian friends and turn to God because even though you feel like he's turned His back on you, He hasn't. Sometimes, it is just part of life. It can get ugly and messy.

Do you have religious or faith practices that helped with your grief?

Faith was definitely very important to me and to my grandparents. I grew up in the Quaker church, and at the time of the accident, I was Quaker. My Grammy would always say, "Where's your heart? Do you know Jesus? Do you know He loves you?" I am not sure how people get through such a time without having God to turn to.

I spent a lot of time talking to God, not necessarily asking why but more about asking for help to get me through this day and get me past this hour. I knew God was ultimately the only one who could pull me through and comfort me. I also had my family. And I prayed a lot and had my devotional book. I had no doubt in my mind that my grandparents were both in heaven; that wasn't a question. But they were so abruptly taken from us that we didn't have time to prepare for losing them.

God felt the need to call my grandparents home.

They were both very healthy for their age. The morning of the accident, Grammy wanted to get off the phone so she could go help Grampy in the yard. They were always working on a house or working outside. However, she had told my mom several times that she didn't want to get to the age where she had to be put in a nursing home or where she had to worry about someone taking care of her. My grandparents always wanted to die together. They got their wish.

Do you have a favorite memory of your grandparents?

Every year, our family would spend a week in the summer with my grandparents. It was usually around my birthday, and we would

celebrate my birthday all week long. One year, they had been working on their house, and Grampy had some extra siding. He cut out
a big heart from it and then painted: "Happy 16 Birthday. We love
you." He had it hanging from their porch when we arrived.

They would come visit us in the fall for a week. They would
bring fish they caught on the lake, and we would have a fish fry.
Grammy would make hushpuppies. She was always baking and
making food. There was never a moment I remember her out of
the kitchen. (Laughs.)

*Do you have any suggestions for someone going through something
similar?*

I would say to pray and try to find people who have similar
experiences who can relate. Talk it out and don't shut yourself
off. Make sure you're surrounded by people who are positive
influences.

I was very angry, and it took me quite a while to forgive the man
who killed my grandparents. Quite honestly, I don't know that I've
fully forgiven him because if I think about it long enough, I still
have very ill feelings toward him.

The guy who hit my grandparents was under the influence of
meth. He had been arrested and had been in trouble with the law.
He walked away from the accident with minor injuries. The trial
was two years later. We were there for the whole trial, and it was a
trying part of the grief process. Just being back in Alabama without my grandparents was very painful.

It was also the first time that I saw the man who killed my grandparents, and lots of feelings came back that I thought were gone.
It was difficult seeing him and not wanting to … (Trails off.) I remember just glaring at him and wishing my glare could hurt him
somehow. Hearing the defense attorney defend this man almost
brought me back to square one. I had to get past those thoughts

and know it wasn't the Christian thing to do, and it wasn't going to bring my grandparents back.

He wasn't convicted of murder but of manslaughter, which is enough to put him away for a while. We wrote letters to the judge about the sentencing. I wrote a letter explaining how close I was with my grandparents, and how I couldn't just call them up and tell them about my day, and see how they were doing, and how that was all ripped away from us. The trial brought closure. But at the same time, it brought back the grief.

There are still times when it's really hard. My grandparents didn't get to meet my husband because I didn't know him yet. They don't get to meet my sons. Sometimes I get frustrated and wish they were here for life-changing events.

My Grampy's name is William, and we named our son after him. I know Grampy and Grammy are in heaven, and they approve.

⇌+ +⇋

Dangerous Addictions

Anonymous Mother (son, suicide)

"The death snapped me into the decision that I have to live." — In our culture, there is still stigma associated with mental health issues, addictions, and suicide. As a result, family members facing this type of loss do not always disclose a relative's cause of death. Because some family members do not have all the details regarding her son's death, this mother asked that her name, her child's name, and their location not be used. In this story, her son is called John (not his real name).

My son John was in his 20s when he died. I can't give you more details because his father and I are divorced, and his dad hasn't told anyone it was suicide. Our son cut his throat.

John did well in high school. But he got into a fight his senior year, and broke some bones in his hands. They had him on pain-killers, and he found out he really liked them — a little too much. That's when this whole thing started to snowball.

He went into the Air Force after he graduated. In the military, he was drinking. That's what they did. The military put him through rehab, but he couldn't stay sober. After two years, he was given a general discharge.

John's a musician. He played guitar. He loved his guitar! He was also a people person, wanting to meet people and wanting them to listen to his music. He wrote music; he wrote songs. He joined a band, but the band fell apart because he had a drug and alcohol problem. He came to live with me to help him get his life straight. He was my child, and I was going to do the best I could by him. I took him to a psychiatrist, who found John had bipolar disorder. He was okay for about a month and really had a desire to change his life. I don't know what triggered him to relapse. One day he left a message on my voicemail. He told me he was going to get a job working for a music producer in a different state, and he left.

He was gone for about two weeks when he called and said everyone took off and left him with no money or food and the water was turned off. I said, "Son, leave." He refused to leave. I said, "I don't understand. Is this really what you want to do with your life? Is this worth it?" And he said, "Yes." And I said, "Okay, then why are we having this conversation?" He got real quiet. The conversation ended. I didn't talk to him for about a year.

When he called again, I had moved to another state. He said he was clean and was starting over. He said he bought his own place, a condo. He sounded like he was doing well. I bought him a guitar online because he had lost everything. The store made a mistake and sent him two guitars. He called and told me that they sent him two, and I said, "Son, one of them has to go back." What he failed to tell me was that he took both guitars to the pawnshop. He had lied. He wasn't clean. He was using. Both guitars were gone, and they were expensive guitars.

It was probably about another year before I heard from him again. I got a call from my daughter telling me that John was freaking out and saying all kinds of weird things about aliens. I said, "Tell him to call me." She said, "He's mad at you. He won't call you." And I said, "Well, there's nothing I can do if he won't talk to me."

When he finally called two weeks later, he sounded like a mess. He was talking about things that didn't exist, and he was saying bizarre stuff about people trying to kill him and how he was going to protect himself. I didn't know what he was capable of doing. He was living far away. I had to call the police to check on him and on the people he had mentioned.

He got into legal trouble. He was driving in a vehicle and got pulled over. They found heroin and brought him up on charges.

After that, John called me and said he wanted to go to rehab. I was thrilled. He said he wanted to go, but he didn't know how he was going to get there. I said, "I'll take you." I drove to his place and spent three days with him before he went into rehab. He completed the two-week program. But he ended up relapsing, and he violated his probation.

Then things got real bad.

I knew he relapsed. He had gotten arrested. I knew he was in trouble. Now, he was looking at four years in prison. He fired his lawyer. His anger was out of control. His mental health condition was in overdrive, and it just took over his life.

He wanted me to pick him up and take him out of state to avoid the legal problems. I said, "No, you have an obligation, and you're an adult. Those are choices you made. Maybe you didn't realize the full implications, but that's what you are faced with now. I'm not going to help you evade your legal responsibilities." He got very upset with me, telling me: "I'm doing really good. I thought you wanted to be a part of my life." He tried to turn that around on me. I did feel bad. I'm not a cold-hearted person. But I had to stick to my guns. I'm not going to help my child or anybody else skirt their legal obligations. I'm just not going to do it.

I had his probation officer's number in my hand. I thought, "Should I call and say that I think he's using and say that they may need to drug test him at home?" But I was torn. If I call, it might create even more problems for him. But if I don't call, can I live with myself? I ended up not calling. I decided to let the law do what it does and not create any more problems for him.

My son always had a connection to cardinals. Whenever a cardinal would come around, I would think of John. He could go a full year without talking to me. Then, I'd see a cardinal, and I'd think, "Okay, here comes John. I know it." And it would always happen that way. And that's what happened when I learned he had died.

I was driving when a cardinal flew past my windshield. The speed it was flying startled me. I've never seen a bird fly that fast in my life, and I'm a bird person.

Within the hour I got a call from my daughter, and she was crying. I said, "What's going on?" and my daughter said, "John's dead." I said, "What do you mean he's dead?" And she said, 'There's an obituary online." So, I got on my cell phone and typed in my son's name, and sure enough, his picture popped up. (Crying.) I was in shock. I couldn't believe it. (Sobbing.) Even though he had spiraled out of control, I still couldn't believe it.

I called the police department, and I explained to them that I'm out of state; I just learned my son is dead. I said, "What's going on?" They said, "We can't tell you anything over the phone. You just have to get here." I said, "You can't tell me anything? I have an 11-hour drive ahead of me, my son is dead, and you can't tell me anything?" They said, "All we can tell you is that you need to get here."

I called the medical examiner. When he heard I was 11 hours away, he told me it was a suicide. I asked, "How did it happen?" He said it was a puncture to the carotid artery in the neck. And I said, "Who does that to themselves?" He said, "I'm just telling you what the results were ma'am." So, I got in the car and drove all night to the police department. The investigator said it definitely was a suicide. My son had been in the bathroom and had used a razor knife to cut his throat. He was in there for five days before he was found.

It's been hard. I still cry every day about it. I have his urn on my ancestor shrine. I have a candle for him, and I talk to him. I try not to talk to him too much because it hasn't been a lot of time. According to my belief system, when somebody passes away, it takes a minimum of just over a year to cross over because it's a process. I don't want to bring his spirit back. I want him to continue on his journey. Right now, I try to strengthen his peace and bring light to his spirit and send prayers to my ancestors to help him. As time goes on, I will talk to him more directly, and I'll have better dialogue with his spirit from heaven.

Do you have any religious or spiritual practices that have helped you?

My spiritual or religious practices are known as Lucumi. It's a Cuban form of Santeria. It's an African nature-based religious philosophy that came to the islands with the slave trade. It blended with Catholicism. I met a Santero (priest) when my son was just a baby. We talked a lot about the Orishas, which are spirits, nature spirits, divinities, deities, and saints because it's blended with Catholicism. I have my Orisha here at the house. I have a shrine to them, and I pray to them. I don't proceed with my day until I go to my ancestor shrine and honor them and ask for blessings.

After John's passing, I had a nine-day litany for the dead. Nine days of prayers specifically for him. According to my belief, a person doesn't pass away and then immediately go to heaven. He may need help to move along. I don't believe in hell or the devil. There's good and evil, sure, and darkness. But there's always a way out of the darkness.

What else have you found helpful with your healing and grief process?

Talking about it helps me so much, but here's the problem I'm faced with. No one will talk to me about it. That has been the hardest thing for me. My friend said it's because people can't handle it or don't know how to handle it. In my mind, it's my son, and I'm handling it! Even my own family, they can't handle talking about it. I talk to a few friends who are there for me and who will listen.

Being alone in nature also helps. Some people may say someone who just lost a son shouldn't be alone. But for me, sitting quietly in nature and listening to birds and watching my cats helps. As simple as that sounds, watching their antics and getting a smile out of that helps me cope and heal.

Before my son died, there were a lot of things in my life that I could have said were tragic. After my son died, something inside of me snapped. But it wasn't in a negative direction. The death snapped me into the decision that I have to live. Not that I was suicidal, but it snapped me out of a depressed state. It snapped me into the belief that I have to do things differently. I have to be positive. I have to look at life as a gift, and I have to be a better person for myself, for my surviving child, and even for my son who has passed away. Energy doesn't die. It just transforms. He's still here. I don't know where. I won't know until I die. It's a mystery. But I'm still his mother, and I'm always going to be his mother. He still needs me to help. His father and I created his energy, and he still needs us.

My ex-husband, who is Catholic, doesn't view it that way. Some in his faith may be thinking his son went to hell. I don't know. Suicide is very bad in the Catholic faith. But according to my beliefs, I created my son, and he's still somewhere, and he needs light, and he needs help. If Catholics want to call it purgatory, okay, that's fine. But in the Lucumi tradition, we see a way for everything. If he is in some sort of darkness, we can find a way through the Orisha and through the ancestors to bring light to his spirit and help him on his way to heaven, which is where all of us go, the ancestor world. There are many different names for it. My son still needs me.

What's your favorite memory of your son?

My favorite memories are camping with my son. We loved sitting around the bonfire and also going swimming. One time, we were sitting in the sand along the coast. He was playing his guitar and singing me a song he had written. It was a beautiful moment. A glorious sunset. I wish I had the lyrics to the song, but I don't. I just remember being moved to tears. That was five years ago now. Seems like it was yesterday. (She pauses.) Thank you for listening.

Did he get any help for the mental health disorders?

I believe he started to exhibit signs when he was in the military. Of course, I don't have any way to know for sure what happened. But he told me he had a problem with drinking, and they sent him to rehab. Then, they put him on a mild antidepressant. He started drinking again. The military might have known there was some mental health issue there, but maybe they just didn't want to deal with it. I really don't know.

He didn't get any help with the bipolar until he came to live with me. I took him to see a doctor who gave him medication. John flushed it all down the toilet. He said he didn't like the way it made him feel. I can't speak for him, but maybe he felt like it was taking away his creativity. For days and days, he would write and play music. But when he took the medicine, he just kind of sat there. He didn't give it enough time to get into his system and level off. He was like an angry person on his medication, and he didn't play his guitar. So, he flushed it down the toilet and said, "I'm never taking that again." But he spun out of control, and he's gone.

He was smart, handsome, creative, musical, and lyrical. He had so many great qualities. He was like sunshine. But I guess we never know what a person thinks or feels. Inside, he had a lot of twisted up emotions. But for somebody to cut his own throat! I asked my doctor: "From the time of the act to the time of unconsciousness, what is that time period?" She said 20 seconds. That's a long time to know that there's no turning back. She told me what he did is *very* painful. It hurts. But you can't change it.

I regret that my last conversation with him was not a good one. I don't regret the tough love part. I regret that I'll never see my son again in this life.

Have you felt any other connection to him since he left?

I had two dreams. The first dream was shortly after he passed away. I dreamed I went to his condo and the whole place was white. He was sleeping on a mat on a floor, next to a puzzle half put together. I could see that the puzzle was dolphins in the ocean, leaping out of the water. His Orisha was Yemaya, the great spirit of the ocean. I said, "Son, I have to use your bathroom." And he said, "Okay," and he pointed down the hall. He was in that groggy state of trying to wake up. I thought what is the significance of that? Maybe I called him away from something he's trying to transition to, and he's trying to put together the pieces of this puzzle.

In the other dream I was outside. I see my son, and he is a child. He had his hands cuffed. I remember being shocked. I said, "What are you doing here?" And he was just smiling. I was yelling, "Are you okay?" He opened up his hands, and a male cardinal flew out, into the bush. I felt like he's telling me that he's okay.

The first dream was unsettling and the second one was letting me know things were okay. I haven't had any dreams since then, and his spirit doesn't feel close to me right now. I want him to continue on his journey. When he needs me, I'll be here for him. After he gets where he needs to be, then I will be able to call on him, and he will be here when I need him.

Do you have any suggestions for someone going through a similar experience of grief?

I might not be able to answer that question right now. It wasn't too long ago that the shock wore off. The shock wasn't just a week or a month. It carried with me for probably almost a year. Somebody might say that sounds weird, but that numb shock feeling is just now wearing off. I don't know how to explain it to somebody who hasn't been down that path. I'm still just trying to get by. I know he's gone from this world, and his energy is not dead. But I'm not there yet as far as the healing.

Are you doing any self-care to help with your grieving?

No. I live in a rural community, and they don't have social services here. I don't have help with grief counseling or anything like that. My dogs saved me, initially and still to this day. I have German Shepherds and a Doberman. I train them and work with them. We have a routine every day. If I hadn't had that routine, I may have fallen into a depression. They give me a reason to get up and keep moving and tend to their needs.

I keep myself busy. I try not to have too much time to get sad. Even though I'm a person who is strong in my faith, I'm still a human being. I'm still a mother, and I'm a mother who lost her child in a very terrible way. I try to be as normal as I can be. I'm not working every minute until I drop. I don't drink. I don't take drugs. I don't smoke cigarettes. I just try to live a good, healthy life to the best of my ability, surviving the loss of a child to suicide. It's not easy.

I always ask myself, "What good could ever come out of something like that? It's brutal. It's sad." I don't know. If anything positive can come out of it, I hope it does. That would be a good thing.

⊷ ⊶

Justin Phillips (son, overdose)

"It's figuring out how not to get swallowed up by grief." — Justin Phillips is the mother of three children: Aaron Kent Sims (who died from a heroin overdose at age 20), an older son who is 23, and a younger daughter who is 14. Justin also has two stepchildren (adult daughters) with her current spouse, Nate Phillips. We met at the one-year anniversary of Aaron's death. When I expressed concern that it might be too soon in the grieving process for our interview, Justin adamantly explained that talking about Aaron is helpful. She spoke with me at the public library, just as the last glints of the October evening sun beamed brightly through a large overhead window.

Aaron was a good kid. He had a heart of gold and was incredibly selfless. He was also naturally talented athletically. He played everything, but football was his love. His junior year in high school, he had a very bad concussion — and probably had more that we didn't know about. He dropped out of school, within six months of his concussion. He did get his GED the same year he should have graduated.

I know Aaron had been an off and on pot smoker. We did a lot for the marijuana thing. We took him to treatment. I did drug testing at home. He may have been doing prescription drugs that his high school friends shared amongst each other, but I don't know any of those details. After he dropped out of high school, he started using heroin and went to treatment. He relapsed once and then was clean for maybe a year. During this time, he wasn't living with me, so I'm not sure when he starting using again. He was living at his dad's house. His dad and I are divorced. Aaron lived with me until he was 18. Then, he wanted to "be a man." He said I "treated him like a baby." I didn't treat him like a baby, but that's the way he saw it.

In October, he overdosed on heroin. When Aaron overdosed, his dad found him, thank goodness. (Pauses.) I don't have any reason to believe it wasn't accidental. It's so easy to overdose on heroin. It's wreaking havoc on that age group.

What's your favorite memory of Aaron?

My favorite memory is of us singing in the car. When he was young, we would sing the Mamas & the Papas song, *Make Your Own Kind Of Music*, really loud together. (Smiles.)

When he was in elementary school, he was big into skateboarding. He pegged his own pants, sewing them with a needle and thread and then pinning them so they would be tight to his calf. (Laughs.)

He did typical teen things. He played video games. He was also a talented writer and had some artistic ability. Aaron was a big-hearted soul with intuitive insight. We had such a challenge because I was trying to keep him from smoking pot and ruining his life. We butted heads a lot, especially when I was disciplining him. We were so much alike. He knew me probably better than anyone. (Crying.)

What, if anything, helps with your grieving process?

I have done *a lot*! When Aaron died, I was in the middle of a mind-fulness stress reduction course. I finished the class and went on a one-day silent retreat. I've since gone on a two-day silent retreat and taken another mindfulness course.

Getting Botox didn't really help. I went to Pilates right away. It helped, but nothing *really* helps. I did a lot of fixing the outside thinking that somehow it would make it better, on the inside. It did keep me busy and distracted. Going to Pilates, getting the Botox, buying more shoes than I needed. I have a new car, a mini convertible. Riding it in is one of the only things that make me feel better. But still, all outside stuff.

I started a parent support group for people who have been affected from deaths by overdose. Because of the stigma, it's different from other ways our children might die. That group has been extremely helpful. Much like the 12-step fellowship, which is where I learned it: "If I help others, then I feel better about me."

I spoke with people who consider themselves mediums and had some experiences early on where I felt like Aaron was present. One friend and I were scheduled to speak on the telephone the day after Aaron died. When my friend called, I said, "Oh, I'm sorry Fred, but I can't talk today." And he replied, "I know, I have a message from Aaron." He said, "Aaron came to me in a vision." I trust Fred. The common theme I heard from him was how sensitive Aaron was, and he couldn't handle it. I know that to be true. Aaron was truly empathic. Things you wouldn't think would hurt someone's feelings hurt Aaron's feelings. Fred also relayed that Aaron was sorry, and that it wasn't my fault. Aaron had no idea how much I loved him.

Do you have any religious or spiritual practices that help?

Symbolism and rituals are helpful for me. I have not been angry with God. I have a Buddha Board that I sit with in the morning and write on. Lately, I've just been writing: *Dear God.*

The day Aaron was found — before I knew about his death — I wrote: *I'm scared.* I knew somehow.

I'm also journaling. I'm doing Reiki (energy healing) on myself. And I pray. Then, I have readings I do from different books. I usually pull a soul collage card. Throughout the day, I try to see what God's plan is: "What is it that we're here for? Why me?" Not "Why me?'" as in "Poor me." But more, "What the hell? Why? And okay, what am I supposed to do with this?"

I go to the cemetery and lie down on a blanket and talk to Aaron. I take food for the squirrels and birds and leave it there. Today I was thinking morbidly. When you're pregnant, you think, "Oh, I wonder what my baby looks like this month." Well I was thinking, "What does your baby look like who has been dead a year?" Crazy thoughts.

I write to Aaron every day, in my morning journal. My therapist told me: "Don't write to him for too long or you'll be stuck in your grief." I don't agree. But I don't know. I didn't know this first year was going to take me by surprise the way that it did.

Aaron was a huge clotheshorse. I took many of his clothes to a homeless shelter because I know that's what he would have wanted me to do with them. I also have a tattoo on my wrist. Toward the end of his life, Aaron was doing graffiti. His tag is: Apex, Pentacle of the best you can be, along with his initials. I did the tattoo early on. Impulsive. I'd probably do it a little differently now.

My daughter did a report for school on traumatic brain injury for football players. There have been a lot of players with concussions who committed suicide or got involved in drugs. I texted the coroner and asked her if there was any of Aaron's brain still around; you can't diagnose the concussion impact until the person is dead. She said, "No, Justin, we put that back." (Sighs.) You grasp at straws to somehow make sense of it.

Is there anything else that helped you with the healing process?

I'm not the same person anymore, and I don't get to be the same person. Each morning I think: "What would Aaron want me to do?" Aaron would not want me to go down the rabbit hole and never come out, which is oftentimes what I feel like doing. It's hard not to want to hide from the reality of how much his loss has shaken the whole family. Aaron and my dad were close, and I can see that it has aged my father and taken something from him.

It's figuring out how not to get swallowed up by grief.

Aaron's dog Cain was just a puppy when Aaron died. If anything happens to Cain it's going to be really difficult because I feel like there's a part of Aaron there.

I try to believe Aaron is in a better place. I do believe he's in a better place to the degree that he's not suffering. But it's *not* comforting when people say, "You'll see him again."

When people don't know what to say, I tell them: "It's okay. There isn't anything you need to say." Saying, "I'm sorry for your loss" is enough. Saying, "I'm here for you." Show up for the person. I was incredibly impressed by my daughter's school. They explained to the kids that it's important to not ignore her, but rather to embrace her.

Do you have any suggestions for someone going through something similar?

Everyone deals with grief differently. I talked about Aaron a lot in the beginning, and I still want to talk about Aaron. I don't want him to disappear.

It's important to have the support of people who understand: people who have lost what you have lost. Only they get it to the depth that you experience it.

Returning to work was also one of the better things I did. It gives you something to keep your mind on.

Find ways to take care of yourself, and don't set expectations for yourself. There's absolutely no right or wrong way to grieve. Sometimes we say to ourselves: "Oh, am I allowed to be feeling this way? Should I *not* be feeling this way?" No one else should tell you how to grieve. You get to grieve however you want.

CHAPTER 2

NAVIGATING GRIEF'S CURRENTS

"Grief is itself a medicine."

— *WILLIAM COWPER, POET*

May I be healed ~

There's a poignant song, "Cradle Me," written by Deborah Dougherty. This song has been performed during numerous healing rituals and ceremonies. I first heard it performed by the Indianapolis Women's Chorus. In times of sorrow, these women sing:

> *"In the morning when I rise, wipe the night-time from my eyes. Plant my feet down on the floor, move myself through daily chores. Giving thanks while breaking bread, and for kind words that are said. Spirit move me through my deeds, cradling me with all my needs. … Earth and breath and sky and sea, all rise up and cradle me."*

In Western culture, individuals and families do not always have access to meaningful ceremonies that adequately cradle them in their grief. Although we may have a worship service or meals brought to our home after a loved one's passing, many people do not receive sufficient community support during the weeks, months, and years that follow. Even worse, some who are grieving are met (directly or indirectly) with an attitude of: *You need to get over it.*

Most of us are not taught how to gently nurture our sorrow or how to simply provide loving space for those who are grieving — even though allowing others (or ourselves) to *feel* the flood of emotions can be enormously restorative. Our culture's focus on productivity and success also may not recognize the lingering nature of grief, which can resurface time and again, especially during significant milestones such as birthdays and anniversaries.

The stories in this chapter address the turbulent, flowing currents of grief. Significantly, the individuals here discuss what it feels like when grief *isn't* lovingly held by friends and family members or isn't expressed through meaningful rituals. Cheri (who lost both parents) states: *"I was just never allowed to process things normally initially. I carried a lot of guilt about a lot of things. I have had to learn how to release that and not claim it."* Karen (whose sister committed suicide) notes: *"It was kind of like existing underwater — doing what I needed to do but pretty depressed. It was a dark time."*

Being fully present to our grief — whenever it surfaces — is itself a path toward healing. With increased collective awareness, perhaps we can strengthen our community practices for cradling intense sorrow. We might also create additional rituals that not only honor those who have passed but also offer greater support for the deep wellspring of emotions that accompany grief.

Unraveling the Layers

Cheri Stephens (parents, car accident & cancer)

"I learned to fake being okay." — Cheri is in her 40s. She lost her mother and her father when she was 13 years old. Her mother (Lorna Walter) passed away on February 16, and her father (Robert Walter) passed away a month later. Born in Roaring Springs, Pennsylvania, Cheri has an older brother and sister. She also has two adult daughters and two grandchildren.

My mom had a car accident. It was a Saturday morning, while she was taking me to my friend's house. It was icy road conditions, and she lost control of the vehicle on a turn and hit another vehicle. I can remember the sun glaring on me, blinding. It was a sunny day but also very cold. It had just snowed and, in the country, the roads are awful. She hit a patch of ice. I was in the eighth grade.

I don't have any other memories of the incident. I only know what people told me. When I was in a semi-awake state, I said, "My mother threw her arm across me." (Softly crying.) I'm sorry. You'd think 35 years later I'd be able to say it. She threw her arm across me because people didn't use seatbelts back then, and my mom begged to God, "Take me and leave her." (Sobbing.)

She was alive until the rescue team came. She passed away as soon as they got her out of the vehicle. Of course, I didn't know what was happening until I woke up at the hospital. I thought, "This will be fun. My mom and me are at the same hospital. We can share a hospital room and be roommates." I didn't realize she was in a morgue. (Crying.) Nobody wanted to tell me. I wasn't happy, but I wasn't sad. I was just looking forward to seeing my mom. I was asking, "Where's my mom? When am I gonna see my mom?" After a while, my grandparents on my mom's side were there. They were all teary-eyed, and their eyes were puffy and swollen. I couldn't figure out what was going on. Oh my gosh, it was hours later. I don't know who told me. But finally, someone told me that my mom didn't make it.

I wasn't injured. Her side of the car was completely smashed and mangled. On my side, you couldn't even tell the car was impacted. I had a little glass on me but no cuts, no scrapes, no scratches. Nothing. The man in the other vehicle wasn't injured either. His vehicle was damaged, but he walked away from it.

I was in the hospital for a few days and made it out just in time for her funeral. (She pauses briefly.)

After my mom's death, we went to live with my grandparents on my dad's side, and they just weren't . . . (Trails off.) They were reserved, very cold and standoffish, let's put it that way. My grandmother never had daughters. She raised seven boys. They didn't know what to do with my sister and me. My dad, who had been diagnosed with lung cancer, also moved in with my grandparents. Basically, he lived on the couch.

My father smoked and had worked at the paper company. At the time he was diagnosed with lung cancer, the doctor told him he'd be lucky if he lived six months. He proved them wrong. He lived five years and six months. But after my mom died, he just gave up. He had already been through all the chemo and radiation and had a lung removed. There was nothing more the doctors could do. He was still healthy enough to walk around and do what he needed to do. It never really got to him until after my mom passed. Then, he just crumbled.

My dad knew he was dying. On that day, after my grandparents took us to school, they drove him to the hospital, and that's where he passed. It was, "Oh, you're a kid. You don't need to be burdened with this." But you can tell. He wasn't getting up off the couch. (Crying.) He could barely hold his eyes open. So, we knew it was imminent.

Do you recall anything that helped you get through that loss?

My grandparents lived in a different school district. So, my sister and I had to change schools. It was awful. My grandparents came to the school and got us when my father passed. That's how we found out. That was horrible. After the funeral, we just went back to school, like any other day. Back then they had no grief counseling at all. My sister, my brother, and I had to find our own way, without any guidance. (Crying.) It was extremely difficult.

When we were younger, before my mom passed, we knew my dad was ill, and we knew he was going to die. We were kind of preparing for that. Then all of the sudden, when mom passes . . . (Trails off while crying.) It's like being blindsided. There were times when I asked my grandfather for help. I told him I needed to talk to someone. He would laugh at me and say, "No, you don't." (Sobbing.) Even when I asked for help, it was denied. My grandmother would call us, "Poor orphans. Nobody wanted you, and we *had* to take you." The love was really rolling in. (Laughs while crying.)

We were Methodist at the time. We went to church regularly. So, that helped me. Just praying. I also had dreams of my parents where they would let me know, "It's okay." I didn't know what meditation was back then; but also, just quietly sitting and thinking about it. I realized there was only one person to take care of me and that was me. (Crying.)

What was your grieving process as a youth?

I didn't have a grieving process. I stumbled through. I cried a lot. My grandparents always chastised me for it. We weren't allowed to grieve in public, and we weren't allowed to grieve around them. I just learned to fake it. I learned to fake being okay. At times, it would overwhelm me. I had to learn to take a step back and try to figure out what was going on, evaluate the situation, how I got to where I am, and realize: *I'm not alone. It may seem like I'm alone, but I'm not.*

My sister and I hadn't even started dating yet. I was only 13. Of course, we had discussions about it with our mom. We were really close with Mom. (Crying.) We'd ask, "When do you think we'll be allowed to date?" When we went to my grandparents' house, we weren't allowed to date, *ever*. Period. Not until we graduated from high school. We weren't allowed to talk to anybody on the phone. We weren't allowed to go to movies. We weren't allowed to be kids. (Crying.) We went to school and could be in school sports or extra-curricular activities if it was school related. If it didn't involve the school, we had to be home.

I started my menstrual cycle the summer after my mom passed. My grandmother didn't know what to do. She cut up a sheet into rags, and I had to wear that. My aunt told her, "You can't do that. You can't make those girls do that." But my grandmother had no idea what to do. Finally, my one aunt stepped in and helped take care of that situation.

We had friends at school but nobody really understood what was going on because how could they? We couldn't see them out-side of school. We really didn't talk about it. We just kept it to ourselves.

What is your favorite memory of your parents?

When he was sick, my dad always liked to take naps. He'd let us lie down with him, and we would cuddle in. And I loved the smell of his cherry pipe tobacco. (Crying.) For my mom, Saturdays were our fun day. We would clean the house Saturday morning. Then, we would go into Altoona, where she worked. We'd help her do some filing. Then, we'd go to the mall and get a soft pretzel.

After their deaths, I used photos to help me remember my parents. I would conjure up memories from my childhood — some happy, some not, some funny. One of my favorite memories of my mom is a vacation we took the last summer we had together. It was a family vacation taken with family friends. During the stay, we were inside the rental house, and a mouse ran across the floor. Mom and her friend jumped on the dining room chairs, squealing like little girls! I can still remember the laughter that brought us. That memory always brings a smile to my face.

But I also had the negative memories of my dad. I had a hard time trying to grieve for my dad because there was no sorrow for him until recently. It was for my mother where I really felt the loss.

I wasn't close to my dad growing up. He was either off fishing or drinking, and he was abusive to my mother, physically and emotionally. We saw that. We were relieved when we found out he was ill because it was all going to end. Then, of course, that adds to the guilt thing: *Why are you wanting someone's life to end?* But, I've come to the realization that people do the best they can with what they have. Sometimes they don't have the ability or don't know how to be different.

Is there anything that helped your healing process as an adult?

I read all kinds of self-help books. I've always known more is out there, another realm. I knew I wasn't alone. (Crying.) There are definitely times I felt alone and lonely. But in my heart of hearts, I know they are still with me. I've learned to maintain a connection. Just talking to them. Thinking about them. I keep their pictures out and have conversations with them once in a while. (Laughs.) I started learning about crystals recently and went and had an angel reading done, which was interesting. I keep that realm open.

I left the church. I liked the minister but the church body . . . (Trails off.) I decided to stay away from the physical aspect of it, but I've increased the spirituality aspect. I've started questioning a lot of my childhood beliefs. I do believe there is a Higher Power, and I've learned to trust that.

I also see a therapist whenever I feel myself going off the track a bit. Just going to talk to somebody who is not involved is helpful. My therapist was amazed I made it out as normal as I did. Of course, normalcy is a matter of perspective. (Laughs.)

I do some meditation, and I love to go for walks — anything that helps me to unplug and just be. Sunshine helps. When I start feeling sad, I go outside. And I have my granddaughters. To me, my grandbabies are a treasure of life.

What might be helpful for someone reading this book?

First of all, grieving is okay. (Crying.) Everybody grieves differently. It's going to be their own time as far as when they need to talk to someone. You can't force it. But when a person decides they need to talk, make sure someone is available — whether it is a family member or a professional.

I've always known that things aren't as bad as they seem. One day, I'll see my parents again and be with them. I can tell when their thoughts are with me. I just have to learn not to beat myself up so much — I'm really good at that one! (Laughs.) When I was young, I thought maybe I wasn't good enough, and it was my fault my mom was in the car. I was just never allowed to process things initially. I carried a lot of guilt about a lot of things. I had to learn how to release that and not claim it.

Before my parents passed and after they passed definitely influenced the way I raised my children. I make sure I don't ever end a conversation without letting them know I love them, no matter what. There are times where I lose my temper or yell, but I always make sure they understand it was not toward them, it was the situation. I want them to always have confidence in the fact that I love them.

❦

Karen Peck (sister, suicide)

"I've learned the rituals of death are important." — Karen has curly, red hair. She is a writer. Originally from New York, Karen currently lives in Illinois with her husband George Peck. They have two young adult sons (Alec and Andrew). She lost her sister, Dara Gail Veder, 35 years ago. She lost her mother, Joan, four months ago.

My sister Dara and I grew up in the Bronx, New York City. I don't have any other siblings. Our mom was a secretary, and our dad was a manager in the garment industry in mid-town Manhattan.

Dara was 17 when she died. I was 20 years old and a junior at State University of New York, Purchase College. The summer before Dara died she was the center of a large group of friends and upbeat and talkative. She came down with mononucleosis. Mono has a long recovery period, and she missed the first day of school that fall. At the time, no one thought of it as dropping out. We all thought of it simply as a late start.

But she refused to return to school. I don't know if Dara was officially diagnosed, but I'm sure she was bipolar and suffered from hypomania and depression. She stopped socializing and refused to go out, isolating her from her friends. Her schedule inverted: she slept all day, and stayed up all night. Although my parents weren't aware of it, she spent her nights inventorying her possessions. She exhibited all the symptoms of depression.

My parents insisted Dara see a psychologist, which was fraught with problems when someone is afraid to leave the house, afraid to take the city bus, and both parents work. No one knew, obviously, what she was planning to do.

Dara committed suicide on December 29. She overdosed on pills, planning it out so she would be dead by the time my parents got home from work. It was winter break for me. I had gone to Europe with friends, a backpacking trip. We didn't have cell phones back then, and I didn't have much money. Consequently, I hadn't called home.

I flew home on January 11. My father emerged from the crowd in the airport. My mother was trailing behind him. We walked over to an empty waiting area, and he sat me down and took my hand in his. Then he told me, "Dara took her life." He was close to crying. My mother was silent. We must have retrieved my luggage and gotten to the parking lot, but that memory is lost. I went into shock, and stayed there for quite a while.

There wasn't a religious ceremony. My parents are humanist Jews. They had a memorial service at the funeral home. Dara was cremated, and my father scattered her ashes at one of her favorite places — Washington Square Park in New York City. By the time I got back in January, all of that was done.

I missed everything.

My parents went back to work, and I was alone. It was awful. My community was at school. So, I went back early and stayed with friends who had remained on campus for winter break.

What did you do to help you cope?

My parents' grief was bottomless, and I was impotent to do anything about it. For sibling grief, at that time, there was less awareness. Sibling grief paled in comparison to what the parents went through, and there wasn't any process to deal with a sibling's grief. I found it difficult to talk to people about my experience. People just couldn't hear it. When you say suicide, people tune out and cannot process the information. People would ask me the same things repeatedly because they weren't listening to my answers. At least that's how it felt at the time.

I dealt with it by not dealing with it. It was like existing underwater — doing what I needed to do but extremely depressed. It was a dark time.

Was there anything later that helped with your healing?

I had started seeing a therapist the prior fall, and it was helpful to continue therapy. In your 20s, your focus is getting through college. Then, you're working, and there are romances. I got married and had my babies. Having children brought up my fears about whether they would be okay — because of the depression history in my family. When my second child was born, I was under tremendous stress. My husband was in grad school, and I was working fulltime and had a new infant and preschool child.

I didn't go back and grieve until I was in my late 30s. I had gone to a therapist with my husband, and I was told that I should see someone separately to deal with the trauma. I said, "Trauma? What trauma are you talking about?" It hadn't occurred to me in that way.

I worked with a therapist who diagnosed me with PTSD (Post Traumatic Stress Disorder). I used somatosensory techniques, cognitive behavioral therapy, and EMDR (Eye Movement Desensitization and Reprocessing) to bring myself "back together."

My sister's death affects every milestone, like my wedding and the birth of my children. I always mark her birthday and the day she died. As a sibling to someone who died by suicide, I lost my future with the sister who would have been an aunt, and I lost the friend I would have had as an adult. That is gone. For years when someone asked, "Do you have any brothers or sisters?" I'd say, "No," because that was easier than explaining it.

Today, I speak about her death if the circumstances are appropriate. If it's the casual chitchat talk at a cocktail party, then no. If it's a more meaningful discussion, I share my story. I do what I can to change attitudes like posting about suicide prevention and awareness on social media. Depression distorts thinking. Suicide is a fatal outcome of a mental disease. Suicide isn't anyone's fault.

There's a unique kind of grief when someone takes her own life. It is an act of violence, and an act that could have been prevented. There's tremendous guilt and a lot of *what if's* and *if only I was* that may not come up with other types of death. We could have done everything right, and still, it could have turned out wrong. Questions will always linger. And there's no getting around the fact that it's an intentional ending of a life. Survivors of suicide loss learn to live with that fact.

I've come to a point of forgiveness because I understand how much pain she was in. I read something my dad sent to me that said, "She picked a permanent solution to a temporary problem." Dara left so much hurt for my parents to live with for the rest of their lives. If she only knew.

When my mom passed away four months ago, it brought up a lot of grief about my sister. My mother's death was a surprise. She had an autoimmune disease, Scleroderma, but no symptoms of imminent danger. It's a progressive illness. She was having symptoms of the illness, but she died from a cardiac arrest. It was a shock. She literally dropped dead in the street. That's a hard thing to think about. I'm finally, after four months, not focusing on that moment. I'm struggling with how sad and terrible this is for my father. It's hard for me, too. But it's much harder for him.

My mom was 78, a little on the younger side. When I think of my sister and my mom, I think: *Not enough life. Not enough time.* Maybe it's different if the person is 98. I don't know. Some people say it doesn't matter how old the person is or how much time in advance you know about it, death is just a tough thing.

Dara was so young when she died. There's little legacy there. With my mom, I have the memories of the joy she had with my boys. That's what I try to focus on: the memories I have, and the love that we shared, and the lives that they've touched.

What else have you found helpful in your healing?

Writing has been the biggest help for me. In both my fiction and nonfiction these themes — grief, loss, love, and renewal — keep coming up.

Talking helps. The whole "better place thing" is ridiculous. I don't believe in that. Or "you'll get over it." I don't believe that either. You don't get over some losses. You learn to live with them. The loss may cease to be something you think about all the time, but when you have lost someone you loved deeply, it will always be there. Like when I see my sister's smile on my younger son's face. It was painful at first, but it is also something beautiful that she left.

My dad is talking which is good because he's of a generation where men don't discuss feelings. When I respond to him, I'll also respond in writing. I can then do so at my leisure without getting upset myself. I don't like letting my grief upset other people and maybe that's not healthy. It's something I struggle with, but grief makes people uncomfortable. The most helpful people are the ones who just allow you to express what you're feeling; they don't judge it. They don't try to make it better. They don't placate it because no one can make it better for you. But we can witness for each other.

Do you have any religious or spiritual practices that helped?

We were Jewish culturally but not Jewish religiously. My parents didn't go to temple. My mother stopped believing in God. God doesn't do this. God doesn't remove a child from a mother or a mother from a child too soon and doesn't damage a father's heart.

My father is an atheist, but he says a prayer for both my mom and my sister. (Laughs.) He says it couldn't hurt, and we chuckle about it. I don't believe in an afterlife, as in a place where people go. It is harder when you can't believe in a place like a heaven.

I envision my loved ones surrounded in light and love. I imagine they are together, though I don't realistically believe that. I try to let go of painful feelings. I don't know if you would call that psychological or spiritual. I think of my sister's ashes all over the world now. I view death in terms of the energy and molecules that remain, being part of the earth and part of the cycle of life. That's a comfort.

I've learned that the rituals of death are important. They offer something to us, especially for me since I didn't have that with my sister. I decided to get two keepsake urns for my mom — one urn for me and one for my Dad. My mom's ashes are in my house, in my garden, and in New York. I want to have a little piece of what used to be her. I wrote something for a memorial we had in my mom and dad's home in New York, and I wrote up my father's thoughts. People heard it and responded. Gathering in community is meaningful. There are reasons people have gathered at the ending of life for ages. It helps you make sense of loss.

I will have a small ritual ceremony at a Unitarian Universalist church I attend. I want to share memories of when my mom was here and have witnesses when we bring her remains back to the physical earth.

Do you have a favorite memory of your sister or your mom?

I didn't get to know Dara long enough. How much do you remember before the age of five? I left for college when she was 15. And she died at 17. Toward the end of her life, Dara was unhappy and angry. I have early childhood pictures, and those are helpful. For years, I talked to my mom about Dara and heard stories because I couldn't remember the good things. My mom would remind me of things, such as, "Oh yeah, you two played dolls for hours." When I lost my mom, I also lost a source of the happier stories of my life with my young sister.

It's easier with my mom. I have lots of memories. I made a photo calendar, and I have other projects involving pictures and writing. That's a consistent for me: documentation. My favorite memories with my mom are with my boys. She loved them and felt joy with them and that comforts me. This woman — who lost her own daughter and went through so much pain — was able to live and love and have joy in her life. And I was able to help bring that to her through grandchildren.

Do you have any suggestions for someone going through something similar?

Getting through grief is a process. I don't think there is anything other people can do that solves it. Every time you revisit it it's a little different, and your response to it is different. But it's a process that will be there for the rest of your life. Hopefully, each time you revisit it there is a little more peace.

Suicide is not easy to discuss. There is judgment and stigma. I actively work to bring awareness of suicide as the result of the fatal disease of depression. Helping others to gain compassion for those who have died by suicide and for survivors of suicide loss helps me heal.

For the people who believe, "Oh, they're off in a better place," that's wonderful for them. But many of us don't believe that. The feelings of hope or renewal come when you take that loss and turn it into something good. In my case, it was learning to value my family. It's showing and sharing the love you have for people because you don't know when they're not going to be here anymore. Our love, both when people are alive and when gone, needs to be cherished. Love transcends time and loss, and it adds meaning to our lives.

Postscript: Fourteen months after her mother's death, Karen followed up with me about a connection she had just felt to her mother.

I had a dream about my mother. In the dream, we both knew she had died. When I awoke, I felt as though I'd spent time with her, as though she told me she was okay, and I've been uplifted since.

I don't know if that means anything more than the product of my mind, but does it matter? I look forward to seeing her again in my slumbers.

⊫⊰⊹⊐

Lori Robinson (sister, suicide)

"Time is the great healer." — *Lori is a gregarious woman with an infectious laugh. Her home is adorned with a buffalo statue in the yard, a bison skull on the wall, and an assortment of drums and Native American blankets throughout the living room. She is self-employed as a massage therapist. Lori lost her sister Carol over 25 years ago to suicide.*

I am the oldest of four. My sister Gail is next in line. Carol was after Gail by three years. My brother Bill is the youngest. Our parents are divorced now.

Carol went to the University of Wisconsin where she was a gymnast. She couldn't compete in gymnastics her senior year of high school because of an injury. As a result, none of the colleges were looking at her. But she walked onto the team that first year and got a full ride scholarship to compete in the all-around the next three years.

After college, Carol came home. She had graduated with a degree in advertising. It became apparent pretty quickly that she was depressed. She was talking to members of the family about depression, saying, "I don't know if I want to be in advertising anymore." I remembered when I went to college thinking I wanted to be an occupational therapist. When I found out I didn't want to be that, I went through the ringer myself because it's that whole piece of not knowing, and it felt so awful. I remember just thinking, "Oh, she's in that place of not knowing, and that's a really hard place to be."

My mom and dad invited Carol to come live back home when it was clear she was struggling.

Carol had wrecked her car two weeks before dying. We found out from her best friend, later, that Carol told her it was a suicide attempt. The friend stayed up all night talking to Carol but then didn't tell anyone — didn't tell a therapist or my folks or a pastor. She must have thought she talked Carol off the ledge. Then, two weeks later, on this friend's birthday when they were supposed to meet up, Carol killed herself. (Lori sits quietly for a moment and then continues.)

Carol set herself on fire, in the garage. Luckily, my mom had parked outside on the street that night and had gone straight to bed. My dad came home late that evening from a bridge game, and he found her. Carol was a perfectionist. Given the fact that she hadn't succeeded the first time, she likely did some research. What I've been told since, by a fire inspector, is that if you take a really deep breath during a fire, you burn your respiratory track and die immediately.

Our minister lived three blocks away, and before my dad went in and woke up my mom, he called the minister to come.

(Crying.) At first, my dad wouldn't tell us how Carol had died. God love our dad, how he … (Trails off.) When my dad said he wasn't going to tell us, I said, "You know dad, that's okay for right now. But at some point, I may need to know. I may need to ask you, and you will need to be honest with me."

I assume it was the minister who convinced my parents to see a therapist. I imagine it was maybe two days later, the funeral hadn't been yet, and there were a lot of people at the house. My dad came in the door after having seen the therapist, and he said, "The family needs to come in the living room right now." He continued, "The therapist told me I have to tell you how Carol died." And he just told us. He did it that way because he knew, if he waited at all, he wouldn't be able to do it.

I'm glad he shared it. Because even having shared it, none of us could carry that burden for him. But at least we know. It's important to know what happened.

Carol had always been this incredibly joyful, positive, optimistic, energetic, and creative soul. She was just a vibrant being. Her death was hugely shocking.

I had gone through periods of depression — when my first boyfriend broke up with me, or I didn't know my career path in college, and you're *supposed to know*. But suicide had never even entered the realm of possibilities.

I think about . . . (Trails off while crying.) I have a lot of compassion for how much Carol must have been struggling. I knew it on some level, but it was mighty how much she was struggling.

What was helpful for you in dealing with Carol's loss?

Several of the gymnasts from Carol's team came to our house after the funeral and told stories about her that we didn't know. The stories were fun and indicative of who she was as a person in the world: that silly creative way she had.

Some things I learned are basic, such as everyone grieves differently. For the most part, our family did a pretty good job of being there for each other. I felt supported anyway. It was harder for my mom and dad. Men and women don't process things the same way.

Also, people who have never been through anything like that will sometimes say just the most outrageous things. You know in your head, in the place where you're a better person, you know that they mean well. But what they're saying is so misguided that it's like being slapped. People feel like they need to say something. Saying "I'm sorry" is enough. One woman I worked with came up and — without asking how I was doing — said, "You know, something good comes out of everything." I was standing at a table, and my hands were resting on the back of a chair at this table. I remember thinking, "Don't take your hands off the chair. Don't take your hands off the chair." Because I knew if I did, my hands were going to go right around her neck. I wanted to say, "You don't get it. There's nothing good enough on this planet that can happen that will make this okay." If God came down right now, and I saw his very being, and he said, "Your sister's all right," that *still* wouldn't make it okay.

While the first week was tremendously difficult, it wasn't until the anniversary of her death a year later — starting the whole month before — that we all went through a new wave of grief and coming to acceptance. You've gone through all the seasons, the birthday, the holidays, and all those things, and the person is still really gone. That's the one thing I try to tell people who have lost someone, whether it's suicide or otherwise: The anniversary of the death and leading up to that anniversary can greatly affect a person.

The first time I kind of felt hope or joy again was two years after she died. That was the year that Garth Brook's 'The Dance" came out and another song, "If Tomorrow Never Comes" about wanting to make sure he told her he loved her. I would be driving and one of those songs would come on, and I would have to pull over and bawl. Then, coming toward Christmas, I'm driving in the countryside heading toward home, and there's a farmhouse with one little lone pine tree with lights on it. I remember looking at that tree and just having a moment of hope. I remember it clearly because I hadn't spontaneously felt something like that in so long. (Crying.)

The other thing I've learned is that time is the great healer. It has been a process of just living each day and finding ways of honoring her memory and also honoring when I'm sad or happy about her. On Carol's birthday and the anniversary of her death we send off balloons to commemorate her. She always really enjoyed balloons, and she desperately wanted to be able to fly. (Laughs.) On the 25th anniversary of her death, mom and I let balloons go by the river.

Just a year ago my dad asked if everybody would write a memory about Carol. We had an email exchange throughout the family. This exchange took place over 25 years later! It was sweet. I was glad to do that, and it surprises me that none of us thought of that sooner. But it was really helpful.

Anything else you found helpful?

I did research on suicide and athletes and how there is such a propensity for athletes to succumb to suicide. They've grown up doing this sport, and it's their whole identity. Also, there's the perfectionist part. Then, they graduate college and what are they supposed to do with all that? It has been their identity for years.

When I was working as an athletic trainer in South Dakota, I was dealing with athletes at one of the high schools, and every athlete I saw was telling me, "I'm really worried about Tony," and I said, "Why are you worried about him?" They'd say, "He's really down, and he's depressed, and saying things he wouldn't normally say." I said, "Well, I'll see him while I'm here today." The students said, "No, he didn't come to school today." So, the guidance counselor and I went out to his house and saw him and talked to him. We asked him what he was dealing with and how bad it was, whether he'd had any thoughts about suicide.

Most people think that if they ask someone if they are suicidal, it will put the thought in their head. You're never putting the thought in their head. And if they are thinking about it, you've now given them permission to talk about it. Whereas, if you don't bring it up, it's still this secret, this hush-hush sort of thing. When I'm dealing with someone who is depressed or someone I have concern for, I start a little more gently, like, "Do you care if you wake up tomorrow?" But what came from seeing

Tony and the outpouring of concern for him is that I ended up doing a talk with the whole school population about suicide, and what signs you look for, and what to do if you are concerned for somebody.

What are the signs of depression and suicide?

The person is obviously sad and down. More often than not, they start taking less interest in life in terms of taking care of themselves and attending to the pieces of his or her life. The person may not shower or change clothes and may not care if their living space is clean. They tend to withdraw. It's no longer important to be social or be with people. Someone who is suicidal will say there's no hope. They feel hopeless. The other piece, if you were to encounter someone like that, is that sitting and talking to him or her for a few minutes is not a bad start. It's not wrong. But it's not where it should end. It ends by getting the person to a counselor or hospital emergency room because people with training know what to do. Some people might say something about suicide just for attention, but wow, you can't take that chance. If you can't get into the room or reach the person, call 911.

It's also important to know that depression can hit anyone. It wasn't just my family saying, "Carol was the last person we ever would have thought." Everybody was saying that: The church community, the athletes, and all her friends. It really can be anybody. Honest to goodness, she was a light being on this planet. Not only had Carol known joy, but she had also been the source of joy. Her death was completely unexpected.

What is your favorite memory of Carol?

The gymnasts had taken a flight for a meet at another college. While waiting to board, Carol set about tearing pieces of paper out of a notebook and writing numbers on them. She gave the girls on the team these sheets of paper, and as guys walked by, they would hold up their numbers — like they used to score in gymnastics before it was all computerized. (Laughs.) It got to be such a thing that, sometimes, when the guy realized what was happening, he'd walk back again and do it a little differently. I can just see some guy walking past and saying, "What do you mean I'm 5.6? Here, let's do this thing again." (Laughs loudly.) She not only got all of her teammates involved in this, she got all the people in the airport doing it. That was her essence. That was how she was.

What has helped with your healing?

About a week after Carol died, I had this vivid dream. I saw Carol, and we ran to each other, and she did this thing she would do quite often. She jumped up on me and threw her arms and legs around me like a monkey. (Softly crying.) That dream was such a huge source of comfort to me. It still is. I know with my whole heart that she was letting me know she's all right.

My Aunt Jean says that after Carol died she woke up and just felt Carol's presence in the room. She didn't see her, but she got the message: Carol was doing well, and that she was okay.

I didn't see a counselor for two years after Carol died. I find that amazing to this day. I have a friend who has a PhD in counseling, and she kept saying, "Wow, that sounds like something you'd want to talk to a therapist about." No judgment, no pressure. Just saying it like she had never said it before until it finally registered with me. I was talking about something I was angry about, and she said, "You know, Lori, this is something you might generally get angry about, and you have a right to be angry. But you're way angrier than you would normally be. You may want to see a therapist about that because it may have to do with Carol." I heard her that time.

That's the first time I'd ever had counseling. It was so helpful. The biggest thing that came out of it for me was when I was talking to the therapist about Carol's friend knowing about the prior suicide attempt. The therapist said, "Lori, you're going to keep finding out more things. More and more things will come out from her journals or stories from friends about her. At the end of the day, it's not going to help you understand it or what was happening to her any better." She said, "You just have to accept because none of the information makes her less dead."

There's no understanding it. As human beings, we always want to understand. That piece of advice, more than anything, really helped me.

(Crying.) I always find it amazing that the hurt and the missing can be so strong. I believe she's in a better place, and I'm glad she's not suffering. Clearly, she was suffering. One of the things that is hard for me is that I don't feel like I should get so emotional and sad about it because I'm not sad for her, I'm sad for me.

Are there any religious or spiritual paths that helped you?

I did a workshop through the Foundation for Shamanic Studies. I became part of a drumming circle, and a core group of seven of us stayed consistent with it. I also attended a workshop every other Saturday. We were learning to tune in and find information. For instance, "What did Hummingbird (a power animal in Shamanism with the ability to heal and bring special messages of joy, love, timelessness, and happiness) have to teach us?" And so on.

Drumming for me is a beautiful way to center and pray. I feel very connected to my drum. We call it a Shamanic Path because we don't know what else to call it. The shamans were the healers. That's what I use it for. I've done sessions where I get information shamanically, depending on what the person wants to know or what his or her concerns are. Pretty much anytime there's drumming now I hear chants. There are two or three songs that come back. I've sung them several times now. Not words, as I know them. A lot of people get caught up in, "I wonder what it means?" That part isn't important to me. I *feel* what it means. I don't need to know what the words are.

That's how it's been along my Shamanic Path. I don't have to know.

Dona M. Robinson (daughter, suicide)

"With grief, you just keep going through the layers. It's amazing how many there are." — After speaking with Lori Robinson about her sister's suicide, she suggested I talk to her mother, Dona. I met Dona at her home. A petite woman in her 70s, Dona is incredibly vibrant with bright, blue eyes and short, white hair.

I was born in South Dakota and married Dean Robinson. All four of our children were born in South Dakota: Lori Lynn, Gail Rae, Carol Ann, and William Paul (Bill). We lived on a ranch for about seven years.

Dean went from being a rancher to a stockbroker. During that process, we moved to Minnesota and then Illinois. Carol passed away while we were living in Champaign-Urbana (Ill).

[I ask Dona about the loss of her daughter Carol. There is a long pause. She wants me to explain why I am writing the book. I tell her I want to share people's stories of loss and what helped with their healing. She makes us a cup of tea and then continues].

What I want to tell you is different from the questions you are asking. When someone in our culture dies, we want to smooth things over. Everyone's focus is to encourage the grieving person to get over it. They want to say something to placate the situation. People want reassurance, and they want to hear the grieving person say, "I'm okay. I'm moving on." And so, we — the grievers — make "moving on" our project. The focus becomes: "How do I move on?" (Crying.) I had good friends. I had tennis buddies. I had walking buddies. They were making sure I kept walking and kept playing tennis. It was a distraction. The purpose was to distract me from my grief.

My grief was so intense. I could hardly breathe for a whole week. My entire body shut down. A friend had been coming over, making sure we had food and checking in on the kids. I couldn't eat. I couldn't swallow. Finally, she said, "All right. We've had enough of you not eating. You either eat by tomorrow, or I'm taking you to see a doctor." Someone told me about a massage therapist who was pretty amazing. I called him to see if I could get in because I didn't want to see a doctor. He said, "No, I'm booked. I can try to get you in to see someone else, but first I need to know a bit about you so I know who to put you with." I told him my daughter had just taken her life. He responded by saying, "I'll see you at 3 o'clock." After the massage, I went home and ate a meal. The massage opened up places in my body that weren't breathing. (Crying.)

I took care of myself by connecting with my friends and being physically active. I would get these phone calls from friends or acquaintances, and I began to recognize a pattern. It was usually someone I hadn't connected with in a long time, and it was always someone who had experienced serious depression. They wanted to talk about it, and I wanted to learn about it. I started to realize that I didn't understand depression, which is what my daughter Carol had suffered from.

My sister came over to our house, and we sat down on the couch. She looked at me and said, "Dona, our mother was depressed." We had grown up with a mother who would shut herself away in her room for weeks at a time with dark curtains over the windows. My focus became trying to understand Carol's depression. Carol seemed to be the antithesis of depression. She loved to make people laugh. But I had seen a change in her, and we had talked about the fact that she was struggling. I tried to understand, to make sense of it. I allowed people to take care of me and appreciated it greatly. I filled my life with a variety of things. But, I didn't really grieve like it's possible to grieve.

Are there any religious or spiritual practices you found helpful?

I had been very active in the church. The minister came to our house when Dean called him the night Carol died. I was also a member of a Women's Bible Study Fellowship; it was fundamentalist Christianity. If you're divorced, you can't be in the group. It's also considered a severe sin if you take your own life. I could not let those teachings influence what I understood and believed about Carol. The incident with Carol drove me away from the church. God was always there, but not the church. Not the teachings. I believe in honoring an all-powerful omniscient presence in the universe that is centered in the heart.

Dean and I eventually divorced. We took different paths. At the time, I wanted to talk about Carol, and he did not. We were both seeing a counselor. The counselor said, "You will each grieve in your own way."

Have you felt any connection to Carol since her passing?

We flew her ashes to South Dakota where Dean's parents have a family plot. On the way, we saw a sunset and moonrise out of opposite sides of the airplane. Later, when Gail was flying home, she was thinking about her sister Carol and wanted to know how Carol was. The words came to Gail very clearly, "Know that I am happy." And that's just the way Carol would have said it.

Carol has also watched out for her brother Bill. One time he was driving on a motorcycle, coming back from the East Coast, and he was wearing a trench coat. It was at night and dark. He felt himself falling asleep. The belt from his trench coat had wrapped around the axel. Suddenly, the belt tore off. It jerked him awake, and he awoke with this clear image of Carol in front of him. I firmly believe Carol helped keep him stay alive that night.

Was there anything you found helpful with your grieving?

With grief, you just keep going through the layers. It's amazing how many there are. My friend Norma, I'll always remember her words. She said, "I wish I could crawl inside you and put a salve on all the places that are hurting." There was something about that I have never forgotten.

Carol's death was 27 years ago. I have been meeting with this incredible counselor. He's an ordained minister and has his PhD in counseling. His first words to me were: "How are you feeling?" I thought about it and I said, "Part of the time I'm feeling anxious. Then, I feel worried too." He was sitting at this huge desk that extended almost the entire length of his arms. He put one finger at one end of the desk and said, "I'm going to make a line across this desk. This is the far past over here, and I'm going to reach over to the future at the other end. And when I get back to the middle of the desk, we're in present time." (Pauses.) He explained that when you start going back from present, you tend to be worried. Worried that what happened before might happen again. And when you go forward into the future, you become anxious about those things that haven't happened that might happen.

I had been teaching yoga for about 10 years. I said, "So, I have to practice what I teach?" (Laughs.) I opened every yoga class with, "The word yoga means the union of the mind, the body, the spirit. You're only doing yoga when you're in the present moment." It was an amazing insight that I could be saying that three or four times a day and not practicing it.

I told the counselor, "It's hard for me to let go." (Crying.) I can't even talk about it. The counselor asked, "Why do you think that is?" In a flash, I realized it was because of the loss of my daughter Carol.

I started to cry, the way I'm crying now, and he said, "You need to go see Sobonfu Somé." She is woman healer from Africa who holds grief rituals. I went home and looked it up on the Internet, and she was coming to my town. Talk about synchronicity!

In the first part of Sobonfu's retreat we spent time getting acquainted. The next day we built altars. During the evening session, someone held space for those who were grieving — like being a loving container around that grief energy. The following morning we were processing and Sobonfu said, "This was a quiet group. If you're really grieving, you're getting your voices into it." It occurred to me that during the prior evening's session, there had been a time when I wanted to scream. (Crying.)

The night Carol died, I remember Dean came and woke me up. He is the one who found Carol. I had been asleep. He said Carol was in the garage. I got up and headed in that direction. He stopped me at the dining room table and said, "I'm not going to let you go in there." The ambulance was already there. I can remember taking ahold of a chair with my hands; probably if I'd tried, I could have broken it. I wanted to start screaming, but I knew that if I started I might never stop. (Crying.) So, I didn't start.

During the retreat, the memory of that night came back to me. I felt like I wanted to start screaming. But I just couldn't. Finally, I owned up to Sobonfu what I had experienced. She said, "Well, why didn't you scream?" I said, "The group had been very quiet; I didn't want to be the only one screaming." (Laughs.) The women on either side of me took my hands, and said, "If you will start, we will join you. When you're ready, go to the altar and we will be with you." And that's what we did. (Nods her head appreciatively.)

These women didn't even know me! Yet, I was free to fully grieve.

CHAPTER 3

CARETAKING

*"When you can think of yesterday without regret and
tomorrow without fear, you are near contentment."*

— SOURCE UNKNOWN

May you be a source of healing in the world ~

Being a primary caretaker for a person who is dying is extremely challenging, even more so if there are disputes with family members or with a loved one regarding treatment decisions. Healing grief in these circumstances may be further exacerbated if unresolved grievances exist after the loved one's passing.

My daughter recently told me a story that her professor shared in class. Various versions of this tale exist — sometimes cited as originating from a Harvard professor, sometimes originating from a psychologist, and sometimes originating from a business lecturer. (As best I can tell, the original source is unknown). In the story, a lecturer who is teaching stress management holds up a glass of water. Everyone expects to be asked the "half empty or half full" question. Instead, the instructor inquires, "How heavy is this glass of water?" Students call out different answers, such as 8 oz. or 16 oz. The teacher then replies, "The absolute weight doesn't matter. It depends how long I hold it." While presented in a variety of contexts, this story serves to remind us that the longer we carry something, the heavier it starts to feel.

Most of us can manage to set down our daily glass of worries without too much trouble. Caretaking for a dying loved one, though, usually includes additional stress that one person may be singlehandedly carrying for months or years. A glass filled to the brim with caretaking obligations is nearly impossible to hold without ample support from friends or family members. The person who accepted the caretaking responsibilities might also need to find ways to empty the glass of any resentment that built up during the caretaking period.

The individuals in this section highlight the complexity involved when grappling with this added aspect of the grief process. As Joe (who cared for his mother) points out, *"If you are the caregiver, just know that you are going to be the recipient of misplaced anger. ... As best as you can, know that the only person you need to answer to is yourself and the person you are caring for."* With awareness, we can learn how to better support those who step into the caretaking role for a dying loved one. We can also practice greater compassion for ourselves if we took on those responsibilities.

Releasing any disappointment between the caretaker and the loved one is likewise valuable. Tom (who cared for his father) made peace with his father — *after* his father passed away. He says, *"I went to the chapel, and I had a conversation with my dad. I told him that I knew we pushed each other's buttons over the years, but I missed him and loved him, and I hoped he realized I did the best I could, even if it wasn't perfect."*

Despite the many challenges, wonderful gifts can come with caretaking. Summer (who lost the man who raised her) says, *"I wouldn't trade the last three or four months with my dad for the world. When people know they're going to die, there's a part of them that loses their inhibitions and fear. They kind of tell you how it is, and how they are. Take it for what it's worth."*

⊨≍╫ ╫≍⊨

A Heavy Load to Carry

Joseph Mooradian (mother, cancer)

"You never hear anybody talk about the caregiver." — Born in Canada, Joseph now lives with his spouse, Patrick Mullaney, in Miami, Florida. A former professional dancer, Joseph now works as a real estate broker. His mother (Mary Monahan) died of lung cancer. During her illness, Joseph acted as a primary caretaker. He recently turned 50 and has one older sibling, Joyce.

My mom and dad met at a party. My dad and a friend came over to Detroit from Canada for the party. My mom is from Michigan, and she and one of her girlfriends were there. Then, when my parents got married, my mom moved to Canada with my dad. That's where I was born. Later, my dad got laid off from the company where he worked, and they moved back to the United States. They eventually divorced.

My mom's health declined after she had a bad car accident. She and her friend were very fortunate the way the car accident worked out. Mom had her seatbelt on, but her friend in the passenger seat didn't. The car hydroplaned and then turned upside down. Mom was upside down, but the seatbelt kept her safely in her seat and kept her from being killed. The passenger side was completely crushed. Fortunately, her friend didn't have her seatbelt on and ended up in the backseat. She was unharmed, too.

At the time, I was dancing for Hubbard Street Dance Company in Chicago. My mom was telling me in a phone conversation about the accident and saying she was fine, but I could tell in her voice that she was not okay. The car accident started a traumatic, emotional breakdown. She went through all these emotions that had been pent up for years. I started hearing stories from her childhood that I had never heard before. It was all flooding to the surface.

She got diagnosed with COPD (chronic obstructive pulmonary disease) and got treated for adult asthma. They put her on steroids, and it was like she was on uppers. To counter that effect, they put her on sleeping pills that were like horse tranquilizers. And then that would have the opposite effect, and you couldn't get her awake. It was like a yo-yo. She suffered from serious depression, which went on for about five or six years. She was diagnosed as bi-polar, but it was likely drug-induced bi-polar.

Then, she got diagnosed with lung cancer.

I had just finished touring with a dance show in New York. She was in the hospital for what I thought was asthma or pneumonia. She called and said she wanted me to come home. She asked my sister to come as well. That's when she told us about the lung cancer.

I remember sitting at the table when she told my sister Joyce, my spouse Patrick, and me. We were all sitting there, along with one of her friends. Even during the drive there I had a feeling that I knew what the news was going to be — not specifically — but I had this weird feeling. From the moment she told us, I remember thinking, "Oh, this is how she is going die." She had been struggling for so long with the depression and had reached a point, a year prior, where she was catatonic. My sister and I had tried to take care of her, but it was far more difficult because mom had been unresponsive. When she was sitting across the table from us, I could see it in her eyes: She was back. It felt like my mom was there, as opposed to this other ghost of a person she had been for the last few years. Our relationship had gotten kind of testy over those years. Ironically enough, after she got the cancer diagnosis, the depression went away, and her personality came back.

She told us she had a very advanced, serious stage of lung cancer. I guess there are different types of lung cancer. She had the terminal one. We met with oncologists and immediately decided to pursue a treatment of chemotherapy. Either the first one or the second treatment was a clinical trial. I don't remember all the details, but we were off to the races. I stayed to take care of her with short trips to New York to pick up clothes or pack a bigger suitcase.

When my mom first started doing her chemotherapy treatment, she did pretty well. The tumor had shrunk considerably. She had radiation later. But the tumor started growing again. I can't remember if she did another bout of chemotherapy again or not. It's all kind of fuzzy. I don't know if that many people die of cancer. Most die from the treatment and from complications that happen because their immune system is completely destroyed by the treatments. When she was doing the chemotherapy, one thing or another would drop, and she'd get very weak. We'd go to the hospital, and they'd put her on IVs, and she'd get stronger again. But it was always that the immune system would get so depleted and weakened that other opportunistic things would happen.

One of the longest experiences of this is when she went to the hospital because her blood pressure was low and her white blood counts were really, really low. She went to the oncology department, and because she wasn't able to eat, they decided to put in a feeding tube. Only, that procedure never healed. As a result, when they tried to feed her, it would come out the opening, and they would take it out. She still couldn't eat because she had to wait for that procedure to heal. She was in the hospital for about five weeks straight and had not eaten any solid food — just ice cubes to suck on. She appeared like this healthy person sitting up in bed, except for the fact that she had tubes coming out of her and couldn't eat.

It was one thing after another. We had specialists who weren't looking at the person holistically; they just focused on their one little specialty. That kind of treatment struck me as being no different than 30 or 40 years ago when my grandmother died of lung cancer. There was also a similar story with my partner's father. The hospital would simply follow their protocol: "The patient is not eating. Let's try this," without taking into account that a feeding tube might work for someone with a healthy immune system, but it's never going to work for the person with a zero immune system because it's not going to heal normally.

It was 18 months from the initial diagnosis until my mom passed. It all went quickly. However, it was a long time from what they had originally given her, which was six months. I was 39 when she passed.

What helped you during the grief process?

During her cancer, I was the primary caretaker. Patrick was good with me staying to help her. He was there off and on for large chunks of it. Financially, I was able to take off time from work. It all just seemed to work out. Not that it was easy. But if she had passed prior to that, from a drug overdose, severe asthma attack, or pneumonia, I'm sure I would be carrying all kinds of guilt and unresolved issues. That would have been far more difficult. I miss her, but we were 100 percent good with each other.

What helps with my grief is knowing that I did all I could for her. Hopefully, I helped her get through what must have been one of the hardest parts of her life. I still periodically burst into uncontrollable tears when something triggers me. But I know she loved me, and I am sure she knew I felt the same. That gets me through the tough times. Also, knowing I did have so much time with her.

What is your favorite memory of your mom?

I'll tell you one story that just cracked me up. This was when she had been in the hospital for about five weeks. Patrick was there. We got to know every nurse who ever came through the oncology department. One day, there's this new nurse who had on these very unusual glasses, and mom was saying, "Well, those are just beauti-ful glasses, really unique, where did you get those?" The nurse is telling mom the story behind the glasses and mom is saying, "Well, I've just never seen a pair of glasses like those," and going on and on. Finally, the nurse leaves and I said, "Mom, what the hell was your fixation with those crazy-ass glasses?" She says, "I don't know. I always try to find something nice to say, and that's all I could think of." (Laughs.) Patrick and I just fell out laughing.

Another time, one of the nurses had this big, cubic zirconia fake diamond ring. I mean it was gigantic! Mom lit off on that, how beautiful the ring was, "Oh my God, how gorgeous!" and "When I get out of here, you'll have to let me know where you got that." She went the whole nine yards over that ring. The next thing I know, within a couple of days, I come back to the hospital and mom has these gigantic fake diamond earrings on. I'm like, "Where the hell did you get those?" She just sits there and doesn't bother telling me. I'm asking her, "Mom, where did those earrings come from?" Finally, she says, "You know the nurse with the big diamond ring?" I say, "Yeah." And mom continues, "Well, I carried on so much about that ring of hers that she brought in a bunch of stuff, and I had made such a big deal that I had to buy something." (Laughs.) I thought they were a gift. But no, she bought them! Same thing: she'd gone down this path of carrying on. But she wanted that nurse to feel good about herself. (Laughing).

Growing up, there were times we could get each other just laughing hysterically. Once, we were at a movie theatre to see a movie called *Far North*. Jessica Lang and her sister start bickering back and forth. Finally, Jessica Lang says, "If you don't shut up, I'm gonna split your lip." (Laughs.) I don't know why that line struck us as funny but we're in the movie theatre, laughing, crying, and then laughing again because we couldn't stop laughing. There were only five other people in the whole theatre, and they were shushing us! Another time, my sister Joyce was there for this one, too, it was the movie, *What's Up Doc?*, staring Barbara Streisand, Ryan O'Neill, and Madeline Kahn. We were watching it and, again, we all started hysterically laughing at one of the lines. Of course, when mom would really get going, she would pee herself, and then that would get it going even more, and we'd be laughing and yelling at each other to shut up, and then laughing more! Those are some of my favorite memories.

Do you have any religious or spiritual practices that helped?

I have my own spiritual beliefs. However, I don't think any of that helped me through the grieving process. I miss her, and that can't be changed. For a lot people, what goes along with missing is regret or wishing you'd had a chance to say something or to make amends or to resolve an issue you never had a chance to resolve. I don't have that. My thoughts are more about being the primary caregiver.

When you hear the stories on "Oprah" or the talk shows, it's always about the person who is sick: the survivor of a disease or the person who has battled an illness. You never hear anybody talk about the caregiver or the pain, anguish, and anxiety that THEY go through.

What did you find helpful in your role as the caretaker?

I had a friend who lost his mom when he was young. He said that when his mom got sick and then passed, his family imploded. It was basically a lot of misplaced anger, either mad at the person for getting sick or mad at the person for dying and leaving you; and then, not knowing how to deal with those emotions. His story helped me in the caregiving because I also experienced people getting mad at me.

When you're the caregiver, everyone comes at you with advice, or how you should be doing this, or why didn't you do that, or why didn't you call me. The same type of things came up for me with the funeral arrangements as well. Understanding it doesn't lessen the burden it puts you through, but it helps to know it wasn't necessarily personal.

When someone gets sick, it challenges us. I'm going back to your earlier question of what helped me get through the grieving process. When someone close to us gets sick, we as adults have to choose: Okay, how much are we going to do? What are we going to do? Are we going to disrupt our lives to go care for this person? Or not? People may not think about it consciously, but in their subconscious that is what they're wrestling with. They're questioning and getting mad at the caregiver. But they're also not choosing to drop everything and come do it themselves. Their reasons might be, "I have kids" or "I have a husband" or "I have a job." Those are all valid reasons. Nonetheless, that person is choosing *not* to be the caregiver.

Also, people say they love someone and want to help. People say it all the time: "Hey, let me know how I can help. I'll do anything for you. Anything you want." That was one of the things I heard all the time. But when I actually did ask someone for something, and it might not be that big a deal, but man, did they fall short! Suddenly, they just couldn't help or couldn't do what they said they would.

A couple of my relatives came to visit at the hospital, and all I wanted was, "Could you just stay here, in the room with her, for 2 hours so I can go home and shower?" I hadn't showered in 48 hours. That's all I wanted. And they were all, "Yeah, yeah. We got her. We'll take care of it. We're good." And then, my mom had to go to the bathroom. She needed help to get out of bed to use a bedside commode. Then, she was going to need help to clean her up and help getting her back in the bed. Right as I was ready to leave, they were like, "We'll get out of your way here." (Pauses.) They didn't get it — that's when I needed them to step up and do this, and they couldn't.

I have a great empathy now for anyone who is a caregiver. I can see it with Patrick's family. All of his brothers and sisters are taking care of his mom. But the bulk of the duties fall on his oldest sister. His other brothers and sisters have an opinion about what should be done. I just say to Patrick, "You know, that's all nice, but everyone ought to keep their mouths shut because your older sister is the one who is stepping up to the plate."

Unless someone else is willing to step up and share the responsibility, my view is that you have to keep your opinions to yourself, and thank the person who is the caregiver. Whether you like the way they're doing it or not, they're doing it.

Do you have any suggestions for someone reading your story?

If you are the caregiver, just know that you are going to be the recipient of misplaced anger or guilt. As best as you can, know that the only person you need to answer to is yourself and the person you are caring for. That's it. Other people are going to make you think you owe them, too, but you don't. If you're choosing to do it and doing it to the best of your ability, then you only have to answer to yourself and the person you are caring for.

The greatest grief I still feel — and certainly felt at my mom's funeral — was the realization that I would no longer be able to take care of her. That I was no longer needed. And that, perhaps when someone truly needs you, it also means they truly love you. I am no longer able to express my love to her by being there to help her anymore. (Takes a deep breath while sobbing.)

During her cancer, I would spend the night with her anytime she was in the hospital. In a way, I felt like that time was a gift because I did have 18 months with her. It didn't matter whether we talked about anything heavy or deep, or nothing in particular, or if we sat there watching TV together. Just spending time with her and helping her through that ordeal was meaningful. I felt blessed that I could do that for her.

⊷ ⊶

Janet S. Brown (parents, Alzheimer's & dementia)

"The gift that came out of all this is calmness in the middle of storms." — Janet's parents are Phyllis and Fred Brown. She is an only child. Our interview took place on the anniversary of her mother's death. Janet was the primary caretaker for both parents, while also raising her own teenager daughter.

My father was from Southern Illinois, a farming community. My mother was fifth generation from Evansville, Indiana. They met at the Oldsmobile dealership. My father started out there as an automobile mechanic and ended up being a service director. He could take cars apart and put them together. I didn't fully appreciate that skill when I was young. (Laughs.) My mom was a bookkeeper at the dealership. They married in 1953 and were married for over 50 years.

As far as their illnesses, it all started in 1999. I went to New Harmony (Ind.) with my daughter Sarah and my husband. We decided that was a nice place to celebrate the millennium change. They had a big celebration with the newly built, granite labyrinth. I was walking the labyrinth that New Year's Eve. My grandfather had recently died, and I was feeling torn about what I was doing for a living. I was at the crossroads in my 40s trying to figure all that out. I remember just letting go and saying, "Whatever this journey needs to be, I accept."

Shortly after that time in New Harmony, my mother was diagnosed with cancer, and she didn't fare well with that news. I shouldn't judge because how would any of us react if diagnosed with cancer? But my mother really struggled with it, to the point of being ready to give up before she even had treatment. I was trying to fix my mom, and I wasn't paying a lot of attention to my dad because I was so concerned with her. My dad wasn't acting quite right, but I attributed it to stress. My mom did go through all the treatment, but there was a lot of angst in the family. I was traveling a lot to take care of them, and that added stress wasn't helping my own family. As time passed, my mother went into remission, and then, I noticed my dad wasn't getting over his anxiety.

As his behavior got odder, we discovered he had Alzheimer's. Then, my mother decided — coming right out of cancer — that she was going to be his caregiver. There were challenging issues around that decision. I had to get him help as the disease progressed. My father did stay at home with her a while. But as he deteriorated, he went into a nursing home. That sent my mother — physically and mentally — spiraling downhill. It really took its toll on her. He went in the nursing home about a year before he died. I tried to get my mom all the support I could through hospice and counseling, in addition to driving back and forth to be with her. Fortunately, my work was supportive.

My dad died right before Christmas Eve. He had Alzheimer's and then got pneumonia. As soon as my dad passed away, I knew I had to get out of my marriage. I filed for divorce on my 20th wedding anniversary. That was another blow to my mother. I couldn't do it sooner because I knew she was already reeling from the news of my dad's Alzheimer's, and how in the world would she be able to deal with my news of a divorce on top of dealing with my dad?

I also spent a lot of time trying to help my daughter through school and just getting her through all the repercussions of divorce and the damage that had gone on in the family while I was trying to be a caregiver and work fulltime.

Meanwhile, my mother is having all kinds of health issues. She fell and broke a hip, and she had a stroke. She went back and forth from hospitals to rehab centers. I made a choice to bring her closer to where I lived in order to care for her. That was quite the struggle because the whole time she wanted to go home. Her mental health was deteriorating. The doctor finally declared that she had vascular dementia from the strokes and the stress from heart attacks. She went into assisted living for those with dementia. It was impossible for her to stay at my house because she was suffering with all the problems that go along with dementia.

During this time, I am also raising my daughter. She is doing well in high school, growing and thriving. I'm a choir mom, and I'm doing all this stuff as a mom while taking care of my own mother. I also had to take care of all the financial arrangements for my parents that they had never addressed. I had to sell their house. I actually hired a woman who specializes in how to navigate the health care system, sort of like hiring an attorney only for elderly care issues.

My mother took a turn for the worse while my daughter was having her open house for high school graduation. The nursing staff at the hospital took over for the day so I could be at the celebration with my daughter. I just wanted to make that day good.

My mother died the day before my daughter's high school graduation ceremony. She did not die easily. (Sighs.) Her death was an intense struggle. While at the hospital, we disconnected her from everything, and we were able to say good-bye. She could only gargle, not talk clearly because of the strokes. She hadn't eaten in three days and hadn't been conscious. Then, 24 hours before she passed, she opened her eyes and looked at me with the clearest of eyes and clearest voice and asked, "Are you okay?" I said, "Yes, I'm okay Mom." And that's the last thing she said.

I fought like crazy to get her out of the hospital because that was a promise I had made to her. She didn't want to die in the hospital. The ambulance drivers were scared they were going to lose her, and I had to sign a zillion papers to take responsibility if my mother died in the ambulance. From there, I got her back to her room at the nursing home. But, she just had all this agitation: sitting up and laying back down and in tears. This went on from noon until 7 that night. All this angst! Hospice was trying to help her, and she had enough morphine to knock a horse out. She wasn't in pain, just full of anxiety. She finally passed out from all the anxiety and then died peacefully, after she was unconscious. It was extremely hard to watch.

That's definitely not how I want to go out of this world. Her death was such an ordeal! I've really taken that into account. I decided after that process, boy, you better make amends while you're conscious, and you've got your right mind about you. I just want to make sure I'm at peace with who I am and what I believe when I die. I don't want to go out of this world like she did. It was quite a life lesson that night.

So, the very next day, I turn around and it is celebratory because my daughter is graduating, and there are all her friends and the parties. It was the most surreal time, and then to go to a funeral right after that. It was symbolic of what life is all about, really.

When I look back on it, it all started out in New Harmony, when I thought, "Well, I'm going to go on this journey to find who I am and the meaning of life and my role in it." Then suddenly, it's like the stage opened and all these events cascaded.

Is there anything that helped with your healing?

The first thing I did was join the gym. (Laughs.) I thought, "All right, Alzheimer's and vascular dementia. These are two ways I don't want to go." Genetically, I'm going to do all I can to take care of myself: watching the food I eat, my physical activity, and my spiritual alignment. Death is a giant wake-up call to your own mortality. It's also a question of, "What are you doing with the rest of your life?" Honestly, I'm 53 and my mom was 83 when she died. That's not a whole lot more time. What am I doing with my life?

Then, I went on a rampage to get all my legal papers in order so my daughter doesn't have to go through what I did. She is also an only child. I got everything set up so that if I die tomorrow, there's a plan for her. It's hard enough going through the emotional side of losing your parents without having to deal with the logistics of money and bank accounts and selling houses. We don't think about those things enough before we go, we just don't.

Is there anything that helped you cope with your grief?

Luckily, we had a dog come into our lives. Her name is Cindy, and she was an older dog, nine years old. She happened to walk into WTHR, where I work, as the Humane Society dog of the week. It was the weirdest thing. I just decided we needed a dog. I'd always had a dog as a child. So, I adopted this dog Cindy from the Humane Society. We definitely needed her as much as she needed us. I felt her to be extremely helpful after my mother's death.

I was also getting my daughter prepped to leave for college. It's an exciting time, but it's like, "Holy Moses!" I woke up the next day, after I've dropped my kid off to college, to an empty house. Thank goodness for my dog. I have friends, and I have work. It's not like I'm living alone as a recluse. But it was just nice to have my dog there to get over that initial hump of being alone. My daughter is the only family I have left.

I also dove into my art again. I'm pretty productive in my art because all this has given me plenty of material to work with. (Laughs.) It has been a long time since I've had any alone time. I focused more on my job, too. That may not be the healthiest way to cope, but it helped.

Do you have any religious or spiritual practices that helped?

I got more serious about a spiritual practice with meditation. Additionally, I worked hard to figure out — now that I don't have family around — what is my community going to look like? I became involved in an interfaith group at the church, Wisdom Circles, and other activities of that nature. I had to redefine what makes me whole and what makes me healthy so I don't just sit in the house and feel sorry for myself.

I've also had dreams about my mom. Finally, after two years, she spoke to me in one of the dreams. In that dream, my daughter and I were trying to wake my parents so we could tour London. My mother got up and said to me, "Well, we were awake all along, but we wanted to make sure you got rest because you look so tired." That's the first thing she's ever said to me in any dream. I thought what she said was interesting.

Do you have a favorite memory of your parents?

Vacations to the ocean were the best, just walking the beach and looking for shells. My mom taught me an appreciation for the natural world, and my dad was more the active one, out in the ocean swimming. He loved history, and we spent time in the historical areas. Going to Mammoth Cave is also something that goes back several generations in my family.

When I visit these places, I find I'm connected to those good experiences with my family.

Any suggestions for someone going through something similar?

On this journey, there was so much problem solving and anxiety. Yet, the gift that came out of all this is calmness in the middle of storms. For example, there might be craziness at work, and I find I can remain calm and not get caught up in the emotion. It's sort of like: I've already been there and done that. I don't want to go there anymore. It's not to say bad things won't happen, but I don't want to react to it anymore like I used to.

You can read all the Buddhism in the world and all the gurus in the world, but there is something about walking through the journey and just experiencing it. You come out the other side so much more whole than when you went in. That's the gift. It sounds hokey, but it's true. It was also important for me to hear other people's journeys while I was going through mine. With the Wisdom Circle I attend, I might find someone going through something worse or going through something similar and hear how that person handled it — not advice but just telling their stories. That's valuable. You want to run away and just cocoon and not share what you're experiencing. I found that my lifeboat through all of it was having friends. They were incredibly helpful.

Also, staying around joyful things, like when I helped with show choir for my daughter. Being around teenagers and their enthusiasm helps you enjoy life. Even if I felt horrible and had just come from dealing with a challenging conversation with health care providers or dealing with my mom having another stroke, I would arrive at the high school and see all these teenagers looking forward to college and singing and dancing in their competitions. It saved my soul.

A good friend took me on a boat in the middle of the Atlantic Ocean. That was good therapy. (Laughs.) Catch fish, eat it, drink wine, and get my sanity back. Then return to the chaos.

It's been quite the journey. I'm ready to do something else in my life at this juncture. I'm searching for what that is. My daughter is moving on and thriving. She's made it through all this, too.

⊫⊰ ⊱⊨

Thomas Robertson (father, lymphoma)

"I had this fantasy that we would have this heart-to-heart moment when he was dying, and I really wanted that moment. When we had the hospice conversation, I realized I was never going to get that." — *Thomas (Tom) enjoys acting and cooking. He is married to Stephanie, a fabric artist. When Tom's father, Gordon Robertson, became seriously ill, he moved in with Tom and Stephanie. Gordon passed away five years later. For this interview, I met Tom at the City Café restaurant, a local favorite for Saturday morning breakfast. As Tom begins discussing his father, Eric Clapton's song, "Tears in Heaven," plays softly in the background.*

My dad was born in Cincinnati. For most of his career, he worked in sales. Mom had died years earlier from a heart attack.

Dad became ill in his late 60s. I was in grad school. We had to do an internship, and I was doing mine at Playhouse in the Park, which is in Cincinnati. I was living at home with Dad, and Stephanie was going to graduate school in Georgia for her MFA. Dad started having sweats, and he had nodes on the back of neck. He was diagnosed with lymphoma. Lymphoma is a long-term cancer. So, dad was able to live at home.

After graduate school, Stephanie starting working at the Indianapolis Art Center, and I got a job at the Phoenix Theatre (both places in Indianapolis). Over time, while we were living in Indiana, dad started having a series of health issues. Some of it was just a matter of getting older. The big thing was that he developed colon cancer and had to have a colostomy bag. He spent a lot of time in the hospital. With his host of medical issues, we felt it ill-advised for him to be living on his own. At the same time, he was having other age-related issues. For example, we would hear from his neighbors that Gordon was having trouble driving. There was that whole issue of should he even continue driving himself, which was an even tougher discussion than where he was going to live. It was such an emotional issue for him because he had to give up his freedom. There were several times where multiple neighbors would take me aside and express concern that dad shouldn't be driving.

It complicated matters that he would be in the hospital so much. I was working. I would leave work on Friday afternoon and drive over to Cincinnati and be there until Monday night. I was in Cincinnati as much as I was home. I was exhausted, and it couldn't have been doing our marriage any good. Once I started staying over, it became a pattern and a clear expectation, which made it hard to say, "You know, I am only going to be staying a day," or "I'm not coming this weekend."

When we started bringing up, "Dad you can't live by yourself. You either need to be in some sort of assisted living or live with us," he was very resistant. Dad would go to great lengths to not change his situation. He has a younger brother who lives in Cincinnati, and because dad was older he could get his brother to agree to things. After one of dad's hospitalizations, the doctors didn't want him to live by himself. We offered for him to stay with us. But Dad told the doctors, "Well, my brother is going to move in with me temporarily and be the caretaker." And he got his brother to agree to this with everyone. At this point, his brother was in his 70s and lived on the other side of town. Turns out, he never moved in with Dad. He stopped by to visit, which isn't the same thing.

One day I went down for the weekend to visit. It was a Friday afternoon around his birthday. Dad had, at some point, fallen and become disoriented, and his colostomy bag had come off. So, there was urine everywhere, and dad didn't have the strength to raise himself to stand up. The house looked like it had been ransacked. He couldn't remember what had happened. He had been by himself a day and a half. That's when we realized his brother wasn't staying there, and also that dad could bend the truth or outright lie to stay where he wanted.

A couple of months later, I called Dad and didn't get an answer. I wasn't aware of any plans, and he wasn't supposed to be driving. It was worrisome. I tried calling all day. I called Dad's brother and just got a real evasive answer. Finally, Dad called back, several hours later. Turns out, Dad was in the hospital, and he just wasn't going to tell me.

When I went to see him in the hospital, I got Dad and his brother and the medical staff together. Unfortunately, I had to do the, "I'm his next of kin and either I'm involved in this or I'm not. Either you do what I say, or I'm not doing this anymore. I don't have medical authorization; all I do is come down here to clean up messes." Once I said I wasn't coming down anymore to clean up the mess, Dad decided not to stay at home. His options were to move into assisted living, move in with Stephanie and me, or move in with someone else. But if he chose to live on his own, then I was out of it.

Dad was extremely resistant to moving into an assisted living facility because of its association in his mind with nursing homes. We looked at a lot of places that I thought were very good options. They would have been close to his brother and close to a girlfriend he had at the time. He had lived in Cincinnati all his life. He loved watching their sports teams and going to the racetrack at River Downs. He could have still done that. I thought it made a lot a sense, but he hated institutional living. So, he chose to live with us instead.

For the first couple of years, he was down in Cincinnati as much as he was in Indianapolis because he had a girlfriend there. We decided to buy a house that had a better layout for someone with an aging parent, with a bathroom and bedroom on the first floor. Stephanie and I had our bedroom and bathroom on the second floor, which gave everyone more privacy. At that time, we merged the households. It wasn't just him living with Stephanie and me. It was more like: This is *our* house.

Gradually, his health got worse. There weren't any big dramatic events for a long time, just a general decline.

Eventually, Dad's physician — the oncologist for the chemo-therapy — said, "There's no point continuing the chemo." The cure was worse than the disease at that point. The doctor said it was time to think about hospice. Concurrently to that, we had a conversation with our neighbor. The houses are relatively close, and our neighbor came over and said, "Do you two realize how sick your dad is during the day?" The neighbor could hear dad vomiting following chemotherapy all the way in the house next door. When the oncologist recommended ending chemotherapy, we weren't surprised. That advice seemed consistent with every-thing we knew.

But Dad went to great lengths to deny what was happening. He didn't agree with ending chemotherapy because he understood what entering a hospice program meant. The expectation was that he would die in six months. He really fought it, and he expected Stephanie and me to find other treatment therapies. His girlfriend wanted him to go to Mayo Clinic, like there was a silver bullet that would fix it. Dad refused to have anything to do with hospice. Stephanie and I were saying to him, "Well, we have to deal with this." Stephanie told me, "You need to have a heart to heart with your dad."

So, one Sunday I stayed home from church to talk to Dad. We sat down to talk. I wanted to help him understand that he needed to enter the hospice program. Stephanie and I knew people involved with hospice care and had contacts through the agency. Dad's reaction was, "Wow, you and Stephanie really can't wait to get your hands on my money." That was the extent of the conversation, and that was his response while sitting at our dining room table. It was devastating. The fact of the matter was that the hospital wouldn't treat him anymore, and how any of us felt about that was ultimately irrelevant.

Stephanie and I did connect with hospice and set that up. They had people come by, and dad would tell them to leave. He didn't use any of the services they offered. Our minister, who is really great guy, made a couple of visits with Dad. Dad was very cursory and made it clear that he didn't want to continue meeting with him. Dad did connect with an odd assortment of people who helped us. We could never predict which people he would click with. A woman from our church would come over during the day when we were at work, and Dad got along great with her. We had other people stop by to help, such as our friends Pam and Judy who are lesbians. Dad was very conservative and did not like gay people, as a concept. But he adored Pam and Judy. They could visit him at his worst. He was very protective of his appearance; if he wasn't looking good, he didn't want people to see him. Yet, Pam and Judy could come over any time, and he had a great time with them. But most people he did not like.

Even while going through hospice care, Dad wasn't in really bad shape until the last week. When the end came, it came quickly and was very noticeable. We knew it was only a matter of time.

By Friday of that week, he couldn't eat or go to the bathroom. We knew it was days rather than weeks left. On Saturday, he wasn't eating, but he was nauseous. We arranged through hospice for medicine to help make the nausea better. There was a place that said they would deliver the medicine. I offered to run up and get it if it would be faster, and they said, "No, no." But they kept getting our address wrong. All day long, I was on the phone screaming with people, saying I could pick it up and them saying, "No, we'll deliver it." We had this daylong battle. It was literally midnight before it got delivered.

Dad was near death when the medicine finally arrived. And it was suppositories! We were in his room at midnight giving him suppositories. It was just the worst day. We sat with him for a while and then went to bed. He died overnight. We found him the next morning. We were feeling like, "Well, we were here with him, and we were the last people he talked to."

Then, we found out that, actually, we weren't the last people he talked to. After he died, we got our phone bill. There was an out-of-state phone bill for a call at 2 o'clock in the morning. We were wondering who would place a call at 2 a.m. We knew it wasn't us because we were asleep, and we thought it couldn't be Dad because he was dying. So, we called the number, and it was an out-of-state bookie. That's the last thing Dad did before he died. He called a bookie to get the horse race results, which seemed very appropriate. (Laughs.) His last day, Gordon went out doing what he really loved, which was betting on the horse races.

What helped you cope with your grief?

Because Dad's illness and death had been gradual, I thought I was handling it well. But about six months after he died, I fell into this horrible depression. It was a great sense of loneliness because I'm an only child, and both my parents had died. I have a small extended family I am not close to. So, I had this sense of being alone, except for Stephanie. I thought if anything happened to her, I would be one of those people eating on a hotplate on Christmas Day, alone in an apartment. Obviously, my relationship with Stephanie is conditional. What if Stephanie comes home and tells me she's leaving, and I'm completely alone in the world? I just felt that tremendously and got overwhelmed.

I ended up seeing a therapist. I went to a number of sessions, and her advice was that I needed a sense of closure because I hadn't heard from Dad what I wanted to hear before he died.

I remember a TV commercial for some laundry detergent where this woman's father moved in with them, and he was rigid and uptight with her rambunctious family, but because she used the right kind of laundry detergent, he came to accept and appreciate their odd lifestyle. I really expected that kind of thing. I thought Dad would come to live with us and ... (Trails off.)

As I got older, there were more things about my life he didn't like and didn't respect. When I went to college and got out in the world, my interests changed. I became more liberal, and Dad was very conservative. That could be a source of tension. I left the church I was raised in, and I don't think Dad was comfortable with that, although he never went to mass after my mom died. But the fact that I was no longer Catholic was an issue for him. But I hoped that Dad would come live with us and meet our quirky, artsy friends and come to respect the choices I made. Only, he never expressed that sentiment, at least not to me. At times, he could say some hurtful things.

I had this fantasy that we would have this heart to heart moment when he was dying, and I really wanted that moment. When we had the hospice conversation, I realized I was never going to get that. It was a real eye-opener. Our relationship was consistent to the end. It was unrealistic of me to expect things to alter. It's not that we had a horrible relationship; he just didn't express emotions easily. Some of that was generational, and some of that was the kind of person he was. He thought writing a check could solve a lot of stuff. I saw him coming to live with us as having a multigenerational family, which seemed normal to me. Dad saw it as a financial transaction, with the decision being, "I can go live in an institution and pay those people to take care of me, or I can keep the money in the family." He was very generous, but it was ultimately a financial transaction, and that didn't dawn on me for a long time.

I took my therapist's advice and went out to Washington Park cemetery, which isn't where dad is buried — he is in Cincinnati — but I went to their chapel. I had a conversation with him. I told him that I knew we pushed each other's buttons over the years, but I missed him and loved him and hoped he realized I did the best I could, even if it wasn't perfect. I found it helpful to have that as our ending.

Do you have any suggestions for others in a similar situation?

I don't regret having my dad live with us, even though it didn't end up the way I wanted. He wasn't a bad person despite the bad anecdotes.

It's important that both people are committed to having someone move in with them. With Dad, I would be the bad cop and Stephanie would be the good cop. I remember I was really concerned about Dad's diet all the time. One day, I made this nice, healthy dinner with vegetable soup. It was a cold wintery day, and Dad didn't have much of an appetite. Two things Dad loved were White Castle hamburgers and shakes from Arby's. While I was cooking, Stephanie had stopped and gotten that for him on her way home, and I was really pissed because I had made this vegetable soup, and Dad needed to take care of his health. Stephanie said, "He's dying, let him eat what he wants to eat." Now, her mom is sick, and she's become the bad cop, and I'm the good cop. Maybe that's a function of dealing with your own parents. It's easier to be the relaxed one when it's not your parent.

Do you still feel his presence?

When Dad was alive, we had to raid his bedroom and drawers because we would find silverware in there. We'd be running short of spoons and wonder, "Where are all the spoons going?" Then we'd find a stash in Dad's room. Periodically, if he dropped a glass or plate, he'd hide it in his sock drawer. So, after Dad died, every once in a while we'd notice, "Wow, we're short on forks. Where did they go?" And Stephanie would attribute it to Dad's ghost. (Laughs.)

I have to admit, the exact day of his death is not important to me. The date that's really important — and this happens every year — is watching the Kentucky Derby. Dad loved horse racing. Growing up, I had cousins in Kentucky, and we would always go down to their place for a Kentucky Derby party to watch the race. Now that he's gone, even though neither Stephanie nor I care all that much for horse racing, we watch the Kentucky Derby. When the first horse steps onto the track and the band plays, "My Old Kentucky Home," we both sit there and sob. Every year, we'll watch the Derby with our Kleenex. Perhaps, that's not the most traditional memorial, but it's ours.

Summer Hudson (non-biological father, cancer)

"Energy can neither be created nor destroyed. Energetically, he is still here somewhere." — Summer is a hairstylist and recovery clinician. She is in her 30s. Originally from Ocala, Florida, she lost the non-biological father who raised her, Terry Hudson, to cancer and disease complications. She has a younger brother Chase and other half-siblings. She lost her biological father when she was 10.

My mom and biological father never married. It's a strange story. My mom dated my biological father, Joe, and ended up getting pregnant.

He told her he loved her, and they would get married. He worked in sales and was out of town a lot. When she hadn't heard from him for a while, she sent him a Thanksgiving card. She got a letter back from his wife. My biological dad was already married, and my mom didn't know!

Then, my mom then met Terry Hudson. They hit it off and got married. Terry raised me from age one. Soon after, my mom and Terry had my brother Chase. That is my family. My biological father allowed Terry to adopt me when I was two years old. When I refer to "my dad," I am referring to Terry.

When I was 10, Joe passed away from lymphoma cancer. He had a son, who is older than me and is my half-brother. Somehow, my half-brother located me and told me about Joe's death. His death was hard for me to grasp. I hadn't known Terry wasn't my dad. My parents said they told me, but I don't remember. It was a lot to understand as a 10 year old.

The year after Joe's death I started having behavior problems in school. I don't remember being consciously aware that his death was affecting me. But it's definitely interesting that right afterward is when my behavior was off the charts. I had the attitude of, "You can't tell me what to do." Maybe it was just too much to process. My half-brother took me to meet all my cousins and aunts and uncles. Here I am, meeting this whole entire family that has already grown up without me. It was a lot of cheek pinching and, "Oh my God, you look just like your father." It was a weird sensation when you don't even know what your father looks like.

After Joe died, I felt no connection to him. I don't even think about it unless I visit that side of my family. It's probably because I had absolutely no contact whatsoever with him when he was alive. My mom did take me to see a counselor. She never gave up on me. I don't know if Joe's death was the reason I was rebellious, but it happened.

The death that impacted me more was my dad Terry's passing. Terry got sick when I was a senior in high school. He fought cancer for eight years.

Early on, I had a dream with my dad's friend, Kean Randall. Kean had passed away from Agent Orange, which greatly affected my dad. I had this vivid dream that I was in my parents' bedroom and everything was gone. There was no furniture except for the bed. I was sitting on the edge of the bed, and a light came in from the ceiling. All of the sudden, Kean was sitting next to me. He said, "Your dad is really sick, and he doesn't know it. I want you to tell your dad that Kean said go to the hospital. It's bad." I must have looked confused because he said, "This isn't a dream. What I'm telling you is really important. I'm going to wake you up now, and I need you to tell your dad."

I woke up, and my parents were at work. The first thing I did was telephone my dad. He didn't answer. But I was so upset that I called my mom. I said, "You don't understand, this is not just a dream." She said, "Well, you know how your father is." Terry's personality was very steak and potatoes. He's from Georgia. He picked tobacco as a kid and worked in a slaughterhouse. She said, "I'll talk to him, but I don't think he'll go." Nothing happened. He wouldn't go to the doctor. Then, he was hit in the back with a bulldozer at work. It wasn't that he got hit hard, but the pain was so excruciating. Well, he went to the hospital, and they found cancer in his kidney. I'm guessing Kean was like, "Okay fine, you're not gonna go to the hospital. I'll knock you over with a bulldozer." (Laughs.)

Terry got his kidney taken out. They did chemo and radiation. He went into remission for a bit. This kind of cancer travels up. So, then it went to one of his lungs. They did a surgery to take a lower part of his lung out. He had tubes and everything. It was pretty bad. He got a spot on his other lung. I don't know if they did surgery on that or not. I do know he went to get Reiki done, which was odd for my dad. I never realized my dad would consider something like energy healing. The cancer changed him. He became more open, willing to try anything.

My dad was stern when I was a kid. Rules-with-an-iron-fist kind of thing. I got my share of paddles. It wasn't until he got sick that I realized my rebellion stuff didn't matter anymore. And he went from being a guy you couldn't really have a conversation with to being very caring and loving. He was energetic and happy. It was like the cancer made him reassess things. Before the cancer, my parents were on the verge of divorce. I believe the cancer saved their marriage.

When my dad first got sick, it was my younger brother Chase who really stepped up to the plate and helped my dad. Then, we kind of switched roles and traded off. For a couple of years, my dad was doing chemo. It was funny, because he would say, "If it doesn't take my hair out, I don't want to take it." I would ask, "Why?" And he would reply, "If it doesn't take my hair, it's not strong enough."

Eventually, the cancer spread to his spinal cord and a small part in his brain. They did a crazy operation where they went into his spinal cord and tried to remove everything. They were able to get a majority of the cancer. They said it would leave him partially paralyzed on his right leg. He refused to buy that. He dragged his leg, but he taught himself to walk.

One story my mom told: My dad was extremely sick, and he *looked* really sick. There was a little girl at the hospital that had leukemia. My mom said my dad burst into tears because he was more upset about the little girl than himself. He was just heartbroken. He said, "Look how sick she is." My mom said, "Are you kidding? Look how sick you are." (Laughs.)

As for the piece in his brain, the doctors said there wasn't much they could do; they would keep watching it. My dad ended up getting spinal cancer again, only this time it wrapped around his spinal cord and was inoperable. My mom contacted one of the nation's top institutes, and my parents used all their savings to fly there and get a second opinion. The doctors did all this research on him and found out there was nothing they could do.

Not long after that, my dad got an infection in his leg. It was MRSA (Methicillin-resistant Staphylococcus aureus). The doctors cut it out so it wouldn't spread. But they forgot to put in the vacuum or suction thing until too late. He got an infection. Then, he got necrotizing fasciitis in his leg, the flesh-eating disease. That's pretty much when everything went south.

At this point, he needed total care. He was paralyzed from the belly button down, he lost all function in his hands, and he was bedridden. We took him home. My mom and I took shifts feeding him and caring for him. We had to clean his wound, and it just got bigger and bigger. My dad refused hospice. He said, "I won't go out that way." His dignity, maybe, I don't know.

We got a lift and figured out how to get him out of bed and into a wheelchair. I'll never forget the first time my dad went outside. He hadn't been outside in maybe eight months. He could still push things with his fingers, and he was just so excited that he took off down the street yelling, "Woo-hoo!" We couldn't catch up. Even as sick as he was, he had the best time.

He liked to sit in the sun. We tried that a couple of times. Then, he started growing this fungus in his leg. The necrotizing fasciitis had eaten almost down to the bone. I've never seen somebody in such excruciating pain. He never complained, not once. He never said, "Why me?" He would just say, "Okay, this is what we need to do. This is God's plan."

When he got the fungus infection, we took him to the hospital. They did a biopsy. The fungus on his leg was a mushroom fungus. It was from when we took him outside. All that wheeling around outside had made him so happy. But that is how the mushroom spores got in and clung to his leg. The doctors gave him pain medication. Only, they didn't realize he only had one kidney. They overmedicated him, and he went into a coma.

Then, that was pretty much it. He was in ICU. When he woke up, he said, "I just want to go home." He still didn't want hospice. We took him home from the hospital, and he was there for just over a week. During this time, my mom was still working and getting about 2 hours of sleep a night. The same for me. We were doing everything. One night, I said to my mom, "You need to tell him that you're okay with him going because he is hanging on for as long as you want him to hang on." He had two oxygen tanks. All the sudden, one of the oxygen tanks blew. We're scrambling to get oxygen back on him and, at this point, I'm like, "It doesn't really matter." I told my mom, "You need to tell him that it's okay to go." She finally told him. She said, "Okay. I really mean it this time. You can go." He took one big old gasp, and that was it.

I didn't realize this before, but when there's no hospice, the police and fire department have to be called. Oh, my God, that was terrible! They came in and my mom's an absolute wreck, and they're like, "Where's the body?" Just the way they handled it was incredibly rough. They were flipping him back and forth in the bed. I said, "What are you doing?" The officer says, "Oh, we're just checking for bullet holes." (Sighs.) Afterward, my mom calls the funeral home to come get him. It's around 3 a.m. The funeral home sends two small teenagers. They can't get him out of the bed because he's gotten so heavy from fluids. I actually had to help them carry my dad out into their hearse because they didn't have the strength. It was just crazy.

My mom didn't sue anybody about the overdose of pain medication. The doctor was such a good doctor, and she just didn't know. She was an infectious disease doctor, not a pain doctor. She cried harder than my mom and was devastated because she loved my dad as a patient. Honestly, I told my mom everything happened for the best in the grand scheme of things. Otherwise, had the necrotizing fasciitis spread … (Trails off.) Can you imagine? Your flesh being eaten to death by bacteria? It's a painful way to go. His death happened the best way it could.

There were lots of people at his service. The church seats 400 people. There was standing room only and a line wrapped around the church. He was a light for everybody. He was always giving good advice. With him getting cancer, he was like a totally different person. He was the strength for everybody else. He was full of laughter all the time. That's why he survived the cancer so long. He treated it like mind over matter. Before he passed away, he had said to my mom, "I can't believe you're giving up on me. I'm not giving up." But she knew that even though he hadn't given up, his body had given up.

What helped with your grief?

My understanding of science: that energy can neither be created nor destroyed. Energetically, he is still here somewhere. As someone reminded me, "He's always with you because he raised you. You have personality traits from him that will never go away." It's true. When I hang up the phone, I say, "Bye" and it sounds like my dad. He has given me the best parts of him.

I don't believe that he's gone. I believe he's in a different space. I'm heartbroken. I miss him more than I ever thought would be humanely possible to miss somebody. I miss him not being physically near. I know people say they're on the other side and can hear you. But sometimes you want that tangible evidence.

As for my mom, I didn't know what she was going to do. They talk about the turtledove syndrome, where one spouse dies and then the other one dies. I thought my mom might die because she was so heartbroken. My dad's death also started a war in our family. Some of my dad's relatives are fundamentalist Baptist. My dad had asked to be cremated, and they weren't happy about that choice. My mom did it the way my dad wanted it, and she respected his wishes. But the relationship with his family has been severed and might never be repaired.

Do you have any religious or spiritual beliefs that helped with your grief?

My parents were Presbyterian and always made me go to church, and I always hated being made to go. Even as a kid, I knew I didn't believe in the church doctrines. I believed in something bigger, but I wasn't buying this man-made definition of God or of the Source. I don't know that my dad's illness influenced my beliefs. By that time, I had found my personal Truth, which made my dad's passing a lot easier.

Spiritually, we're all still here afterwards: Guiding each other, watching over each other. I never felt my dad's presence. I feel like he was such a different spirit that when he passed, he skipped a level. Like he's not here watching over me, he's on to do more important things.

Sometimes when I miss him, I'll say, "Hey, come visit me," and he will in dreams. In every dream, in every circumstance — even if it's us passing in a mall — he always comes over and gives me the biggest hug.

I think about the kind of person he wanted me to be. Had he not gotten cancer, our family would have turned out differently. I may not have been the type of person I am now.

Do you have a favorite memory of your dad?

We lived on a farm when I was younger, and my dad used to drive me to school every morning. It was a 30 to 45 minute drive, and he would get up really early and take me to school. My dad loved country music and was a phenomenal singer. I know people say that about their parents. But my dad really could sing. We didn't talk very much on those rides. He would sing, and I would watch out the window. There were these electrical pillars, and they were perfectly sequenced. They had eagle nests on top of them. I don't know why that memory is vivid.

One of my other fondest memories is when he came over to my place in Florida. I was 23 years old and had just bought a house. It's the one time I really looked at my dad differently. I was engaged to the guy who I was supposed to be buying a house with. He cheated on me. I found out two days before I was supposed to close on the house, and I decided it was cheaper to buy the house anyway because it was less than rent. I finished my closing, signed the papers, and drove to my new house. I'm sitting in my driveway with my keys in my hand, and I just started bawling. I thought, "What do I do now? I own a house. It's a three bedroom house, and I don't have anybody else but me and my dog." Then, my dad's car pulled up behind mine. He came up to my car and said, "Hey, new homeowner. I'm so excited for you." I just started crying, and I said, "This is terrible!" And he said, "No, no. It's part of the journey. It'll be okay. I want you to understand that you never need a man to depend on. No man will ever complete you. You need to complete yourself." He reassured me, saying, "You'll figure it out. You'll meet somebody who is good for you. Don't ever be afraid. I'll be here for you if you ever need anything." And he was. If something broke, he'd come over and fix it. (Laughs.) That was probably one of the more important conversations in my life.

Do you have any suggestions for someone going through something similar?

Anger is part of the grief process. But I wish people could take the anger out of it. It's not worth the energy. Everything happens for a reason. It doesn't seem like it, and it doesn't feel like it. The circumstances suck, and you can't get that person back. But there's no point in wasting your energy being so angry because it just eats you up. It's like that Buddhist saying, "Anger is like holding onto a hot coal and expecting it to hurt someone else." I was angry, too, for a hot minute because you're angry at the universe or God. But actually, if we all lived forever, this planet would be overrun.

Spend as much time with that person as you can if you know they are sick or dying. The moment I got off work, we just sat together. Sometimes I typed my work notes, and it was understood that I was just spending time with him. He knew he wasn't going to be around much longer. People get this feeling with someone who is sick, like: "I don't want them to know that I think they're going to die." Well, they know. It's not a surprise. You'll kick yourself in the butt afterward if you don't spend time with them. I wouldn't trade the last three or four months with my dad for the world. When people know they're going to die, there's a part of them that loses their inhibitions and fear. They kind of tell you how it is and how they are. Take it for what it's worth.

I wish loss was easier for people. So many people believe in heaven or the afterlife or reincarnation. Yet, they grieve terribly, as if they'll never see the person again. Just be patient, no matter what your belief system.

⟩⟨ ⟩⟨

Barry E. Childs-Helton (parents, Alzheimer's & cancer)

"The Long Goodbye" — A tall man with a deep voice, Barry Eckersley Childs-Helton (Barry) is married to Sally Childs-Helton and plays guitar in the musical group, Wild Mercy. He lost his father (Orlo Eckersley Childs) and then his mother (Elizabeth Catharine Childs). Barry is in his 60s and has two siblings. He and his siblings became caretakers for their mother after their father passed away.

My grandfather died in his early 50s of a heart attack. Dad was always watching to see if he would pass that particular milestone. He lived to age 82, although he did carry nitroglycerin. But it wasn't his heart that proved to be his undoing. It came from a completely unexpected quarter.

Dad was park ranger as a young man and worked at the Grand Canyon in 1940. As a family, we always considered the Grand Canyon an axis point, the center of our family universe. We kept coming back to it for significant things, like my brother's graduation from business school. My sister also worked in the gift shop there in the early '70s. My father's last trip to the canyon was in 1995, the year before he died. He was fighting renal cancer but was still well enough to get around and drive around the canyon's rim. At that visit, he took us to all the places where he used to give group lectures as a ranger.

My parents met when my mother was an English major at the University of Michigan. U of M had just hired this fresh, young PhD who had taken his doctorate there and whose name was Orlo Childs, my father. My mother was his student in his geology class. There are two family legends, only one of which is probably true. One story is that at a mid-term exam, he laid out a sample of minerals, and the last one was rock candy. He had all the students identify the rock samples, and at the end of the exam, after they had turned their papers in, he picked up the rock candy and ate it as he left the room. He always had a high-level sense of humor.

The other family legend was a joke. My dad would say, "I told your mom I'd give her an A if she'd marry me." Only that's not true. He didn't start dating her until after she graduated and was doing her student teaching at Connecticut College. He played by the book. He was respectful of the academic institutions and their mission throughout his life.

This period that I think of as the long goodbye began in November '93. My father had some blood show up in his urine.

One of his kidneys was completely engulfed in tumor cells. The doctors took out all the tumors they could, including the kidney. In January '94, he was diagnosed with an aggressive form of renal cancer. The doctor gave my father six months to live. He lived for two more years. That allowed us to get him out to the Grand Canyon for that final visit.

Meanwhile, my mother started to have problems with her memory, and dad was covering for her. It was all they could do to deal with the fact that he was under what amounted to a death sentence. My parents didn't take any steps to close up the house or get their will revised. They were mostly just clinging to each other and trying to protect each other. During that time, the siblings would take turns jumping on airplanes and visiting them. My parents had settled in Tucson, Arizona, for their semi-retirement. I say "semi" because dad was still working on a geological project, and mom was intensely and diversely involved with public service. She had graciousness down to an art.

In October of '95, my parents celebrated their 50th wedding anniversary by doing what they called a round robin. My parents got on a plane and visited the households of each of their children, which took them to Missouri, Minnesota, and Indiana. They had a chance to visit us in our settled houses and appreciate that they had successfully launched all three of us.

By the spring of '96, my father's cancer had started to metastasize. My brother's family, my sister's family, and my wife Sally and I went to Tucson to celebrate what turned out to be my father's last birthday. There were a couple of times when he needed help getting to the bathroom. I was still fairly healthy then, and I picked him up and helped him get on and off the toilet. I'm grateful that I was able to offer that assistance.

In the third week of April, everyone returned to Tucson. My parents had set up a hospital bed in the den, and dad was essentially in at-home hospice. My parents had healthcare givers to bathe dad and feed him and take care of him. Because the cancer was spreading to his brain and his lungs, he was having trouble breathing. My mother was trying to comfort him and minister to him, even trying to feed him applesauce at the very end when his body was trying to shut down. At that point, feeding him could have possibly resulted in compounded stress if he had aspirated. Dad had passed into the stage that I now understand is palliative care, where you just try to make the patient as comfortable as you can while they are exiting this world.

Anyway, that's what I tried to do. I had my guitar, and I played him a couple of the songs he liked. The day before I had to go home, my sister was on a plane to land that afternoon. I read passages to him from Khalil Gibran's *The Prophet*. It's a book that both he and my mother loved. He fell asleep while I was reading. I sat at the foot of his bed and told him that we loved him and that my sister was on the way and would be there soon. By the time my sister landed, he had died.

When I returned back home, it was okay to howl and cry for a while. So, I did. The next morning, because I had interviewed and gotten a job, I went to my first day of work editing computer books. It was okay. Trust me, it was *really* and thoroughly okay because this was, in a strange way, honoring my father. He had bought one of the first personal computers and taught himself how to use it.

After our dad died, we all gathered in Salt Lake, Utah, to decant the ashes into a handmade box that his father had built and covered with a copper relief. That was the last time I saw some members from his side of the family.

My mother was 74 when my father died, and he had just turned 82.

Mom developed this pattern of calling us long distance and telling us she was having gastric problems or headaches or backaches. One of us would get on an airplane and fly out to Tucson. I did this a couple of times, and my sister did it a couple of times.

And Mom would greet us at the door with this cheerful smile and bake us an apple pie. It became clear that it was a way of getting family out there, even though we had hired caregivers to be with her in the house.

She followed this same pattern from her apartment in Ann Arbor (Mich.), where we eventually moved her. Except now instead of getting on an airplane, I could get in a car and drive. It would be the same thing: "Oh, hi," very cheerful. She was most content when she had her family around her.

Later, I moved my mom into an assisted living unit where I live. Then, my sister wanted to take a turn watching over my mom's care. So, we moved my mom to St Louis. For about three years, I'd get in the car, and sometimes my wife Sally would drive with me, and we'd go to St Louis and provide respite care for my mom while my sister got some things done or took a break.

And mom went through one of the stages of Alzheimer's where she got intensely paranoid. By paranoid, I mean she was aware that things were being taken from her, but mistook what was being taken. I remember I had exactly one argument with her during that phase. It was about what we called, "The Rubber Band Lady." My mother would take her letters and wrap them up in rubber bands and put them away to make sure they were safe. Then, she'd find them later and forget she'd put the rubber bands around them and assume that someone else had done it. Mom would leave these threatening notes around the room addressed to the Rubber Band Lady.

This was just the tip of the iceberg. My sister had a couch that my mother had given her, and then my mother forgot that she had done so. When mom saw the couch, she accused my sister of stealing it. This got into a horrible and intolerable dynamic between the two of them, such that my sister could not take it anymore. Her academic responsibilities were increasing, and it was interrupting her teaching and writing.

So, Sally and I moved Mom back near us. We still had not determined that she was beyond what assisted living could provide for her. We spent a while finding that out.

Meanwhile, more things happened. Mom broke her hip. She'd turned wrong and fallen. This is sometimes typical of Alzheimer's: Any injury will be the signal that the disease has reached its next stage. It became apparent that we would have to move her again.

In September 2006, we moved my mom to an appropriate care facility that had an intensive memory care unit — the only one that accepted Medicaid. My brother helped immensely with that process. He has an MBA from Stanford, and his handling of the money went way beyond anything I could have done. The siblings would have periodic meetings. We called them "Sibling Summits," where we would eat together, discuss things, catch up, and decide the next thing to do with Mom.

Mom would have this period of curling up into a semi-fetal position and breathing through her mouth, which I learned to recognize as potentially a signal that the body was shutting down. Each time it happened, I went to her bedside and just told her a long story, everything I knew about her life and the life of the family. I gave her as much of the family history as I could remember, partly so I could speak to her but mainly so she would still hear a familiar voice. That's something that stays with you. Also, her manners stayed with her amazingly late. She would say, "please" and "thank you" for as long as she was verbal, and she would smile at people. Even in later years, now and then her face would light up, and she'd say, "That's wonderful," in exactly the tone I remembered.

In February 2011, she had another one of these incidents of curling up in a fetal position and breathing through her mouth. It was starting to look like this was it. I called my siblings. That winter was brutal. We had ice an inch thick all over the driveway that was as solid and opaque as milk glass. We broke it up with a sledgehammer just to get out of the driveway. My brother drove down from Minneapolis through a blizzard. My sister had her adult son Will drive her over from St Louis. The weather was horrible the whole way. But we all got where we were supposed to be on time and in time. Sally and I had been playing in a band called Wild Mercy, which was Celtic folk rock. Our Celtic harp player Jen came and played for 4 hours on the last day of my mother's life. The last thing mom heard was harp music. Jen greatly eased my mother's passing that way, and I also brought my guitar and played to her. There was music for the last time.

After my parents' deaths, we spent a lot of time in the intervening years distributing the possessions we felt we wanted and deciding what we could let go back into the world. There were those decisions to make and financial matters to clean up. During that time, a lot of other things happened. My nephew Will went off to college. My nieces grew up, graduated, got married, moved away — all over the country — the way we'd done.

But we all came together again at the Grand Canyon for my father's centennial. We managed to coordinate it from various places. Nieces and nephews were asking, "*Where* are we going?" And the answer was, the Grand Canyon. The last family visit to the Grand Canyon had been in 1995. Twenty years later marked the long goodbye coming to a close.

We had Dad's ashes in a small container, in silk a glove from his pipe, and my brother sailed the ashes into the canyon. That was a major part of the closure. One of dad's last requests was that some of his ashes go to the Grand Canyon.

After we had done the observance, Sally and I took my mother's ashes to Salt Lake City and arranged to have them buried with a portion of my father's remains. We had a new stone placed, and my parents now have two duel gravesites: one in Salt Lake City, Utah, my father's family plot, and the other one is in Ann Arbor, my mother's family plot.

What helped with your grief?

Life is always messy, and end of life is just as messy. I think my siblings and I did well. All of us operated as a team, and all of us were consciously grateful that our siblings fully participated in taking care of business during this time. It probably helped to keep a strong bond among us as siblings. As long as you can make an effort, then the teamwork to deal with the really important things is possible.

I kept journals the whole time. That's been a great help. Martial arts also helped because it gave me a place to put the energy. There is something about physical activity that helps to process stress and give it a focal point and discharge some of it. Karate is useful because you realize there is so much you can't do, and you just try to put it in front of you and beat the hell out of it. That was valuable.

My attempts to help my father did have a physical component to it and that helped me about as much as anything. There's a kind of odd male bonding that happens in that situation. My father would never have turned to my mother to help him get up off the floor. The male bonding aspect of the whole thing was kind of a father-son dynamic that said, "We're guys. We're gonna try to fix the situation and handle the situation, and the parts that can't be fixed, we're going to be strong about those parts."

Do you have any religious or spiritual practices that helped?

My family has a history of being on a kind of a religious walkabout. My maternal grandfather converted from Catholicism to Presbyterian to marry my grandmother. Our parents had what the Mormons would have called a mixed marriage with my father's Mormon background and my mother's Presbyterian background.

My brother is in a different faith group with born-again Christianity. I believe my sister still attends a Presbyterian church, and my wife and I have found Unitarian Universalism the most compatible with our view of the world. Apparently my father, during his geological studies, had a discussion with my Mormon grandfather. Geological time did not sit well with Bishop Usher's 4000-year timeline for the creation of the earth. They had discussed this topic and reached a gentleman's agreement not to discuss it again. They got along fine after that. To my mind, that is a valuable lesson in itself.

My current place and challenge is to be a humane nontheistic: someone who sees the world in terms other than those that require a concept of deity, but still has the absolute dictum that you must treat each other decently, and you must try to live a humane life. Connecting with a caring community helps. Friends also help, especially if they understand where you're coming from and don't try to change your view of the world.

Anything else you found helpful?

Talking about it is giving it a coherent shape in memory. Human beings organize experience by telling stories. Speaking as one who studied folklore for years, I'm aware that it's an important factor in orchestrating our relationships and also moving us on from one stage of life to the next. It seems to matter the kind of care you put into the story, trying to get it right and trying to honor those who figure in the story, and that's probably a moving target. I'll be doing that the rest of my days. That's okay. I'm proud of us for getting through it the way we did. I like to think that my parents would be, too.

CHAPTER 4

THE PRECIOUS GIFT OF TIME

"Joy comes, grief goes. We know not how."

— *JAMES RUSSELL LOWELL*

May we be at peace ~

Along the muddy creek beds of Kentucky, Indiana, and Illinois, it's not uncommon to find geodes. In the western United States, geodes are often located in the deserts of California, Arizona, Utah, and Nevada. In Iowa, the geode was designated the official state rock. Many states and places throughout the world have geodes.

These bumpy, oval rocks are plain on the outside but contain bright crystals inside. Geodes are created in hollow areas of soil and are also formed in the bubbles in volcanic rock. Dissolved minerals seep into a hollow area and harden into an outer casing. Over time, the minerals continue to form on the inside walls of the shell, growing towards the center. When the hard shell is broken open, beautiful crystals shine within.

Similar to the inner workings of the geode, grief changes us in ways that are not necessarily visible on the outside. Like the geode, we may form a hard protective shell while our inner healing work takes place — over an extended period of time. When we're ready, we may break open to reveal our most precious, sacred gem: the enduring love for those who have passed.

The stories here convey both appreciation for valuable time shared with a loved one before death, as well as the anguish felt at watching someone undergo pronounced physical hardships from an illness or the treatment of a disease. Lia (who lost her mother) and Bonnie and John (who lost their daughter), express gratitude that the extensive suffering finally came to an end. Bonnie says, *"I have never cried over it. I know that's odd. But I feel grateful. We talked after the funeral. We were all just so relieved for Annette that her suffering was over. She had been in hell, multiple times."* Deb (whose father died from a stroke) says, *"I was so happy for him because he really loved God, and he was free. If he had lived, with his entire right side was paralyzed, it wouldn't have been good for him. He would have hated us for keeping him here."*

This section further emphasizes the importance of living life to the fullest, as well as the astonishment at unexpected gifts that arrive after loss. Ralph (who lost his wife) says, *"I am profoundly grateful for the way things have turned out, and the life I've had with Ellen. Every moment is a good deal more precious now."* David (who lost his life partner and is now in a new relationship), says, *"I open my eyes every day, feel my heart beating, and realize I have a purpose."*

The luminous, bright crystals within each person's story have formed not only from experiences of penetrating sorrow but also from a vast capacity to love — through life's heartaches as well as life's joys.

Letting Go

Lia M. Guerin (mother, leukemia)

> *"My mom would want me to keep going." — Lia works as a flight attendant and is from Dearborn, Michigan. She is in her 20s and has two younger sisters. Lia lost her mom, Gina Maria (Belissimo) Guerin, to lymphoma. Her mother was married to Robert (Bob) Guerin (Lia's non-biological father). Lia's biological father died from a drug overdose.*

My mom died at age 46. Three years prior, she had her regular yearly gynecology appointment, and the doctor felt a lump in her neck. It wasn't bothering her, and he said, "Well, let's get it checked out." They did more testing, and that's when they found out she had lymphoma. It was Non-Hodgkin's Lymphoma. I was 19 when she first got diagnosed.

My parents tried to keep my mom's illness from us. My sisters were young and, even with me, my parents didn't tell me too much.

She started having chemotherapy at this place in town. But they had caught it too late. It was Stage Four. The doctors said it was too risky to do anything more than the chemo. My mom was researching it and asked about bone marrow transplants. The doctors said they didn't recommend it at this stage, and it would be a big risk. She got a second opinion, and the other hospital said they could try the bone marrow transplant. It all went downhill from there.

When I was in my teenage years, my mom and I didn't have the best relationship. We didn't get along too well. But when my mom got diagnosed, we became like best friends. With her illness and trying to help her out, we got closer. She was kind of a private person, and she became more open. She was always positive, like she was going to make it, and it wasn't a big deal, just going through some hurdles. But it was horrible. With the bone marrow transplant, she went through hell. I could see how much pain she was in. She went through a total body transformation. She almost didn't even look human.

If it happened to me, I would probably just do chemo. The bone marrow transplant was too much. It got rid of the cancer, but she had so many other issues. She got diabetes and had to take a lot of pills. She was super thin, but her belly was bloated because her liver was having problems. My mom's hair was gone, and her skin was yellowish. She looked so cancer-stricken. My sister Jade was around 8 years old when my mom got diagnosed, and she was 12 when our mom passed away. Jade says she doesn't really remember our mom looking normal. She only remembers how she looked going through cancer.

For six months after the bone marrow transplant, my mom couldn't leave the house. She sat outside. She liked to be outdoors. Eight months after the bone marrow transplant, she passed away.

I was 23 when she passed. It was two and half weeks after my birthday.

What helped with your healing?

When she died, I felt a relief for her because she went through so much pain, and she did all she could. That's how we dealt with the grief, too. It was horrible that it happened, and she was still young. But she did every single thing she could to stay alive, and it just didn't work. It was good that she was out of the pain. She is not suffering anymore. That's how I looked at it.

Bob helped. He stayed strong. I would be a wreck without him. My sisters and me lean on him and each other. Also, because of my mom's condition, I prepared myself. It wasn't a shock or a surprise. I was prepared for my mom to pass, and I had time to process it. That helped.

We all felt it was unfair. But she went through so much agony that we kind of accepted it. I don't think my sisters have acted out or gone rebellious. They are both good girls. My dad is a strong figure, and he makes sure we stay on track.

Me and my sisters and our dad have become extremely close. We ask, "What would mom say?" and we talk about her. He keeps her pictures in the house. It's not like we got rid of pictures or anything like that. We still have pictures of her up, and we have her jewelry. We keep her with us that way, and we remember the good memories.

Do you have any religious or spiritual practices that helped with your grief?

I follow some of the Catholic rituals and beliefs. I believe in God. My mom was angry with God. She wasn't too religious. She didn't really want to deal with all of that on top of everything else. But I believe in a higher power.

My biological father passed away last year. Drug overdose. I was not raised by him and was never close to that family. I found out I have half siblings, but I never knew about them and didn't grow up with them. His daughter found me on Facebook, and that's how I found out he died. She's around my age. We went out to lunch, and I got a lot of information about my biological father. With my mom, I knew that conversation was off-topic with her. She got divorced when I was really young, maybe around a year old. I met my biological father only a couple of times.

When I found out about his death on Facebook, I cried. I just felt sad for him and the choices he made. Not sad for myself because I have a dad. My mom re-married when I was around six. I never called Bob stepfather. He raised me. But as for my biological father, I just felt sad for him. I cried for him. The choices he made, and now it's over.

I guess, technically, I'm an orphan. Both my parents are gone. But I don't feel that way because Bob is my dad, and I never felt like I was without both my parents.

Do you still feel a connection to your mom?

My mom loved music. When a certain song comes on the radio, I feel a connection to her, especially in the car because my sisters and I would always sit in the back. She used to listen to the Pretenders on the radio. On a nice day, when a song comes on from nowhere, I feel a connection to her.

I also feel a connection to her when I go up north where her grandparents had lake property. It's on Saginaw Bay. She loved going by the lake. My mom would dance around with us on the beach. That's a favorite memory.

Are there any other favorite memories or things that helped you?

My mom was so pretty. She was just gorgeous. My guy friends from high school would come over and hang out, and my mom would put out cookies. Everyone was like, "Lia, your mom's so hot." (Laughs.) My sisters and I liked that she was beautiful and had a good personality. She liked music, and she liked to joke. She had a nice laugh. People always say I look like her, and sometimes they get freaked out. (Laughs.)

My mom was creative, too. She liked decorating the house. Her decorating skills were great. She was a hairstylist. She did different hairstyles with my sisters and me and gave us fashion tips. Mostly, she raised kids after she had my sisters. She only did haircuts for close friends or family, not an on-going thing. And she only did my dad's hair during her cancer.

I'm enjoying my flight attendant job. Sometimes we have layovers for a day; we had one in Boston and another in Mexico. I met the actor, George Clooney. He was doing that movie, *Up in the Air,* and they were showing him at the airport. I called my mom, and she said, "Go up to him and talk to him. Put him on the phone!" And I was like "Mom, I can't put him on the phone!" (Laughs.)

Like I said, the healing is just thinking of her and keeping the good memories. I don't talk to anyone, and I kind of keep my emotions deep down. I hold it in. I think I've dealt with it. I didn't do alcohol or drugs or anything. I know my mom would want me to keep going.

Do you have any suggestions for someone going through something similar?

At some point, you'll feel their presence again. It's not like they're gone forever. Maybe not now, but you'll feel it again. A song comes on or a certain thought will come to you and you'll feel that connection again. You have to know life goes on and to cherish the really good memories that you have.

You can remember what made you happy about being around the person. And if you have kids, you can tell them how awesome their grandma or grandpa was. Keep that alive. That's what I'll do if I ever have kids. I'll tell them how awesome my mom was. The only way to heal is that time goes on, and it gets better.

⊷ ⊶

Debra L. Lambert (father, stroke)

"You have to learn to cherish the moments that annoy the crap out of you ... because you don't get those moments with them again." — Debra (Deb) is in her early 50s and is married with two adult children. With a great passion for dogs, she volunteers after work at an animal shelter. She lost her father, James (Jim) Carey, from stroke complications. Deb's mom Shirley and Deb's three younger sisters survive him.

My parents met when my grandpa took my mom to buy her first car. My dad was a salesman at Hare Chevrolet. When they were looking at cars, dad had told her, "You buy this car, and I'll buy you a steak dinner." The next day, they went back to the dealership, and my mom ran all over the place trying to find dad — to get her that steak dinner. (Laughs.) And that was it.

Mom was a charge nurse for years while we were growing up. Dad was a jack-of-all-trades. He was a salesman, a farmer, a mailman, and whatever else he could do. Mainly, he was farming and then had others side jobs.

At the time of his stroke, my parents were living in Arkansas. Dad had a stroke while driving, which caused an automobile accident. It wasn't a bad accident, thank God. The other people just had glass scrapes. Being a nurse, Mom recognized the stroke signs. They always carried a cooler of water bottles in the car because it was such a long drive to the store. When the accident happened, mom saw that things weren't right with Dad, and she got out one of the water bottles from the cooler and poured it on a towel and put the towel on the back of his neck. An off-duty EMT guy happened to be driving behind them. Immediately, as soon as he saw the accident, he called it in. Those two things saved my dad. They got dad life-lined to Springfield, Missouri, and he was a very lucky guy.

The family drove to the hospital, and the doctors told us that if they had to go in and operate, that meant it was serious and getting dire. We were scared to death. I called my church and had everyone praying. Fortunately, the blood had pooled to the outside, and the doctors were able to drain it. The damage for him was much less severe than it could have been. Afterward, he had disabilities, and his left-side vision was affected. But he was able to recover. He came out of the stroke pretty good actually. All this came about because he had high blood pressure and an enlarged heart, and he refused to do what the doctor told him.

Later, he had TIAs, mini-strokes. It finally got to the point where the doctor said to him: "It's time you got your wife back home with her daughters." The doctor told my dad, "You're not going to get any better."

That was the beginning of the end. My parents moved down the street from my sister Jenny and her husband John, who is a Battalion Chief, EMT. Having that extra medical attention close by was good for Dad.

From the time of Dad's first stroke, Mom was the caretaker. She cared for him for 12 years. She'd spend one day with him while he was acting like an adult and the next day with him acting like a child. He did get everything set up for Mom. He got the investments done — trying to make sure she was provided for. He planted fruit trees that bore fruit that next spring after he was gone.

One day, Mom knew something wasn't right. Dad was not himself. Normally, he would sit in his recliner. But he was slumped halfway in it, like a teenager, with a leg up over the arm. He was talking different. He kept telling Mom stories of this guy who had been dead for years. It was a guy Dad used to go to cattle auctions with. He said, "Yeah, Floyd and I went to the auction this morning, picked up a bunch of cattle." Mom was like, "Really?" Then, while looking out the window, he said, "Those trees out there look like ours from the house we had on Hague Road." Mom said, "We are in the house on Hague Road." So, she had to call my brother-in-law John, and he called an ambulance. John told them which hospital to take Dad to. But Dad got in and told the driver something else. The ambulance driver listened to my dad, and John was angry. (Laughs.) My brother-in-law isn't vocal, but he just has to give you the look and you know you're in trouble. That poor driver. (Chuckles.)

Dad ended up having a golf-ball size bleed on the front right portion of his brain that was affecting memory and the way he acted. The other stroke clot had been in the back. It affects personality and mood when it's in the front.

Dad was in the neuro-trauma unit for at least a week. That's when he started seeing people who had passed. I stayed with him a couple of nights in the trauma unit, and he would say, "Uncle Lefty is standing there," or "Aunt Emma Jean is standing there." I'd say, "They are?" And he'd say, "Yep." I tried so hard to see what he was seeing, but obviously I wasn't in that place. It sounds weird, but it's normal for those passing.

Dad ended up improving, and they took him off the neuro-trauma unit and put him on the neuro unit. Then, he went to a nursing home rehab center.

At the nursing home, he was angry with Mom and yelling at her because he thought he was going home. The doctor tried to explain it to him. Dad couldn't control his bowels; he sat there and wet himself and would have no idea he'd done it. That was hard to see. He just didn't understand what was going on. There were times where he'd just get angry for no reason. Probably the TIAs had something to do with it, but it was hard. Normally, my dad was a joker, a real card. He liked to pick on people and tease. If he didn't tease you, then you knew he didn't like you.

In mid-March, Dad was at the nurses station and said, "I'm gonna go to bed now." He turned and fell to the floor. He was having a grand mal seizure. My brother-in-law called me at work. He never cries. He called me in tears. He said, "You need to get there." They took Dad straight to the hospice section.

I visited Dad with my parents' dog, Maggie. He loves Maggie. I had to leave earlier than I wanted because Maggie started barking, and I knew we were gonna get in trouble. Dad had on one of those censor things that let off a shrill beep, and dogs don't like those kinds of noises. I don't remember if I told him I loved him. (Weeps.) I did tell him I'd see him later. I did see him again. But he didn't know I was there the next time. (Crying.)

Dad died the day after my nephew's birthday. We were all praying that he wouldn't pass on my nephew Noah's birthday. That was difficult.

When he actually passed, his eyes flew open, and he looked up, which I guess is a normal thing for the dying to do. My sisters and me ran to his bed. We told him, "It's okay. We're going to take care of Mom. She's gonna be okay, and we're gonna be okay." I told him, "I love you. If you see Jesus, just go. Go to Jesus." Oh, my God. It was incredible. I was up near his head. I actually felt him leave. I turned around, and I was excited for him. I looked and everyone was crying and sad. But I was happy. I was like, "Yes, Dad. You did it!" I had to talk to two different pastors to make sure there wasn't something wrong with me. I was so happy for him because he really loved God, and he was free. If he had lived, with his entire right side paralyzed, it wouldn't have been good for him. He would have hated us for keeping him here. The preacher told me that God wants us to be happy. God wants us to be excited.

I went home after that. I had to pay a bill, get stuff done, and I thought, "Well, I'll pay a bill and then get back up there and help with the funeral plans." I had to call about the bill because the on-line system wasn't working. That poor lady who took my call; I feel bad for her. I said, "All I'm trying to do is pay your damn bill, and this site is so stupid." I just went off. Then I said, "I'm sorry. I lost my dad." She said, "I totally understand." And then, you know how that anger starts. I knew Dad was better off, but I was angry. I've never been so angry, screaming and hitting the furniture. I felt better after. But my poor dog sat there looking at me like, *It's okay.* I think I scared her.

After dad passed away, I was worried about my mom being alone in the house. My sisters and me were trying to figure out, "Okay, what do we do? Do we take turns with Mom? How do we keep Mom busy?" I held up a good front to get through it all. I'm the oldest. There's more stress being the oldest one.

Dad was 76 when he died. God blessed him with 12 more years after the first stroke, and he got to see his grandkids. He got to know them, which was a good thing.

What helped with your grief?

There were a lot of cry sessions, especially with my daughter Amy. My son Danny and his cousin Tyler would drive out to the country. They'd sit and have a beer for pappy and talk. They'd listen to certain songs on the radio and that was their therapy. Amy goes to visit him regularly at his gravesite, and she sits and talks to him. We went for his birthday this last year. Danny and my husband Randy and I took a sip of beer and gave pappy the rest of it. Dad liked having a beer with the boys, whether he was supposed to have it or not. (Laughs.)

Songs on the radio helped me through it. I listen to K-Love. Those songs remind me that he's better off. There are a couple of songs, like "I Drive Your Truck," and when they came on the radio, I turn up the volume as loud as it can go and just bawl like a baby. You think grief will go away, but it doesn't. Last week, we were sitting in the pub, and this man comes in and walks right past me. His gait and the back of his head were just like my father. I have not, since the day Dad left, felt that urge to want to jump up and give a hug to him. Of course, a strange person would think I was nuts if I did that. I was weepy the rest of the dinner. Seeing that guy set things off again.

Having a strong immediate family helps, too. Both of my kids help me, and I couldn't have done it without my husband, that's for darn sure. He lost his dad when he was 11. My dad's passing dug up things with him. Then, Mom started cleaning out Dad's stuff and gave us all of Dad's fishing tackle. That's when it hit my husband Randy. It brought back a lot of memories. When I was a kid, Dad and my grandpa would go fishing. When Grandpa passed away, Dad rarely went fishing until Randy came into the picture. When my parents moved to Arkansas, they were on the cove of the lake. It was a little bitty house, perfect for them. It had a big, old porch where you could sit and watch the sun set on the water. Fishing is all they did when Randy visited. They'd be out there all hours of the night.

Do you still feel your dad's presence?

I definitely feel dad's presence. Right after he passed, that next summer, my sister decided to take Mom out to Montana. While they were gone, I thought, "I'll surprise Mom: I'll clean the house and have it ready." Luckily my son Danny went with me. He was down the street at my sister's house. As I'm cleaning, I go into my parents' bedroom. Something didn't feel right. I felt like someone was over my shoulder. I left the bedroom with my vacuum cleaner, and then I said to myself, "You're being stupid, go back in there." So, I go back in, and the vacuum starts acting up. It had been working fine. Then, I started feeling weird again. I ran out the front door and called Danny on my cell phone. I said, "You have to come over here. Now!" He thought I was losing it. I said, "Pappy's in here, and he's playing a trick on me. He's thinking this is funny, I know he does."

Danny walks in, and he looks in the bedroom, being all "Mr. Serious." I said, "I mean it. You have to stay in this house. Don't go anywhere." Danny sat at the breakfast bar, while I'm the bedroom working. Danny had gotten the vacuum cleaner to work again and was on the phone getting insurance quotes for a car he wanted to buy. Then he yells, "Mom!" He said he saw Pappy sitting in his recliner. I said, "See, I told you he was here." Danny says, "Can we leave now!" That was the fastest cleaning job I ever did.

My mom saw him, too, and one time heard his voice. Within a few months of when he passed, Mom was in the garden and she heard, "Shirley," and there wasn't a soul outside. Another time, she told me, "I woke up, and I turned my head over toward the bedroom door, and there was your dad looking around the door frame with that impish smile, like when he's up to something."

My sister also saw Dad. She is living with Mom now. My sister was sitting in the recliner one day, and Dad was standing right there, looking at her. A few months later, the doorbell to the garage started ringing. My sister Jacquie was the only one home when that happened. She said, "Dad was being a brat the other day."

That's my dad, always up to something. (Laughs.)

Not too long after Dad passed away, Mom had this cardinal that would tap on her bedroom window. We called the bird Ruby. If Mom was on the computer in the front bedroom, there would be this, tap, tap, tap on the window, driving Mom crazy. She would go to the other end of the house, and she'd still hear it. Ruby would come around to the window on my mom's side of the bed and do the same thing. I said, "Mom, what if that's Dad? What if he's doing this?" Well, I was up there one day when Ruby started on the bedroom window. I said, "Mom, did you talk to this bird?" She says, "No, not really." I opened the blind, and the bird flies to the bush. I started talking to it. I told it, "Everything is okay in here — even though you can't see in." I talked to the bird like it was my best friend. My mom looked at me like I was crazy. But you know, that bird never bothered her again.

My dad loved eagles, too. The guy who is in charge of the cemetery, Mike, was telling us about the day he was digging the plot for Dad, and he hears this noise and there's this big eagle in the tree. Mike was telling us this story and Mom and I both got goose bumps. Now, every time we go, we look to see if we can find Dad's eagle. We feel like it was a sign from Dad to let us know he was there.

This past Christmas was hard. Mom bought all of us Christmas ornaments with Dad's picture on them. I was fine until I got home and put the ornament on the tree. Then I burst into tears. My son Danny said, "Mom, come here." I sat on the sofa and put my head on his shoulder crying. He can be sweet when he wants to be. (Laughs.) I couldn't have made it through without my kids and my husband.

Do you have any suggestions for someone going through something similar?

It gets tough dealing with the in and out of hospital stuff. Also, the things that seem to annoy the crap out of you, you need to learn to cherish. Take a step back, breathe, and cherish the moment because you don't get those moments with them again. We were lucky to have a little bit of time with him, but we didn't realize how close it was to the end. (Crying.) We didn't take advantage of it. The thing is, we knew that he loved us — even though he wasn't real forthright in showing it.

It's funny, when Dad was on the neuro unit, I had been walking in to the hospital to spend the evening with him and telling my cousin on the phone to get there. I was getting ready to go on the elevator, and I hear this woman's voice say, "Debbie?" And I thought, *Who in the world is that?* No one has called me Debbie since I was a kid. Everyone calls me Deb. Well, it wound up being a childhood friend I grew up with. I told her about Dad. Then, after I spent a couple of hours visiting with Dad, she went to see him. Dad remembered her and everything. We were surprised. God worked on that one because there's just no way. People say it's a coincidence. But I don't think it was because it brought her back into our lives again.

⊷╬╬⊶

John & Bonnie Bittner (daughter, leukemia)

"We are proud of our family. We drew our wagons in a circle, quick." — John is a farmer. A good-size man, he speaks with a slow drawl and has a deep laugh; his wife Bonnie is petite, quick-witted, and assertive. They lost their daughter Annette to leukemia. Annette was 32 when she got sick. She died 5 1/2 years later.

BONNIE: Annette went in for a standard gestational diabetes test when she was six months pregnant with her third child. The doctor told her that she had leukemia, and without medical treatment, she would be dead in 90 days.

She was working at Mead Johnson, a division of Bristol Myers, as a nutritional sales representative. She worked in Bowling Green, Kentucky; Tennessee was also part of her sales territory. That's where she met her husband Allen Meier. She met him at a fitness center. She called me and said, "I met the man I'm going to marry." And I said. "I'll be down there, and we'll see." (Laughs jokingly.)

Anyway, she and Allen got married and had two children: Adrienne Nicole and Alex Joseph. They moved closer to us when Bristol Myers asked Annette to work in the home office in marketing. Three years later, she got pregnant with her third child, Allison Marie. Then, after the leukemia diagnosis, she was given 90 days to live.

Annette and Allen stopped by to tell John the news and then left because the kids had a game. I got home from work, and I saw an open bottle of whisky on the counter — and John's not a drinker! He was sitting in a chair with a glass of whiskey and looked horrible. I said, "What's wrong?" He told me. And I said, "I'm quitting work. She's not going through this by herself." I called work and they said, "Do what you have to do. We'll work it out. You're not quitting your job."

The hospital Annette selected was about 3 hours from where we lived. Alan and I alternated weeks to be with her so we could both keep our jobs. She went through high-dose chemo, and the doctors told us the chemo probably would not cross the placenta.

When Annette was 26 weeks along in her pregnancy, she developed a bad infection, and the doctors told her they had to put her into a medical-induced coma to keep her alive. If the baby wasn't born by morning, they would have to abort it. She told me she lay awake all night and prayed.

JOHN: Annette told me she talked to God and got pretty stern with him. The doctors gave her injections of steroids to help the baby's lungs develop. The next morning, Allison was born feet first, with no doctor there.

BONNIE: Her sister Julie was there and she kept telling the doctors how fast we have babies in our family. Allison Marie was born in the bed, and Julie called the nurse, wrapped the baby in a blanket, and walked with the nurse through the tunnel to the children's hospital section.

JOHN: The baby's body was as big as my hand: a tiny, cute baby.

BONNIE: She weighed 3 pounds and 3 ounces. Perfect for me, didn't wear my arms out like my babies.

JOHN: Annette was in the induced coma for three to five months. It was a long time before they brought her out of it. Everyone went to visit her because we didn't know if she *would* come out of it.

BONNIE: Julie's husband Joe came to visit when Annette was in that coma, and you've got to have a little fun, otherwise you could go nuts. Some of our other kids were there, and they said to Joe, "If Annette needs you to wipe her butt, would you?" And they were serious; they weren't laughing. He said, "Of course I would." I told Joe I wouldn't trade him for anything.

JOHN: While we were at the hospital visiting Annette, we all took blood tests to see if there was a match for a stem cell transplant. They didn't give us the results right then.

BONNIE: Meanwhile, the baby went home first and stayed at Julie's. Then, when they brought Annette out of the coma, she went home to be with the baby and her children.

When we went back to the hospital for Annette's check-up, the doctor said, "We need to talk. Sit down." I thought, "Now what?" He said, "None of you matched when we took the blood tests." The doctors were wondering who Annette's father really was. And I said, "You thought I was having an affair with the milkman out on the farm!" (Laughs.) But what happened was all those drugs had messed Annette up, and once they got it balanced out, our youngest son Nick was a perfect match.

JOHN: Nick had to give himself a series of shots in the stomach in order to stimulate growth of stem cells, and then it was a matter of a needle in one arm where they harvest stem cells and a needle in the other arm to return blood. It took over 5 hours.

Annette had the stem cell transplant. Then, she was behind that doggone plastic in isolation because her immune system had been wiped out in the process.

This whole chemo treatment would knock her down, and her food would taste like metal, and she'd lose her hair. It's a nasty old thing. Then, just when you think, "By golly you got it," her white blood cell count would come up, and then they'd say no, the cancer showed up again and we'd go back. We did that … (He glances over at Bonnie.) How many times?

BONNIE: At least three times. About half way through the illness there was a divorce between Annette and Alan. I sensed there were problems before the diagnosis, with the stress of fulltime jobs, and then all this. The middle time she had total body radiation.

JOHN: That's where you get sunburned from the inside out. I had a picture of her at Christmas, she was sitting at the end of the table, and her skin was black.

BONNIE: She lost her hair, and I told her, "When it grows back, I hope you're a redhead and have some fun when you get over this." (Laughs.) She got herself a pretty red wig to surprise me. The last time she went back for treatments, and every time, I said, "You don't have to go through this again Annette." And she'd say, "Yes I do, for my children." I'd say, "Okay. Let's get started."

JOHN: It was just a matter of time before the doctors said we couldn't do anymore and to just keep her comfortable. She was coming to that stage.

I was there when they gave Annette red blood cells, and her blood pressure shot up, and the technician panicked. They called another nurse and stopped the transfusion. Her high blood pressure caused a stroke. The next morning, the doctor called and said that Annette didn't respond to pain anymore.

BONNIE: The doctor called me and wanted to know if they should keep Annette on life support or take her off. I said, "If it was your wife, what would you do?" And the doctor said, "I wouldn't let it go on." I said, "Well, I'm glad you agree with me because I don't want to argue with anyone."

JOHN: Annette had an advance directive, and Bonnie was her appointed person for medical decisions.

BONNIE: I called our close friends who are counselors. I said, "How should I handle this with her children, and I need to know quick. I don't have time to figure it out. Tell me what to do." The counselor said, "Go get them and take them to see her." I called our sons, Patrick and Dan, and they came right over. As they pulled up, I said, "Go get Adrienne, Alex and Allison, we're going to the hospital immediately." They said, "You shouldn't take those kids up to the hospital." I repeated: "I said go get her children, we're taking them up there and I mean business. Do it!" And they did.

We drove to the hospital with all three kids. When we arrived, Annette's doctor cried in my arms and so did her husband Alan.

JOHN: We went from the hospital to the hospice center that day with Annette. Julie arranged all that. Our whole family was there.

BONNIE: We sat up with her all night. The next day, Julie said, "Can you leave Adrienne and me alone with her?" I said, "Whatever you say daughter."

Julie told Adrienne: "We need to tell your mom that she can let go." So, they did. And Annette died. She stopped breathing.

What has helped with your grief?
BONNIE: I have never cried over it. I know that's odd. But I feel grateful. We talked after the funeral. We were all just so relieved for Annette that her suffering was over. She had been in hell, *multiple times*. When they checked her bone marrow, I would sit on the floor, at her head; I would rub her arm and talk to her through the procedure. It was so painful, but they gave her a pill that made her forget. We did that several times.

JOHN: It was like your hands are tied, and your child is being tortured, and you can't do anything about it, from being on ventilator machines to all kinds of trachea things and learning how to swallow. What a mess. But the stroke that evening, after a pleasant day, probably just shut her down. She didn't have to agonize over knowing she was going to die.

BONNIE: That was a blessing too. While she was sick, people would ask me, "Why aren't you angry?" And I said, "I don't have time to be angry. I have to take care of her. I can't change it. Why be angry? That would just wear me out."

JOHN: Who would you be angry at anyway?

BONNIE: Well, a lot of people would be angry with God. You can't change it; why worry about it. Just do the best you can. Our motto is: *Two mules pulling together.*

JOHN: You have to be a team.

BONNIE: As for her children, Annette had them well-prepared and looked after with nannies. When she died, Adrienne was 11 ½ and Alex was 8, and Allison was 5 ½. Julie is like a mother to them. Annette's insurance was set up in a trust for her children. The trust will help them through college.

During the funeral, at the end of mass, Allison got on my lap and she asked, "Grandma, what happens to my mom now?" I said, "Allison, that's not your mom anymore in that casket. She's up in heaven already looking down on you. They're just gonna bury that box with that body in it." And she said, "Oh, okay."

What helped you cope?
BONNIE: You just keep going. And hang on to each other. I kept working; I never ran out of leave. I had wonderful people I worked with who supported me.

JOHN: How do you cope with anything? You sit down and figure out what you can do. And do the best you can. It's not easy to sit there while you watch someone who is dying. You put on an apron and gloves. You watch them put the chemo into her veins, and you say, "Boy, that's a good thing." She's losing her hair and stressing about what will happen to the kids when she dies. It's not as hard on the person watching it, nothing like the patient. But this ole world, we're not in charge of it. We come into the world, and there's a lot of fun stuff, but we certainly don't control it, not everything at least.

BONNIE: That last night, Annette had said she thought the kids would be okay because we'd see to it!

JOHN: She was at peace. It was disappointing because she was one of our children who would be stressed out about a test and the next day you'd ask her how she did and she'd say, "Oh, I got an A+." She was a perfectionist and always did things over the top. Then, there were 90 days to live, with no signs. It would be a shock to any person. But I am proud of our family. We drew our wagons in a circle, quick, to care for Annette.

Do you have any suggestions for someone going through something similar?

BONNIE: Take one step at a time.

JOHN: You only live until you die. Once you're born, you're heading toward your grave. Annette gave it her best her shot, and medicine gave it their best shot. From a spiritual perspective, it gives you time to reflect on anything you did wrong and get it straightened out. You can see the glass half empty all the time rather than being glad you got something in the glass at all.

BONNIE: And her kids are doing great.

JOHN: If you didn't want to expose yourself to some real hurt, you'd probably never get married or have children or any friends. Any time you have a relationship with anyone, you have a chance of losing it. If you only concentrate on that, you'd never do anything. We have 12 grandchildren and 2 great grandchildren. And the chance of those folks having troubles … (Trails off).

BONNIE: So far, so good.

[While we are talking, Bonnie telephones her son Nick. She says I need to speak to him because he can explain the stem cell transplant. She puts Nick on speakerphone and I introduce myself.]

≈+ +≈

Nicholas J. Bittner (sister, leukemia)

"Our family was able to have 5 ½ quality years with Annette." — Nicholas (Nick) studied to be a chemical engineer and then received a MBA in finance. He is Annette's younger brother and the youngest of five children. He was a stem cell transplant match for Annette.

From the first moment Annette found out she had leukemia she took an optimistic side of the situation. On one hand, she had leukemia. But on the other side, the doctors had caught it early because of the routine pregnancy check-up. Knowing she had the earliest start of diagnosing and treating it, she wanted to fight it and win the battle. She was completely upbeat, asking, "What's needed next to beat cancer?"

Annette went from knowing about the leukemia to getting quickly hooked up with some of the best doctors in the country, leading experts in leukemia. We felt like she had great doctors.

If she had been diagnosed two years earlier, her odds of making it six months would have been dramatically reduced given what science had learned about the disease and where they were in the medical field on treating that disease. There was a lot of reason to be optimistic.

We all got tested for bone marrow matches. I was a perfect match. It was a great thing because you only have about a 20 percent chance between siblings. If you don't match, it's a tougher route. The match started her ability to do stem cell transplants.

For my part, there wasn't anything to being a stem cell donor, no different than donating blood. Annette was started on chemo to buy time for her baby to develop and to prepare for an eventual transplant. It was at that point where they thought they might have to abort the pregnancy in order to save Annette, and the next day Allison was born. Fortunately, the same hospital had some of the best premature infant care.

Annette went septic right after Allison was born, a near miss with that. Annette could have passed away then or Allison as well.

Annette had two stem cell transplants. Her third time at the hospital, she was in good spirits but all of us were fearful of how much a body can take. It's worth taking the risk to see if you can beat it, but shortly thereafter she slipped into a stroke. They transported her to hospice so all of us could be with her before she passed. It was nice from our family's perspective for everybody to be with her.

What has helped with your healing?

Both Annette and her baby made it through the initial diagnosis. Allison was able to know who her mom was and get the benefit of growing up with her mom until she was 5 years old. A lot of things got set in place that gave Allison a good start in life. Adrienne, Alex, and Allison have family who were able to provide them support — before, during, and after. They are doing as good as any of my nephews and nieces.

I felt fortunate that our family was able to have those additional quality years with Annette, which allowed time to say goodbye and, more importantly, to share all the good memories that we had with her in those 5 ½ years.

Life Lived Well

Franklin D. Oliver (grandfather, stroke)

"He lived with a lot of joy in his life." — Franklin is 41 years old. He is a tall man who teaches social studies at Brebeuf Jesuit Preparatory High School. He lost his grandfather, who was 86 years old, from stroke complications. Franklin is married to Rachel Sipes and has a teenage son, Jacob (Jake).

My grandfather is Moses Jenkins. He was born in 1928. He is from rural Georgia; that's where he was born. But he moved around a lot as a kid. He was orphaned by the time he was two. Basically, he went from relative to relative. I'm not certain his father ever knew he was born. His mother had heart problems and died in her 20s. It's hard to imagine the kind of medical care available to her as a poor black woman in a rural setting in the south in the 1920s.

Jenkins was my granddad's last name, sort of accidentally. The typical practice was that everyone took the last name of whoever was the head of the household. At a certain point in his life, my grandfather was called Ponder, and at another time, he was called Whitefield — that happened to be the name of the relative who was head of the house. I don't think he knew his birth last name. Then, it was Jenkins.

He married Annie Ruth Bell. They worked together in Atlanta, Georgia at Tom-A-Toe Company, a tomato processing plant. My granddad took a shine to her. The story she tells is that he said, "One of these days, you're gonna be my wife. I've already seen it in a dream." She was 13 or 14 years old at the time and laughed it off. Later, she was being harangued and berated by a supervisor at work, and my grandfather intervened — at some risk to himself. She never forgot that and was really taken with him. It wasn't much after that they got married and had their oldest child that they moved north in the 1950s. The company sent him to help set up a new facility. Granddad's expectation was that it would be a two or three week startup. It turned into an opportunity to have a permanent job, and he decided to stay. They had eight children. My mom is the second oldest. Her name is Belinda.

Our family is a pretty diverse place. In some ways, our family portrait is representative of the world. (Laughs.) It's a huge variety of colors, shapes, and sizes. One of my uncles in 7 feet tall and one of my cousins is around 4 ½ feet tall. Lots of folks have a variety of tattoos or piercings and four or five people are openly gay. All of them felt very loved by my grandparents. I would not have guessed that my granddad would become an advocate of marriage equality. His church is a very conservative traditional church. He did though because he thought it was a right that everyone should get to marry who they love. I didn't give him enough credit I guess.

Even though Granddad is black, three of his eight kids married white people. I am black but my wife and son are white, and my granddad loved them both. He called Jake the roadrunner. I have great pictures of them together. He always wanted to know what Jake was doing in school and if he was practicing his violin or taking up the guitar now. He wanted to know about everyone, and he always seemed to keep up. He always said, "I just don't have time for hate." To him, that felt like the most obvious and simple thing in the world.

My grandfather died last year from the effects of a stroke. My grandmother had died three years prior. In most important respects, my granddad was my hero. He really epitomized my ideal of what a person should be, and I admired those characteristics. I tell people he was so strong that he could always be gentle, and he was so firm that he could always be kind.

Do you have a favorite memory of your grandfather?

To me, my granddad seems like a character in a movie. He was about 6-foot-1 with massive hands and absurdly wide feet. Once when I was finishing grad school and starting to go on job interviews, I didn't have any nice shoes. My grandfather gave me a pair of shoes. I had to wear three pair of socks! (Laughs.) My feet were as long, but his were quite a bit wider. I wore tube socks under the fancy dress socks. I forgot about that until I pulled out his shoes to wear to the funeral and thought, "Oh my God. I can't do this." (Laughs.)

As a very little kid, of course, he's my grandfather. My mom and my sister and I lived with him for a little while. So, he had these mythic proportions for me. It wasn't until I was a teenager that I started discovering it was real. He held those kinds of proportions for many other people as well.

My grandparents lived in an evolving neighborhood, and he and my grandmother were two of the few constants. I have no idea how many dozens of people who weren't actually related to them called them Ma and Dad, or Grandma and Granddad for those in the younger generation. My grandparents were continually busy with kids. If a kid in the neighborhood had a date for prom and couldn't afford to rent a nice car, he'd ask my granddad to borrow his car. My granddad always said yes. It happened multiple times. I don't know how many pregnant women my granddad drove to the hospital to give birth. It was a large number to the point where it was almost an expectation: If you're waiting and the bus is late to arrive and your family doesn't have a car, just call Moses and he'll drive you. (Laughs.)

We had a tradition of Sunday afternoon dinners and that meant going to his house after everyone finished church. We'd have dinner and sit and talk, often for hours. There was something he called praise reports, where someone gave updates on something positive in their lives, and that usually evolved into a whole host of things, a worry or issue going on. There was time to talk about it and have an informal help session and ask folks for prayers about a certain situation. That was a standard part of my life for decades.

My granddad did not graduate from high school. He worked, retired, and raised eight kids. He was about 13 years old when he quit school. Astonishing to me, after he retired, he started going to a literacy program. My mom and her siblings didn't know until they were adults that he was a functional illiterate. For a decade, he had the same reading tutor. I was on "Jeopardy," once — so you know the outcome. (Laughs.) But that was the thing I mentioned in my 20 seconds with Alex Trebeck. I talked about my granddad learning to read after retirement. He was in his late 60s. He didn't have a need to read anymore. He just wanted to improve himself.

Do you have any suggestions for someone going through loss?

I can imagine someone in my granddad's life situation being very negative. He grew up as a black man in the depression in really bad circumstances without parents. He was sent from place to place, sometimes in a very unpleasant fashion. He'd hear them say, "It's too hard for us to feed all these kids. You have to take him now." He was unwanted or felt unwanted a lot. Yet, he lived an ungrudgingly positive life. He was physically affectionate, which is rare for men of that generation, and he drew a tremendous number of people into his orbit. His funeral was amazing because it had this hodgepodge of people from across the city. There were tough looking white biker guys, lots of little old church ladies, and a surprising number of young people who knew him as one of the elders of the church community.

My grandfather went into the hospital after his stroke and had some time with us afterward. He went into a couple of different rehab facilities. But he did not recover. He could communicate a bit, but his speech was always poor after the stroke. I saw him lots of times before he passed away, which was really helpful. I was lucky that I went to visit him probably two days before he had the stroke, and we had time together. He told me a couple of stories he'd never told me before. That was fantastic.

In some respects, the difference in him after he had his stroke proved helpful. It didn't feel that way at the time, but it helped convince me that death was the best option at that point. He wasn't himself any longer, and he made it clear to multiple members of the family that he was ready to go. As a result, my family isn't reeling in the way we thought we would.

He missed his wife and talked about her consistently. But he had also started dating. He developed a great relationship with another woman that was hugely helpful for him and for the family at large. I was very worried that after my grandmother died, after 60 years together, he would wither. He refused to wither.

What has helped with your grief?

One thing that's helpful for me is having no pretense about it at all. I don't use euphemisms. I don't try to pretend that I'm 100 percent fine. I would worry if I didn't miss him. I would worry if I didn't feel sad. About a month ago, I was driving on the highway, and I saw the street sign that made me think, "Oh, I should go visit Granddad." It felt like a gut punch. I had to pull over and cry. That helps more than pretending to be distracted or acting as though nothing was happening. Something important was happening.

Additionally, I do something physical that helps. When someone important to me dies, I shave my beard. I've always had a beard. It feels like part of my identity in a sense. When I'm clean-shaven, every time I touch my face it feels weird. It gives me this moment of pause. I have to think about why my face feels different. After two or three weeks, I let it start growing in again. It felt like that was enough. Like the power in that moment of touch was gone, and I could let that go.

I meditated a little bit more right after his death. That was a conscious decision. I just needed it more. My wife Rachel checks on me; she asks how I'm doing, and she monitors. That helps. A student of mine gave me a prayer when Granddad passed, and it turned out to be a consolation. I also went to dinner with one of my aunts. We talked about a wide variety of things and Granddad came up multiple times. And we shared stories about him, and she told me some I hadn't heard, which was nice.

It helps me now that he lived so well. Not financially. (Laughs.) He joked that he had the taste of a rich man. But no, I don't mean he lived well financially. I mean that I don't feel badly about his life in any respect. He lived with a lot of joy in his life. He helped bring people and communities together in different ways, which is a great model for me. Long-term friends of mine were devastated by his death. People felt that Granddad loved them.

I told people that if I ended up being half as good a human being, I would be doing very well. I'm getting there. (Laughs.)

⇒+ +⇐

Ralph H. Lovberg (wife, leukemia)

"Every moment is a good deal more precious now." — Ralph is an intelligent, thoughtful man who grew up in Montana and lives in San Diego, California. He is 89 years old and has eight grown children. He lost his wife Ellen. They were married 56 years. His adult daughter Emily joins us for the interview.*

I met Ellen in the fall of 1952, while I was attending graduate school in Minneapolis. I was renting a room in a house there and had gone home to Montana for a short vacation that summer. While I was gone, the owner had rented rooms to a pair of nurses. When I came back, I walked into the house, and Ellen was the first person

132

I met. She said, "You must be Ralph." I said, "Yes, I am." And the rest is history.

Ellen worked as a nurse, up until we married and started having babies. We both came from working class backgrounds and that affected both of our outlooks. Her father worked for General Motors in a factory, and my father worked for a construction company as a builder. I decided I really wanted Ellen to be the mother of my children. It's kind of strange. That assumption just grew on us, and I never actually popped the question. It became obvious we would marry.

I went to the University of Minnesota for graduate school to get my PhD in physics. We married in June of 1953. By the time I got my degree, we had our first child. I've had a career in physics ever sense. I mainly worked in nuclear energy fusion or propulsion.

Later, we moved to New Mexico, and I worked at the Los Alamos national lab. Afterward, I agreed to go to San Diego because General Dynamic wanted to work on propelling spacecrafts. By the time we moved out to San Diego, we had five children. We decided to stay in San Diego. I joined the University of California at their new campus, and I got an offer of full professorship and spent almost 30 years there.

We had a lovely place in San Diego, an old turn of the century house, and it has become a family center

The thing that killed Ellen was leukemia. She collapsed one day on the front lawn. When we took her in, the analysis was severe anemia. It was the type of leukemia that they said only responded to very vigorous chemotherapy, which she had, but it was not sufficient. After the leukemia, the routine consisted of blood transfusions, frequently. She had transfusions, at least every week, maybe more toward the end. We spent a great deal of money.

At one point, Ellen made a conscious decision to stop the transfusions. She told her daughter, "It costs the price of a vehicle every time I get a transfusion, and I can't do it anymore." Ellen said there were too many people who don't have that ability and, morally, she couldn't do it while others did not have the ability to pay for it. She lost all her hair with chemotherapy but stood up very well and maintained her spirit through all of it. She never became morose or discouraged. Her faith really buoyed her up. She certainly taught us all how to die.

EMILY [*joining in*]: My mother was the mother of eight kids, and she was constantly trying to save a buck. I remember mom going to the dented can store, and we would buy dented cans. She would get them cheap because they had the labels off. So, our pantry was full of these cans without labels, and she'd say, "Go get six cans." We'd get them, and she would make a dinner out of it. Anyway, when she was dying, and this is from my brother Peter, the hospice nurse said to everyone, "Okay, she is transferring over right now. She's in a deep coma, and she probably won't come out, and it will be soon." Meanwhile, a call came in from the mortuary, from the people who prepare the body. Peter came back and was talking to one of the siblings and he said, "The mortuary said they're going to charge another hundred bucks if we don't bring her body downstairs." And mom, who is in a deep coma, sat up and said, "You don't pay them one more cent!" Then she lay back down and that was it. She died. (Laughs.) Peter said, "She got the last say." (Laughing.)

[*Ralph continues*]: She died at home, exactly as she wanted to, in her own bed and with us around her.

Our house sits on top of a high hill in the midst of this forest of eucalyptus trees. Ellen always admired the big red-tailed hawks that sailed across the fields and perched in the trees. The day she died, as her body was being taken away, the family gathered together, sort of stunned, the way you are when your wife and mother just died. We were out on the rear patio, and here came a group of hawks. Now they are solitary birds; they normally do not fly together. They're usually quite silent. But they came directly above us, and flew in a circle, around and around and around. And they cried and cried and cried. It was absolutely not hawk-like behavior. It was squarely over our heads, which is strange. Then they flew off, and I have not seen one of them since. I do not share this story unless I have a witness who can confirm it is true. (He glances over at his daughter Emily).

EMILY: Yes, that is exactly what happened. It was amazing.

What helped you cope with your grief?

After Ellen died, I was not torn up in the sense of weeping and wailing. I was kind of numb. A lot of the color went out of the world. It was greyer. I had the blessing of the kids and good friends who gathered around. My very best friend, who I've known since college, lives on the East Coast. He called me when he got the news. He said, "You come out here right away." He has a place around Martha's Vineyard, a nice place in New England. I went out there for a couple of weeks. Also, I'm still working in my profession, doing science and physics. My photography, which I've done all my life, is still there. There were things to keep me busy. Time going by really does soften things and heal.

In some ways, I had a new freedom I never had before. With a large family, whenever I found something fun to do, there was always hanging over me the issue of whether I was neglecting Ellen or the kids or things I should be doing. There was always unease. Now there is no unease. That has been a terrific thing. It's a little lonesome maybe — more than a little lonesome a lot of times — but I can spend any amount of time doing anything and not feel guilty about it. It wasn't that Ellen ever made me feel guilty about doing things I enjoyed; she was nice that way. But still, one feels that way oneself.

Now there is time to go into unanswered questions in physics and do my photography. I am also dabbling in poetry. I never had a notion that I could do a thing like poetry. I simply tried it, and it didn't turn out too badly. So, my days are pretty full.

There are times that come when I miss her severely. Times when I'd like to share an idea. Even times when I need my back scratched. (Chuckles.) But not being able to share things makes it most lonesome.

I will mumble things as I go past the memorial, like, "Dear Ellen, if you're there, say a prayer for me." I don't talk to her as if she were literally there. With this poem, on the occasion of that, I did feel her presence very much there. The occasion of it was just going outside and looking back at the house. We used to go and sit out on the patio, and each one of us was full of the sense of this life that finally came to us. It was way more than we had a right to expect. How did this happen to the likes of us? Maybe it's our working class backgrounds or something. But we had this sense of gratitude for the life we had. That's a wonderful feeling.

What are your favorite memories of Ellen?

One of my favorite memories is from during the time we were raising the kids. We'd go back to visit our parents: her mother in Wisconsin or mine in Montana. In either case, it was a long trip, 1,500 miles to Montana and 2,500 to Wisconsin. I bought a big Chevy van, and I took out all the seats and built in a set of bunks in the back.

EMILY (with excitement): That's my favorite memory, too!

[*Ralph continues*]: There was room for all the kids to sleep back there. We would travel overnight rather than during the daytime: from midnight to noon. We could always find a motel to stop mid-day and let the kids swim around in a pool in the afternoon, have something to eat, and then all go to bed around 5 or 6 p.m. and then get up at midnight and put the kids to bed in their bunks. Those overnight drives are absolutely one of my favorite memories because we could sit there and chat without interruption for hours. There was the smell of coffee and a little bit of music in the background. That particular music is another of my absolute favorite memories. All of the major radio stations had this overnight classical music. It transports me back whenever I think of it. Those memories are really, really good.

Is there anything else that helped with your healing?

When I'm really, really missing Ellen, those times come unbidden. Every now and then it just hits me. I spend that time missing her ferociously. There's nothing you can do about it. It passes. The world is full of interesting things to do and people to know. It passes, but it does hit from time to time. I never know when.

The question is how to get through missing routines: dinner, coffee together. You have to accept it, and feel the pain if it's painful. There's no fix for it. I don't have any prescription for, "Now I'm feeling this way," and "Now I will respond by doing something else." With me, it doesn't work that way.

I always had this dream that if I was strictly on my own, I would get in the car and drive up to the canyon country. I love that place. But what happened was that it developed that I finally couldn't drive. I had trouble with my eyesight. I had to give up driving. That's a bitter pill because having the car gives one a real freedom. Suddenly, it's not there.

Do you have any spiritual or religious practices that helped?

I am spiritual. There is a strong bias by scientists for the scientific method and the idea that the findings of Darwin, molecular biology, and theoretical physics will lead us to complete knowledge of ourselves — not only our bodies and structures but also in our minds, our cells, and our personalities. The scientific presumption is that knowledge will be all we ever need. Recently, Steven Hawking said flat out that we would learn all we need to know by applying the laws of science. Well, no, I firmly disbelieve that.

Pierre Teilhard de Chardin, a paleontologist and a Jesuit, influenced me in my thinking. My belief is that we occupy a realm of reality that is just as real as the material realm we live in. Our physical or material reality is subject to the laws of biology and physics, but that other realm is not. It's simply different.

It doesn't bother me that my life will end, and I don't know what comes after. I'm in the dark about what happens afterward. I don't have much time left, and I'm kind of on borrowed time now. I'm not scared or worried about it. The life I've led has been exceptionally good. I'm quite satisfied. It's been a good show. The way I'd like to die is to simply drop dead while doing something I enjoy.

Is there anything else you found helpful?

Creativity, I have to say, has been a surprise to me. Talk about mystery. This one poem came out in a single afternoon; it just rolled out easily. The photography and poetry have kept my mind active and sharp. The thing about the poetry is that it's a new adventure. A whole new door has opened that I never knew was there. It's fun. A thrill actually.

I am profoundly grateful for the way things have turned out, and the life I've had with Ellen. Every moment is a good deal more precious now. I know there are not going to be as many of them. That's another reason why it's been such a joy for me to write the poetry. Suddenly, these moments are really useful in a new way. I have created something that is complete. That goes for other things as well, taking photographs or working on a piece of physics. Anytime you can strive to complete something and finish it and set it there and say, "This is beautiful." That's what you want to live for.

Postscript: Two years after our interview, Ralph passed away.

⊨+ +⊨

David Traylor (life partner, rapid onset MS)

"I open my eyes every day, feel my heart beating, and realize I have a purpose." — David has a sharp mind, kind heart, and keen sense of humor. He lost his father (Eddie), his life partner of close to 30 years (Bruce Osborn), and his mother (Doris Ettinger). At the time of Bruce's death, gay marriage had not yet been legalized. As a result, David was not legally permitted to make medical or burial decisions for Bruce. After Bruce died, their home went to Bruce's mother.

I was 10 when my dad died. His name was Eddie. My dad was a mixologist; if you called him a bartender you would get a scolding because he went to school to learn his trade and, therefore, deserved the title. I had only met him a couple of times when I was really young and didn't know him. He and my mother were married but not to each other. Polite people didn't discuss things like that in the 1950s. On my 18th birthday, my mother told me Eddie was my father. I always thought I looked like my mother, but when I was finally able to access my father's obituary in the newspaper, I saw his picture come up, and it explained a lot, like why my mom's heart always broke when she looked at me.

I also learned that somewhere I have two half-sisters. Very few people know my story. But it's something you walk around with.

My partner for 28 ½ years was Bruce Osborn. We met at a restaurant where I worked as a waiter. He was straight-laced, three-piece suit, very business-like. I was kind of a crazed punk rocker. We had absolutely nothing in common. He was older, very buttoned down, and I was a free spirit. His friends hated me, and my friends hated him. He was Republican, and I was Democrat. I was the artistic, outgoing, gregarious personality, and he was the wind beneath my wings. He stood in the background and the shadows and was supportive. It became what I thought of as the perfect union.

We were together six months before we decided to consolidate households. My first love was Patrick. I stayed with him past the point of hurt, and I lost a lot of self-esteem in the process. After Patrick, I had a lot of trouble trusting anyone. On a physiological level, I was impotent for almost a year. At 27, that's kind of devastating. People always said about Bruce, "He's such a nice guy." At first, I was taken aback by that comment. After Patrick, I didn't think I deserved a nice guy. But Bruce was the most kindhearted, gentle, loving, rational person that you would ever want to meet.

After Bruce and I got together, Patrick showed up on our doorstep one day, saying, "I love you. I made a mistake. I want you back." Bruce told him, "You've chosen your path. I suggest you walk down it."

Eighteen years ago, Patrick died of AIDS. When he got desperately ill, Bruce said, "Go, be with him. He needs you." That meant the world to me. I was the only one there in the end, and he died in my arms.

Bruce's illness was horrific and unbelievably devastating. It started as a headache, double vision, and neuralgia (nerve pain). He went to the eye doctor and also his primary care physician. He was ill for 4 ½ years before they were able to get a diagnosis. They tested for Huntington's and ALS. One of the doctors said, "What about HIV?" I said, "I've always trusted Bruce, and I've always been faithful. You know what, do the test and get it out of the way. It'll be one more thing we can rule out." Of course, the test was negative. Bruce began to lose mobility, and then he would get confused, like early-onset Alzheimer's. I lost a little part of him every day for almost five years, and no one knew why.

The last nine months of his life, Bruce's health insurance ran out. He had to go to a learning hospital. That is where we finally got a diagnosis of rapid onset MS (multiple sclerosis). It took 12 neurologists, 7 hospitals, 14 different doctors, and countless MRIs, CT scans, and spinal taps to find out.

At the same time, my mother's health was deteriorating. Normally, I talked to her five or six times a day by phone. One day, I couldn't get hold of her. I had just brought Bruce home from the ER. I had to go to my mother's apartment complex to find out what had happened. Turns out, she had fallen and had been lying there for about 5 hours. I took her to the same ER the same day. One of the techs looked up and saw me and said, "Are you still here?" I said, "Different shirt, different patient, let's do this." And that's just how it was. She recuperated, but the doctors determined that dementia had set in for her.

Then, without my knowledge, Bruce's mother had Bruce placed in a nursing home on July 21. My mom was admitted to a nursing home on July 22. The doctors told us that they didn't expect Bruce to last until September.

Each morning, I would get up and go take care of my mother at her nursing home and then get on the interstate and drive to take care of Bruce. I would go back home and take care of the house and our animals and try to make some sense of all the paperwork and bills. Afterward, I'd go to work where I served people for a living.

This back and forth went on every day for a year. Bruce's mother, I believe, never really approved of our relationship. I was trying to keep her happy and keep Bruce happy. Everything was in Bruce's name. Through this process, she got our life savings and our home.

I was truly left homeless. It didn't matter because she did one perfect thing in her life when she had Bruce. I showed his mother nothing but kindness for close to 30 years. I would tell anyone who asked why, "No matter what she does, no matter who she pisses off, that man in the bed is her baby." That had to be my mantra.

The day he passed, Bruce had gone to the hospital for a spinal tap. It was April 28, 6:35 in the morning. The doctors called his brother, and his brother called me. The hospital staff said Bruce had experienced complications, and they didn't expect him to make it. I do not remember getting dressed. I do not remember driving to the hospital. All I know is that I arrived there in about 7 minutes.

I walked into the room. All of the machines were off. It was quiet. The nurses and doctors were standing around. Somebody took my coat. The nurse said, "We gave him morphine, and I don't know if he'll recognize you." I said, "That's okay." I sat down and took his hand. I told him that he had been strong and brave and if he was concerned about me, that I would be fine. That he needed to be free of pain. And to just let go. Bruce turned toward me and opened his eyes. He took a very deep breath, with a smile. He didn't exhale. It was quiet. I looked up at the caregivers. I said, "I'm not an expert, but I think he's gone."

Shortly thereafter, his mother arrived. I said to her, "Bruce tried to be strong and wait for you, but he just didn't have it in him." I pretty much crumbled in a corner.

I went home with his belongings and made my obligatory calls. That night, I was feeding the fish in the koi pond. I looked up at a full moon. It was round and brilliant and bright. Bruce had been a corporate photographer for over 40 years, an amazing photographer. I said out loud, "That son of a bitch waited until the lighting was perfect before he took his last shot." Then I realized, I'm home alone and I'm talking to the moon. I started laughing like a madman.

The next day, I met his mother at the cemetery for the arrangements. I took Bruce's neckties with me. I had never been through the process and wasn't sure what to do. His mother had bought the two of them side-by-side crypts at the mausoleum. She never inquired if we had plans for his memorial or what I wanted for him.

I decided to go over to the nursing home and clear out the rest of Bruce's things. What a difference! Every kitchen staff, nursing staff, front office person and so on, came in to tell me what an impact we had made in their caretaking and how amazed they were at the love Bruce and I shared and my resolution to be there for Bruce. What should have been a 45-minute process took 3 hours. It was 3 hours of packing and weeping and personal testimonials. The last three people in the room were the maintenance men who said they never knew what to make of us. These maintenance men said, "But we loved him, and we love you." That was the best testimonial.

Later that afternoon, Bruce's mother telephoned me. She had gotten a pastor and planned a memorial service, a two-day event. Again, I breathed: *her baby.*

The pastor called me. She was a Quaker who, turns out, was rather progressive. She was very friendly. She said, "I want to know your story. What can you tell me about Bruce?" I said, "The best story I can give is of the 500 valentines."

Bruce had created a holiday he called the 14 days of St Valentine. Every day, for the two weeks leading up to Valentine's Day, there was a numbered card and then the actual Valentine's Day card itself. I thought it was a little cuckoo. But I adored it. Not everybody gets treated that way.

The last year Bruce was home and ill, as Valentine's Day was approaching, he asked me for a lap desk and a piece of paper. I knew he was doing something. His coordination was off, and his vision was going. But he had drawn a Valentine's Day card. It looked like it was from a first grader, a Valentine with our initials and our years together. He said, "I didn't have any money." I said, "That is the most precious Valentine I have ever received."

When he passed, I realized that in boxes, in bundles, tied with red ribbons, there were approximately 500 Valentines cards, and I felt the enormity of that coming from the same person. So, I told the pastor the story of 500 valentines and other tidbits about Bruce.

The day of the funeral, Bruce's family sat on one side in the chapel and my little band of angels sat on the other side. As people were arriving, I notice this guy, and he's wearing this glittery-pink, heart-shaped, stick-on heart. I thought, "Oh, that's interesting." Meanwhile, I'm busy, busy, busy greeting people. Then, I look up, and there are more people with hearts on their lapels; the hearts are different colors and sizes, and some have the glitter pink. I'm thinking, "Okay, this is kind of unusual."

So, I step out into the front hall where the greeting table is located.

The pastor had taken it upon herself to provide a basket of these heart valentines, and a sign that said: "Please take a Valentine in honor of Bruce's love for David." Her sash was crusted with tiny hearts. That was the theme of her eulogy: The 500 Valentines.

What helps you cope with your grief?

I open my eyes every day, feel my heart beating, and realize I have a purpose. When Bruce passed away, my friends expected me to go into a dark period. My resolution was to become a survivor. My logic was that I mourned his passing almost every hour of every day for nearly 5 years. I saw a piece of him slip away and the hollow shell that was left. I was grateful his suffering was over.

In coming to terms with my financial situation, my coping mechanism was to take Bruce's wishes into consideration. I was the sole beneficiary and was able to hire a lawyer, and the first thing he did was fire off a letter to Bruce's mother saying, "Thank you for allowing David to remain in the home." With the help of the attorney, I did not have to leave immediately.

Bruce's mother called and said she was coming to the house to get some of Bruce's things. Now, remember, this is close to a 30-year relationship. Bruce and I had over 28 years of memories there and artwork and collectibles. That was the last time we spoke.

I visit the mausoleum about once a month, sometimes more. His mother's name is carved next to Bruce's name. The day she passes will probably be my last visit because I doubt Bruce will get any rest in the hereafter. (Laughs jokingly.) I get a ladder and change his flowers. I sing our song. I'm not a vindictive person, but when I visit Bruce, I do have a little ritual. I always chew gum and, while I'm singing our song, I take my wad of gum out and leave it on the ledge under his mother's name. It's kind of like spitting on someone's grave. It's passive, but after 4 ½ years, you should see what the ledge looks like. (Laughs.)

Anything else that has helped you cope?

I'm in a new relationship now, with Jonathon. About eight months into the relationship, I decided it was time to introduce him and Bruce. Being an orthodox Jew, Jonathon is familiar with rituals and traditions. I took Jonathon to the mausoleum. I got the ladder and went through my little ritual, and Jonathon had walked away. When I came down, he said, "Would you mind if I go up?" I've never shared that ritual with anyone. I said, "Of course you can go up." He went up for a few minutes, and I gave him his privacy. When Jonathon came down, he had tears in his eyes. I said, "I have to ask. What did you say?" He replied, "I said, *Thank you*." (David sighs deeply.) That meant the world to me.

During the first year after dating Jonathon, possibly the person I could consider spending the rest of my life with, I sold everything and moved into his home. I met a lady one night in the restaurant and turned out she is psychic. I'm somewhat skeptical. There are certain things I believe in. But, I began to talk to her, and she read me in a manner that rocked me to my soul. She said, "You were with someone for a long time." I said, "Yes." Then she said, "And they left you." I said, "Yes." She continued, "You've recently met somebody new, that's making you smile." (Laughs.) I said, "Yeah." And she said, "Bruce wants me to tell you that he sent Jonathon to you. Let go. Be grateful." Meanwhile, I am openly weeping.

The more time I spend with Jonathon, the more I can see that if there is indeed someone that was meant to step into that position, he's certainly it.

Do you have any religious or spiritual practices that helped?

I've relied on my own internal spirit and knowing right from wrong. My mantra has been, "Make people happy, and you'll be happy in return." I've always been a giver, and I keep a sense of humor. I wake up, my eyes are open, and my name is not in the obits. Chances are it's going to be a good day.

"Blessed again," is my mantra. I was incredibly blessed with Bruce in my life, and I am positively ebullient that I am blessed again. Jonathon is amazing. The feeling I had after Patrick left me, my first love, was one of abandonment and abuse. When I met Bruce, I couldn't believe he was real. I had trust issues for quite a while, and then I let go and was grateful for every day. It was about eight years in when I realized how tremendous our relationship was. That is true of my relationship with Jonathon. There are days when I cannot believe he loves me as much as he does.

My mom passed two years ago. Her wishes were for a cremation, no services. Honoring those requests is the easiest thing in the world: no flowers, no casseroles, and no family coming over to do the dishes. But the residual effect is that you realize there's not much closure. You're just alone with your mom and a box of ashes.

I had my mom's ashes with me for a year, and on the anniversary of her passing, one year later, I said to her, "Okay. We're going for a road trip." So, I put mom in the car. I took her ashes to this little country cemetery, next to my grandmother's grave. Jonathon gave me a red rose to place on the grave, and I spread her ashes on top of my grandmother's grave. It was a beautiful day. It felt right in my heart. It was kind of windy, and I tried to spread the ashes in a heart shape because it's artsy. Then I looked down to see her ashes all over me. I said, '"Holy crap, mom! This is one of my favorite sweaters." Again, I'm laughing. If you can remember someone's passing with laughter, there's no better way.

Sandra G. Harris (husband, brain tumor)

"When we gather as a family, we tell stories. It helps to know we're not alone in missing them." — Sandra is in her 70s. She lost her daughter Edith to suicide and her husband, W. Edward (Ed) Harris to a brain tumor. She and Ed were married 56 years. Sandra is a professional storyteller, and Ed was a beloved minister.

I met Ed the summer before we went to Birmingham Southern College, a liberal arts college in the Deep South. The boy I had been dating told Ed, "I got a girl for you I think you'll really like." So, Ed and I went out. But he was wild and irreverent. He just seemed too much for me. The college was Methodist and served as a training ground for ministers. After dating a few of those young men, I found them too serious and earnest. I decided Ed might not be too wild after all.

I let Ed know I was interested when I saw him perched on a railing outside Munger Hall where we attended classes. He was sitting in the sunshine, in May. I had bought an ice cream cone at the student café and was climbing the hill to go back to class. When I got to the top of the hill, I reached out and offered him a lick of my ice cream cone. I like to say when I tell this story that I couldn't even spell Freud and had no idea how provocative that might seem. (Laughs.)

Once we started dating, we discovered we had a lot in common. He wasn't really quite as wild as I thought. We married in 1956 and had three children: Edith, Mark, and Phillip. Ed continued on to theological school and became a minister. He worked at a church in Boston and later at a church in Urbana, Illinois. He then worked as a minster at All Souls Church in Indianapolis. After eight years at All Souls, he became an interim minister at a church in Bethesda, Maryland.

That was a good year for us. I was invited to tell stories at the White House Easter egg roll. I got back from lunch with a friend, and Ed was pacing up and down, about ready to jump out of his skin. He said, "You'll never guess who called! Guess who wants you to tell stories?" I said, "Who?" And he said, "THE WHITE HOUSE!" I called, and they told me there would be 7,000 people at the Easter egg event. I said, "Well, that's a few more people than I've ever told stories to before." (Laughs.)

Later, Ed went to another interim job in Evanston, Illinois. At that point, I told him I wanted to retire from being a minister's wife. He said, "That's fine. Wherever I go, I will just tell them that I'll come, but my wife is retired from being a minister's wife."

Then, our daughter Edith died. It was a terrible blow.

Edith struggled with depression and the disease of alcoholism. She went into treatment and got good care. In treatment they asked her what she wanted in her life that she wasn't getting, and she said, "I want to get married and have a baby." She found a wonderful man to marry, and they had a daughter, Tabitha, whom they both adored. But Edith continued to suffer from depression and also had two back surgeries that left her in constant physical pain.

After her first suicide attempt, we brought Edith home to care for her. In retrospect, I thought it was too soon for her to be discharged from the psych department. She had not been happy about being found and rescued. When she was at our place, she felt a little better. Then, on a beautiful day, when she seemed to be feeling pretty good, she said, "Mom, you know I may not be able to see you and dad through your aging." She was a social worker; she knew that when people make a suicide attempt, they often do so again. After she left our place, someone else took her in. She wasn't able to find a job, and it was just bare survival. It got to be too much.

It almost goes without saying that all of these issues are hard on a marriage. The divorce was going to go through on the very day Edith took her life.

Was there anything that helped you with the loss of your daughter?

With grief, there's a process you go through. We absolutely cleared Edith's husband, Steve, of any blame. He has been like a son to me and an amazing father to Tabitha, who was only 11 when her mom died. I attended a suicide survivor group. This whole business of facing into what you're feeling: it's territory women live in from the get-go. We know there's no avoiding our feelings.

I found the works of Byron Katie, a spiritual teacher. Ed said, "I think you need to go to her workshop. I'll go with you." We went together. It was an enormous help to me.

I went on a six-day silent retreat led by Adyashanti. I told Adyashanti my daughter had died, and I was afraid of losing more of my children. He said, "We ask questions here that sometimes take people aback." I replied, "Yes, I know. That's why I'm here." Then he asked me, "Has anything beautiful happened as a result of your daughter's death?" I told him, "Yes, lots of beautiful things have happened." And he said, "None of that takes away from the tragedy of your loss, but it helps you to see the larger picture of what is unfolding here." I found that tremendously soothing.

After that retreat, I bought a small portable recorder and contacted eight or ten of Edith's close friends and asked them to meet with me to talk about Edith. That process was tremendously healing for me and for them as well. We laughed and cried together, and those recordings will be available for Tabitha one day if she wants to learn more about her mother.

When did your husband pass?

Four years after Edith's death, Ed died. We started out thinking it was a urinary tract infection. But when treatment for that failed, the urologist sent him to a neurologist. The doctor told us he thought the message was not getting delivered from Ed's bladder to his brain. The neurologist immediately ordered an MRI. By that time, our son Phillip had come from St. Louis to be with us, thank God.

As we walked in the door after the MRI test, the phone was already ringing. The neurologist said Ed needed to check into the hospital that very evening. We were in shock, but none of us had eaten. So, Phillip and I began putting together something for dinner. Ed, who was exhausted, said, "Hon, let me do that. It may be the last thing I can do for you." (Crying.) It was a completely unrealistic offer, but I think he knew then that he probably wasn't coming home again. *He knew.*

The doctors had seen a large brain tumor. Ed had been in the hospital just two or three days, and the doctor said, "It looks like brain cancer, the type that progresses fast in people his age." Ed was 76 years old. He had been telling people on the phone he had a small tumor on his brain. I told Ed, "We heard you say the tumor was small. It's not small, and you're probably going to die from this. The doctors aren't going to be able to fix it." (Crying.) That was hard.

Ed was in the hospital two weeks. He asked me to bring his book of Chinese poetry. One of his doctors was born in China. Ed and I had been to China, and Ed had bought a book of Chinese poetry. The doctor came in and the two of them sat, and he got the doctor to read him these poems, in Mandarin, and then translate for him. It was not the kind of thing doctors usually do with dying people.

My son Mark said we needed to get his ex-wife Debra there. She's an occupational therapist and absolutely fearless in taking things on and asking questions and pressing. She loves us, and we love her. She was extremely helpful.

Ed was smart, and he was losing his speech. He had this beautiful voice and now he had to whisper what he wanted to say. There are so many sweet things about that time.

The discharge social worker told us we needed to take Ed to a nursing home. Picking out nursing homes isn't something you need to be doing when you're a wreck yourself, but that's what had to be done. My friend Ken Oguss helped me find a nursing home.

A good friend who is a therapist had said earlier, "You are geared here for sprinting. But you don't know how long it will go on. You've got to take care of yourself." I had begun to let other people stay with Ed so I could get away a bit, and I went to my yoga classes. I was at yoga when the nurse called and said it was time to look at hospice. Well, I had been thinking that for some time, but I didn't know how to judge those things. I said, "Good, yes, that sounds right."

Two days before he died, an occupational therapist came to work with Ed. It was a beautiful day outside; the August heat had broken. She got him in a wheelchair and invited me to go outside on a walk. While walking, she talked to Ed about the breeze on his face and asked if he could hear the water in the fountain. We came to a gazebo and sat there. I had told her that Ed liked all music, but he *loved* Van Morrison. She pulled out her recorder, and she had Van Morrison music on it. She said, "Ed, listen to this." He was sitting there in his wheelchair, and he had turned inward; we weren't always sure if he was tracking what we were saying. When she began playing that music, he started tapping and rocking to the music. I was so touched. It was wonderful.

The occupational therapist said, "We want to keep people alive, in this world, while they are here. Anything you know he loves from home — scents or textures or tastes — bring it." Phillip stayed that afternoon, and I went home and rested.

That night, I thought about ice cream and wondered how I might get a tiny bit of ice cream to Ed when there's no refrigerator in his room. The next day, I went into a drugstore and bought one of these little frozen ice cream cones. When I got to his room, they had taken him to the dining room. He was just sitting there. He couldn't feed himself. I fed him this ice cream cone with a spoon. That's the last he ever ate.

The next day they told me he had just days or hours left.

I left to call my sons to tell them how close it was. When I walked back to the room, Ed was gone. I didn't realize it at the time, but the ice cream cone had brought us full circle, back to when we were kids who had just started dating.

What has helped you with your grief?

Losing Ed was excruciating. I was desperately in need of help on all levels. I asked the minister at All Souls Church to do a small family service right away. I didn't want to put pressure on us because I knew it would be a big brew-ha-ha. None of the family was in any shape for a large gathering.

Also, I let people help me. I had learned from all those years of being a helper that there comes a time when you need to let people help you. Sometimes, it's a service you do for them.

I have a spiritual group that meets in my living room once a month, and I have a circle of women who have been meeting for close to 30 years. Getting anchored by those monthly meetings really helped me. Ed would have wanted me to make it through this. My friends told me, "Ed would not want you to throw yourself on the funeral pyre." I said, "No, but that would have been easier." That's kind of the truth of it. My storytelling helped me through it, too. I hope to do more of that soon.

Do you have any suggestions for someone going through something similar?

In my early stages of my grief, it was hard to plan. I'd get to feeling better and then never know what would trigger it. You have to know that you can cancel. People won't sue you for not showing up. I got comfortable knowing that whatever plans I made had to be tentative.

Pay attention that you're not doing only things to just distract yourself — things that are not getting you anywhere. Find what really nurtures and helps you, whether its music, meditation, yoga, or singing. If you pray, then pray. If you garden, then garden. If you dance, then do it with all your heart. For several months, I wrote letters to Ed almost every morning. If you're trying to hold grief at bay, get over that. It needs to be welcomed, not wallowed in, but welcomed.

I rode my bicycle and that took me outdoors. I could see people, and that boosted my spirits. Stay connected to people. If you are open to things getting better, then beautiful things happen in the wake of devastation.

My grandchildren help. I have three. When we gather as a family, we tell stories. We tell stories about Edith and Ed and anyone else who has passed. We think that telling their stories is a good thing to do, and it speaks to the fact that the people we love are still with us. It helps us to know that we're not alone in missing them.

⊷+ +⊶

CHAPTER 5

BALM FOR THE SOUL

"The artist vocation is to send light
into the human heart."

— GEORGE SAND

May we know the beauty of our own true nature ~

Following our true calling in life may not seem like a path toward healing, but such a decision can make a world of difference — in our happiness and in the happiness of others. In the wonderful children's book, *Miss Rumphius,* by Barbara Cooney, a little girl named Alice lives with her grandfather, who is an artist. He tells Alice that she must do something to make the world more beautiful. When she grows older, Alice decides to scatter lupine seeds throughout her village. Initially, the people in her village think she is crazy. Later, when the seeds grow into vibrant, colorful flowers, Alice becomes known as The Lupine Lady. This story beautifully illustrates how our small acts can greatly benefit the world.

Doing what we love in this world can bring enormous healing to our hearts and provide healing for others, as well. Meredith, (who lost her husband and father) acknowledges, *"With photography, I find I can engage in a way that is healing for the world."*

Grief and loss in this section have blossomed into a calling. As Sophia (who decided to study nutrition after her father's death) says, *"I feel like I have helped some of my friends become healthier and taught them some of the things I've learned. It's just really cool to see the chain reaction. I'm thankful to my dad."*

Through creative outlets or vocation choices, the individuals here express their lasting love for the person who has passed and carry that love forward in meaningful ways.

Bonnie (who lost her baby three days after his birth) states, *"I believe Tommy transformed my life. He came here to set me on my life's path as a woman, as a person who's legally blind, and as an advocate for people with disabilities. I carry Tommy's wisdom and love everywhere and always, in my heart."*

⋙ ⋘

Creative Expression

Katharine J. Oberreich (father, heart attack)

"The thing that helps me most is doing what I love." — Katharine (Kate) is in her early 30s and maintains a youthful sense of wonder. She is a mixed media artist. Her artwork was used on the set of the movie, The Fault in Our Stars. Kate lost her father (Stephen Oberreich) when she was in college. He was 54.

Dad was primarily a photographer, involved in photography sales for as long as I can remember. He did a lot of media photography and also his own fine arts work on the side. When I was 11, my parents divorced. My mom worked for a couple of advertisement agencies and then started doing pottery when I left for college. She's a full-time ceramic artist now.

My dad had a very sudden heart attack that came out of nowhere. It wasn't until after he died that I learned he had visited a hospital in Iowa a few months prior. We were going through his apartment and finding paperwork for hospital bills and half-used medications. It spoke to an ongoing health issue that he just didn't tell me about. In hindsight, I suspect more was going on because that summer he was changing his will and making sure I had power of attorney. He always put it in the context of, "Should anything happen." Looking back on it, I think he knew.

He was just shy of turning 55.

At the time, I was in college. I was 22 years old. It was the end of fall semester. I had just taken my last final the day before and was getting ready to pack up and come home for winter break. It was one of those non-stop days, and I finally got back to my dorm room around 8 or 9 p.m. My roommate was gone. It was the first time I had to sit down all day. I sat down to eat and got a call from the residence hall front desk that I had guests.

When I got down to the front desk, my mom and stepdad were there, which was completely out of nowhere. I was expecting to drive home the next day. We went into my hall director's office, and my mom told me. My roommate was kind of hiding out because she already knew. I saw her afterward. She is a sweet, wonderful person, and she was great. She is the first person I saw after I knew.

It was so sudden. The coroner said it was so fast that my dad probably didn't even know what was happening. Just gone. Then, there were all the phone calls to pertinent people. My mom wanted to tell me in person. It wasn't something she wanted to do over the phone. It helped having my stepdad, Mark, there. His dad died when he was young, and his grandfather not too long after that. Mark had been 11 or 12 when it happened. So, he was sort of the only person who exactly got how it felt for me.

I don't think I processed anything immediately after my dad's death. He had made me an executor of his estate, which was the paperwork he had been anxious to have me sign. I was on a holiday break from school. So, I just dove into the business of his life. I went to court, hired a lawyer, and did all the stuff that comes with emptying an apartment and selling a car. I had great help from my family and relatives. But I was so focused and business-minded at that point that it felt like a full-time job. Every day something had to be dealt with. I don't remember specifics. I just kind of kept going. His memorial was a month later because we didn't want to interfere with the winter holidays. I only vaguely remember the memorial service. I realized later there was this gap in my memory, and that was a little scary.

I considered not going back to school after winter break. In my head, I was keeping myself busy and thinking, "There's more to do, there's more to do."

I did go back to school after break. I would have regretted it had I not. Education has always been important in my family. The message was: "Even if you don't do what you went to school for, you're going to college."

At school, I had a series of ... (Trails off.) I tried to concentrate on being in school because it's what my dad would have wanted. (Pauses and then continues.) I had a series of panic attacks that semester. I was taking art classes. One happened in class when we were watching a movie about the painter Jackson Pollock. There was this scene where he dies in this horrible car accident. I sort of flipped out and had to leave the room.

What helped with your grief?

It was probably a good year before I felt like I was grieving because the estate closed, that stuff was dealt with, and I finished out the school year. I might have done summer school that year. I don't like to sit still. I process things by not processing — by staying busy. Then it comes out in different ways. I don't necessarily approach things directly when it comes to grief. I'm also not sure that I need to or that it would benefit me.

I never felt the need to sit with a therapist. I'm not saying that I won't at some point. But I've not been one to sit down and talk it out with someone. I might talk about it over several conversations. Not in a "Let's sit down and hash it out" kind of deal. That may lead me to holding onto things longer than I should. I hate to say, "should" though.

Before I realized I was processing, I started seeing changes in my artwork. To some degree in school you're making things based on the assignments you're given. Only, I noticed the way I would do those assignments was very different from the previous semester. A lot of anatomical hearts started showing up in my artwork. Also, there was more open space in my work, which hadn't been there before.

There are still times when I put a heart in a painting, and that for me will always be his symbol. Sort of a way to say, "He is still around." I did this painting for a show and the title is, "Portrait of an Artist." It's meant to be a self-portrait, symbolically. The painting is of a tree with a paper airplane nailed to the tree. Hanging from the tree branch is a heart dangling on a string. The heart sort of snuck in there again.

Do you have any religious or spiritual practices that helped?

I have a women's circle group that I came into shortly after my dad's death. I was going to a Winter Solstice celebration with my friend Stephanie, who I've known since I was 14 years old. She introduced me to the other women in the circle group, and they invited me to join them. Being with those women the first year after his death helped me let go of a lot of things, crying through most of the retreat weekend and doing extensive talking about my dad.

My spirituality is something I'm always working on and investigating. I'm not Christian and I'm not Jewish, although both are part of my family's religious orientation. I believe in a spiritual power, but I don't put a name or face on it, and I don't really want to. Pagan seems to fit the best because I have a strong sense of personal responsibility, and I feel like others should, too. I believe in the principle of karma, but not in terms of punishment. I don't identify with an All Powerful God ruling over us and directing our lives. Not to say that there isn't some being. But I believe she's a woman.

In some ways, I pray through my artwork. And I meditate through my artwork. There are periods where I am working on a painting, and I will lose complete chunks of time, and that's what I needed at that moment.

Have you felt any connection to your dad since he left?

My dad worked as a photographer for the Indy 500. So, race day is a tricky day for me. Last month my basement flooded, and I was trying to pull everything out, including a camera bag of his that I distinctly remember him carrying on track days. I used to go into the racecar pits with him without a media pass. Sort of like, "She's my assistant, pay no mind that she's 12." (Laughs.) That was our thing that we could do together.

Occasionally, I had these weird moments. His nickname for me was Babe O, which stood for baby Oberreich. He called me that his whole life. Not too long after his death, I was in a store and heard — or thought I heard — someone say, "Babe O" to a child. I burst into tears and had to leave.

The semester after his death, I took a photography class. It was an easy class because I grew up with a darkroom in the house. But

I needed the credits. During that semester, I had a dream that I was in the school's darkroom, and I was processing film. My dad was standing behind me telling me that I was doing it wrong. I was trying to tell him that this is the way my teacher said I was supposed to do it. He said, so clearly, "Well, your teacher is a moron." (Laughs.) Which is totally something he would have said. I was like, "Okay, I'm going to do it the way you taught me." Then I woke up. The dream was reassuring. I felt like: *Alright, he's still here.*

Is there anything else that helped with healing your grief?

The holidays are hard. My dad's death was in December, and his birthday is December 30. That time of year is difficult. Last December was the 10-year anniversary of his death. At that point, it hit me really hard. I thought, "It can't be *that* long." (Crying.)

I struggle with him not telling me what was going on with his health. I try to be understanding. I was at school. He didn't want to worry me. Then, I also think, "Why couldn't he trust me enough to tell me or let me help?" Maybe he had this sense of: He's the dad, and he's supposed to take care of me. (Crying.)

It worries me a little that I don't think about him every day like I used to. I've reached the point where I can't remember his voice anymore. That scares me.

I don't think the grief is ever completely gone. You don't get over it, and I don't think you're supposed to. In the same degree, I can't let it be my whole life. (Crying softly.)

Do you have any thoughts or suggestions for someone who is reading this?

My dad told me a lot that he was proud of me. I think he would still be. I was never discouraged from pursuing art. I was never told: "You can't make a living or you should consider a *real* job."

Putting myself into what I love, which is making art, helped immensely. I could get some feelings out, whether I knew it was happening or not. My artwork was my healing and my catharsis. So, that would be my suggestion: Get out what you need to in whatever media — art, music, talking to people, or whatever it needs to be. The thing that helps me most is doing what I love and what he knew I loved, and not putting life on hold.

I'm also really grateful that he said, "I love you," every day.

⊫⧾ ⧾⊨

Ellie M. Siskind (husband, heart attack)

"George taught me so much about life." — Ellie is an acclaimed, award-winning professional painter. She lost her husband George to a heart attack. They were married 20 years. Ellie has two adult sons, Larry and Chris, from a prior marriage.

My first marriage was when I was 19 years old. I divorced at age 23 and had two adorable boys from that marriage. After the divorce, I moved back home with my parents, and my dad sent me to Kansas City Art Institute. I was a risk taker, and my father supported me in the pursuit of art. This was in the 1950s and there was no such thing as "a single mom." It was considered, "boys without a father."

I eventually got a job at an advertising company. We all had desks behind big drawing boards. I had brown paper on my board, and I sketched everyone in the office. My boss walked by and glanced at my sketches. Well, the next day, this ambulance pulls up and then leaves with someone. I got called into the boss's office. I thought he was mad about the sketches, and I was getting fired. I figured my goose was cooked. He said, "You're the only one left here who can sketch." The man in the ambulance had been hired to do the company's sketches. That's how I got my start as an artist.

During this time, I began going to a therapist. When the therapist was moving his practice, he recommended me to Dr. Siskind. That was my husband to be, George. I went as a patient for a year or two. No hanky-panky, just as a patient. Then, I stopped seeing him. He said, "I've taught you all I know." Really, he taught me how to grow up.

A year or so later, he was working with a group on an alternative newspaper. This was during the Vietnam War. They needed someone to do sketches for their political cartoons, and he remembered I was an artist. So, we started working together on that project. He was married, and his youngest was in high school. I decided I would not do anything to precipitate a relationship. We just worked together.

George started dropping over more frequently. He and his wife got a divorce, and he moved into an apartment nearby.

We married in 1970 and were married 20 years.

One night, George got up and went to the fridge. That was unusual because we were already in bed. He came back to bed and said, "I'm either having the worst heartburn I've ever had or I'm having a heart attack." So, I drove him to the emergency room. It was awful. He was in so much pain that he couldn't talk, and I was asking, "George, you all right?" and trying to drive.

The physician told him it was a mild heart attack and likely he wouldn't have another. George took that news as an excuse not to change his behavior. A few months later, he had a second heart attack. I called an ambulance. George was taken to the heart critical care unit. My son Larry worked a few blocks away, so he was there with us.

They moved George to another room and had put him in a chair. I think the nurse was going to take him to physical therapy. Larry happened to go in and saw George gasping for breath. He got the nurse and told her to take George back to critical care. The nurse said, "I'll need to check with the doctor." And Larry said, "I know how to roll a bed. Either you take him there now, or I'm going to roll him there myself."

George was in intensive care for 15 days. I could have sued the hospital. I didn't though.

I visited him every day, and he remained conscious until the end. I had just gone home to rest and the phone rang. Larry said, "You better come up right away."

The hospital had a new chaplain, a big guy with a farm-like accent. I was running down the hall, and he stopped me. He put his hands on my shoulders. I said, "He's dead, isn't he?" And he said, "Yes."

What helped you with your grief?

First, I will tell you what didn't help. My husband had a private practice in psychology, and every one his patients was grieving his loss and calling me. The phone rang constantly! I didn't want to tell them I didn't want to talk, but I'll never forget that because the phone rang all the time, for weeks and weeks. So, what I want to say is: It made a difference that George improved a lot of people's lives, and these people were trying to tell me how much he had meant to them. But, I already knew how much he meant to me, and I was grieving.

I also got a bucketful of sympathy cards that said, "I know how you feel." I thought, "There's no way you know how I feel." His death was very sudden. I was expecting to bring him back home.

I saw my family doctor and took medication to settle my nerves. That helped. Both of my sons were very helpful in getting me through all that.

Dogs are extremely important in my life. When George and I were getting married, he said, "No pets." (Laughs.) We ended up having dogs *and* cats. After my first divorce when my boys were young, my dad said, "Come with me, I have something to show you." He had gotten us a police dog. I learned from my dad, "You can solve a problem with a dog." I'm still doing that today. I can hang tougher with my dog nearby.

My grief was not any worse than other women who are widowed, but George — being 13 years older and being a psychologist — taught me so much about life. I had been busy raising those two boys and just managing to cope and all of a sudden, I had someone to help lift me up.

Do you have any religious or spiritual practices that helped?

Judaism has been very valuable. George and I had been married a few years before I decided to convert. When we married, I started going to temple with him. Then, I went even when he didn't go. The thing I like about Judaism is that there is a belief in God, whatever that means, but it's more about the energy that fuels the universe.

Judaism has a whole different approach to death. This is going to sound very blunt, but in Judaism it's believed that when you're dead, you're dead. It's the end of the road. That helped me with the acceptance of George's death. It was so final. Stories make death easier for people. If you believe the person is in heaven, it is easier. For me, Judaism is a practical way to deal with life. You can have wonderful memories, but the person doesn't come back to visit you. I liked that about Judaism because I'm realistic.

Anything else you found helpful?

After George died, I was a basket case. I saw a counselor for about two years. Finally, the counselor said, "Okay, you're done. You're in good shape. I feel I've been able to help you, anything more would be us just visiting."

I went to a writer's group, and I started teaching art. That helped me tremendously. It was a bridge for me.

My art has always been about my life. Only, it didn't appear to be about my life because it addresses big questions. I never painted George while we were married. I didn't want to use him as material. Besides, he would have been telling me stories and never would have sat still. But George made it possible for me to paint. When we got married, he said, "I don't want you to get a job. I want you to paint." And he was adamant about that. So, I got a studio for the first time while we were married.

George was such an important part in my becoming a successful painter.

My work is displayed in museums now. It is just amazing the way your life turns and turns in different directions.

⟨⟩ ⟨⟩

Meredith A. Eastwood (husband, cerebral hemorrhage & father, suicide)

"We express the healing in some way, and by expressing it, we put it to work in the world." — Meredith has long, white hair and wears a red heart necklace. She lost her husband, Thomas (Tom) Eastwood, and her father, Carl Grey. A former schoolteacher and school counselor, Meredith now writes children's books and enjoys photography. She also leads Active Dreaming workshops. She has one adult son, Kent, and three grandchildren.

My father was in World War II, and I was born while he was in England. When he came home, we traveled to various states with the military. After high school, I attended the University of Florida for my undergraduate degree in secondary education, which is where I met my husband.

Tom and I got married in 1965.

After we were married, I taught for a few years and then we had our son Kent. When Kent started school, I went back to teaching sixth grade social studies. During this time, I also got a master's degree in secondary education. Meanwhile, Tom had become vice president for a public relations and advertising firm. That was the job he had when he died.

He had been on his way in an airplane to California. He was in charge of the advertising and public relations for a new animated feature film about Raggedy Ann and Andy. They had to land the plane in St Louis and take him off the plane.

Tom had a cerebral hemorrhage, which was a combination, unknown to us at the time, of several strokes. He had experienced personality shifts, and we were having difficulty in our marriage at the time. He had a lot of depression.

There was no hope of recovery because the hemorrhage had blown out the major portion of his brain stem. He was 39 years old.

He was in a coma for several months and never woke from that. I had him moved to a hospital near our home. He spent four months there. Every time they tried to do a brain scan, he would go into seizures. It was an incredibly tough time. I was at the hospital every day and also had to leave to go get Kent from school. Then, a miracle happened. One afternoon a woman who worked for Tom went into his room, prayed with him, and told him it was okay to go, and he died. (Crying.) She was a very compassionate Christian woman.

My son was only 6 years old when his dad died.

What helped with your healing?

I was left raising Kent without his dad, and there was a lot of anger. When I sought counseling, I was told, "Get your anger out." Counseling was more confrontational back then. I needed peace, someone to just hold me and be sweet to me and not yell at me. So, I gave up on the counseling. I thought, "Well, I'll take care of this whole thing myself."

We had some rough years. But I'm not one to give up. I got a Masters in counseling and psychology. The kids in the classroom would come to me with their problems, and it seemed like a natural fit. It took me a few years to get my counseling degree because I was involved in coaching tennis, and busy raising Kent, and trying to keep a job. I was a busy woman. Starting with books was easy though because I didn't have to deal with the emotional piece.

After I had lost my husband, had gotten my counseling degree, and had started moving forward with my life, my father died.

Here's the rough part. (Pauses.) I was still teaching at the time. I was driving to school the day it happened. While driving, I was thinking I wanted to buy a new car, a BMW, just imagining frivolous things. I got to school and the secretary said, "Your mom is hysterical." When I spoke to my mom, she said I was to come home immediately. Apparently, she had already told the secretary what happened. My father had gone out into the garage, taken the German Luger he had brought back from WWII, and shot himself. A German Luger is a heavy, thick German handgun. Our family background is English, Scottish, and German, and we do repress a lot. The note he left just said he couldn't stand the pain any longer.

My mother had found my father. One of the men with the janitorial service, who also did yard work for us, came over and cleaned out the garage. He was a fireman, too. So, he was familiar with all of that.

My dad had complications from diabetes, which was neuropathy — severe pain in the leg. He was experiencing incontinence, and lots of physical things were happening to him. He was retired and in his late 80s. He was in emotional pain and physical pain. I believe his emotional pain manifested in physical pain.

Do you have any spiritual or religious practices that helped with your grief?

When I retired from teaching, I started on a spiritual journey. My counseling background gave me the tools to go forward in a more spiritual way.

My background is Christian Science, and I follow *A Course in Miracles*. I also studied at the Deepak Chopra Center where we were asked to address a painful family issue. The things my dad went through growing up colored his outlook. I revisited all of that at the Chopra Center in meditation.

I felt I was healthy, emotionally, and had dealt with the loss. In the meantime, my son got married, and I have my grandkids, three boys.

I started studying with Robert Moss through the school of Active Dreaming. At the time, I had been studying with him extensively for three years. But I realized something was wrong. I didn't want him to know about my history. I was thinking, "No, I'm not going to tell him anything, tricky shaman." (Laughs.) I finally wrote Robert a note. I said, "I need to share something I've never told you. My father committed suicide." I immediately broke down. I'm thinking, "How many years has this been!" (Crying.)

Afterward, I had a dream about a very large dark monster that has been trapped inside the hull of a ship. When I get to the ship, the top of the hull has been blown off, which is why I can see this creature. It scared me of course, and I woke up. I said to myself: "I need to re-enter this dream, through shamanic journeying." I returned to the dream, and I also wrote everything down. In the dream, I slipped down into the platform next to the watery container where the creature is and I asked: "Who are you? What are you here to show me? Are you in pain?" I discovered in my conversation that it was my father's dense energy, still very present in this level of reality. I needed to turn a red dial next to a platform so that the dense energy could be dispersed into the water. Only everything was rusted, so I had trouble turning the dial. My father said, "Well, you have to use magic." I asked, "What magic?" and he said, "The magic of love."

The ending is beautiful. (Crying.) I cried and cried through this whole process, wiping my face and just saying, "I love you Father. I love you."

I'm not crying from the grief. I'm crying from relief. I've been carrying around anger and concealment. When we conceal our pain from the people who are our helpers — our therapists and our shamans — we don't give them the tools and information they need to help us because we're too afraid. We pick fear instead of love.

Do you have any suggestions for others who are experiencing grief?

It's important to follow our dreaming and perceptions with an action plan. We don't just dream it. We do something. We write it, we express the healing in some way, and by expressing it we put it to work in the world.

Healing can be art or anything you do in the world where you have a romance with life. I'm writing children's books now, leading Active Dreaming workshops, and doing photography. Through my photography, I can focus on what is good and beautiful and experience a loving relationship with life. It helps me see life from a place of gratitude.

Those we love are always with us. We draw on them, and they come to us. We carry them in our hearts. We dream about them. And they do love us. Our ancestors are lining up behind us, and I can feel their love.

Without soul healing and heart healing, I don't think we can access our creative source. It's an ongoing process, not just one effort. It's also not necessarily over. We have to address things again and see them in a different way. When we're ready, we can see how loss has impacted our life and is preventing us from living authentically and lovingly. Then, we tell the story, again and again, until it no longer holds any power.

So, how much more healing is there? I believe this is a big one. I had no idea I hadn't dealt with my dad's loss in that way.

I had that dream yesterday. It's like I was meant to have that revelation to share. It still feels raw, but not painful raw. Poignant.

⊷ ⊷

A Meaningful Vocation

Sophia Stockamp (father, brain tumor)

"I still carry him with me." — Sophia is friendly, tall with long, blond hair. She lost her father, Clifford (Cliff) Stockamp, during her senior year of high school. He was 49. At the time of our interview, Sophia is a sophomore in college.

My dad got sick the summer right before my senior year of high school. He had always worked out and played sports, especially racquetball and tennis. But his health focus really increased when he got sick. He was reading all kinds of books and learning more.

In college, he had majored in general business and, afterward, worked with companies that offered life-coaching services. Later, he started his own business as a life coach. He would give advice on how to change your life. He was good at it and enjoyed it. He loved helping people.

My parents got divorced when I was in fifth grade. The divorce was hard on my dad. He wasn't good at being alone. His business struggled, and then he lost his business. He was a very disorganized person, which probably had something to do with it. He ended up losing his house, too. I didn't see him all that often. He got a new job as a mortgage broker.

The summer before my senior year of high school, I got a call at 8 in the morning. It was the mortgage office where he worked. They told me that my dad had fainted, and his words were jumbled. He wasn't making any sense. They had called an ambulance, and I was my dad's emergency contact. My brother was away at college. I was the only family in town. I was 17.

I went to the hospital. My dad hated doctors and hated hospitals. He was incredibly uncomfortable being there and kept saying, "Take me home." He had passed the mortgage broker test and had been up studying a lot. He said, "I haven't eaten well. I'm just tired." He can be extremely hardheaded. I was the only one who could handle him. The doctors said, "We will leave you two alone." I said, "Dad, the doctors want you to get a CAT scan. Why don't you just do it? Either you're fine and can walk out knowing you're healthy. Or, they catch something early and treat it. It's a win-win." He finally said, "All right. I'll do it, and then we'll leave."

Turns out, my dad had a softball-size tumor in his head. The doctors were astonished that he was still functioning. Because it was so large, they thought it must had grown slowly over a couple of years. That made sense because my dad had been acting bipolar, moody. Some of the doctors wanted to do surgery, and some of them were saying, "We can't touch that thing. It's wrapped around the hypothalamus; if we operate, it will leave him without any quality of life."

After the diagnoses, my dad got obsessed with health, reading book after book and learning everything he could. He was taking supplements and pills. He honestly was getting better. He had days where he was coherent and still driving. He shouldn't have been driving but he was. (Laughs.) How do you tell a 49-year-old man what he can do? He didn't listen to anyone. But he was doing really well. I moved in with him and was helping take care of him.

When high school started up again that fall, I stayed with him every weekend so he would have someone there. It was tough.

Some days my dad couldn't get out of bed or talk right. Other days, he would be fine. It was on and off again. He would have regular checkups and talk about whether the tumor was growing or shrinking, which was pretty hard to tell in a couple month's span.

Around Christmas, we all went to my aunt and uncle's house. My dad's brother was a doctor. While we were staying there, my dad got another CAT scan. His brother told him the tumor was growing, which was devastating to my dad who was trying to do all these things and figure it out. I think it was just past the point of no return. Had he done all that he was doing earlier, with a smaller tumor, it might have been fine. But it was so massive. I don't think anything could have helped it, traditional medicine or alternative medicine.

My dad passed away at the end of my senior year, in April, during final exams. I missed a lot of school. The teachers were all really understanding. But it was hard to get caught up that late in the school year. My brother and I were trying to plan the funeral. My brother was amazing. He closed the bank accounts and talked to the phone companies and had to deal with everything. He had just graduated from college and was trying to get his own life in order while closing somebody else's life. My brother handled it exceptionally well, even though it was a very painful time.

I took my high school exams and graduated. I had already taken the SAT and ACT and applied to college. That part worked out well.

What, if anything, helped with your healing?

I talked to a good friend whose dad passed away and to my other close friends. My friends' parents even helped. Everyone's family was there for me, which was amazing. My friends are a huge support system for me. I don't know what I would do without them.

Looking back on it, the way I can explain coping is that whenever anything difficult or bad happens in your life, you can either let it consume you or you can kind of push it in the back of your head and keep going with your life. That is how I took it. I dealt with it, and then tried not to think about it. I just tried to stay busy.

There are times, of course, that I think about his death. It's a weird thing to know that he is not here anymore, especially since it has only been a year and a half.

A lot of my friends told me diaries and journals were the best way to cope. But I never got into journaling. For a while, I kind of moped and felt sorry for myself. Then, I realized that no one is going to take pity on me. People have had hardships much worse than someone they knew dying. Dying is a common thing.

What else has helped with your grieving?

I am in college now. It was nice to be in a new environment and in a completely new change of pace. I joined a sorority, and there are girls in my sorority who have lost parents, too. It helps to have friends who understand. College has helped me grow into my own and not dwell, which is good for me.

I played sports in high school, softball and tennis, and my dad and I used to play tennis. So, I have always fallen back on that also. The girls in my sorority play tennis all the time, and we go to the gym together. I started going to the gym regularly. I love working out. It keeps me happy, focused, and energized. I'm healthier than I've ever been. I feel like my dad is a huge part of that.

Do you have any religious or spiritual practices that help?

My grandparents on both sides are very religious. I didn't know this until after he passed, but my dad was religious growing up. He didn't raise us religious or spiritual at all. It was kind of hard when he passed because I didn't know where he was going or what was going to happen. My grandparents are a great support system, and I love them. After he passed, my grandmother was praying for me and looking out for me. It's a good feeling to have someone care and to feel loved.

Sometimes, I feel my dad's presence around me. I think about him a lot. After he passed away, I became more spiritual, though not necessarily religious. I believe good things attract more good things, and so I try to stay positive. That's my spirituality right now.

Do you have any suggestions for someone going through something similar or thoughts for the parents of a young adult going through this type of loss?

A good friend told me that when her dad passed, she would feel his presence, and it would scare her. I don't know what I expected after he passed, but I felt him all the time and weird things would happen. Like my radio would randomly turn on. I would almost laugh because it was like he still wanted to be around and wanted to be there. It's comforting to know he's with me. He's watching over me now more than ever before. Knowing that he's there and still cares is what any parent would want for you to know.

I loved when people would talk about him. I didn't want people to forget and not talk about it. I didn't necessarily want pity. I just loved when people talked positive about him, like "Your dad was a great man," or "Your dad was a really great guy."

Kids learn how to grieve in their own way. Adults should make the resources available for their kids, give them a journal or a diary or tell them they can go to their friends. Encourage them to do whatever they need to do. I don't think parents should push or force something like counseling. I'm glad my mom never did that.

My suggestion to adults would be: Don't push your kids too much because it takes time. That's the main thing: Everything just takes time.

Do you have a favorite memory of your dad?

He was a great dad. When I was little, we had a trampoline. No matter how tired he felt, he would go and jump on the trampoline. It became the neighborhood trampoline, and all the kids would come over and he would put speakers outside and play music. He loved having people around. That was the number one thing about him. At his funeral, all his friends spoke about him and gave memories. He was just a lighthearted, goofy guy. He loved messing around and having fun. That is what I remember about him.

He used to coach my sports leagues. Other parents would say, "Oh, it's just for fun." And my dad was like, "Winning is fun." (Laughs.) He was not afraid to go after what he wanted. I learned that from him. If you want to pave the path, you have to do it on your own. Nobody is going to do it for you.

My dad is awesome because even though he is gone, he continues teaching me new things. I carry him with me. That's an important thing to remember: When someone passes, you can still carry that person with you. You don't have to hold on to material items because it's not necessarily the material things that we remember the most. I just remember him.

After everything my dad went through, I decided to major in dietetics, nutritional science. I feel like he's always pushing me to try something new in health and fitness. Eating the right foods and taking care of our bodies is not something we learn about in school. We're taught that medicine, pills, and chemicals kill everything. So, nutrition has become an interest of mine. I have helped my friends become healthier and taught them some of the things I've learned. It's just really cool to see the chain reaction. I'm thankful to my dad.

⟫⊹ ⊹⟪

Amy M. Walker (father, cancer)

"The memories will never leave you." — *Amy is in her 20s. She lost her father, Dennis Walker, to cancer when she was 7 years old. She has one older brother, Andrew. Her mother, Holly, is married to Amy's stepdad, Tom Stratman. Amy is finishing up her Master's Degree in Social Work.*

My dad was diagnosed with colon cancer when I was 6 years old. They didn't find the cancer right away. He had complained of aches in his abdomen, and the doctor ran tests but didn't find anything. So, he took Maalox. But he kept having problems. It wasn't until later that they decided to do a colonoscopy. He was only 40 years old. They did the first colonoscopy, and it came out normal because the tumor was at the end of the colon; they thought they had reached the end, but really it was the tumor blocking.

Eventually, the doctors did another colonoscopy and found the tumor. It was Stage 4. They did surgery on the parts that were operable. It had spread to his liver, as well. When the cancer is there, you can't do a lot of surgery, and some spots were too small to remove. I remember my mom and dad going to New York for one of the surgeries.

They had scheduled an appointment in Houston, Texas, for a clinical trial. It was for a drug not yet FDA-approved. He was scheduled to go June 12, but he passed away on June 10. That was about a year and a month after he had been diagnosed.

Do you have any favorite memories of your dad?

He was my fishing buddy. I caught my first catfish when I was with him. It was 10 or 15 pounds, which was really big for my first fish, and we cooked it for dinner.

We would go to Sanibel Island every summer. That was our favorite vacation spot. This was during the age of camcorders, and we still have the videos of us kayaking. There's one time where the camera is on me and I'm saying, "Are we done yet? Are we gonna go back now?" Being out in the sun that long, a 6 year old gets kind of restless. (Laughs.) When he passed, we had him cremated. One of his requests was to have his ashes scattered on the beach at Sanibel Island. So, we did. His parents wanted a place locally where they could visit his grave, and some of his ashes are in the tombstone in town.

What helped with your healing?

In the beginning, I didn't really know what was going on. My first grade class made get well cards and sent them with me when I visited him at the hospital. My brother was 11, and I was 7. The stiches from his surgeries looked like an arrow pointing up. I would tell my mom I thought it was cool because it was giving us hope, like it's pointing up to heaven.

Toward the end, he had in-home hospice care. We had a bed in our living room, and I was like his little nurse. He would tell me the different medicines, and I would go run and get it. He would say, "I need the medicine that begins with the letter B," and I would find it and bring it back to him.

I remember the talk with the hospice nurse. We had a family meeting, basically telling us that we didn't have much longer with him and should spend as much time with him as he had left. My mom already knew, but she wanted us all to be there: me and my brother and my mom's mom. When you're that young, it doesn't sink in.

At this point, he would just mumble and talk about his child-hood. Most of it didn't make sense. We would be there and just nod our heads. We said goodbye to him before he went to sleep because we didn't know how long he had. That night, before we went to bed, I hugged and kissed him. I said to my mom, "I have this weird feeling that dad is going to die tonight," which was probably unsettling to her.

The next morning all my family was around his bed and my mom told me he had passed in his sleep.

I remember the funeral, standing up there with my mom. Being that young, you know what's happened, but you don't know how life's going to be afterward. I remember telling my mom later, "I know it's bad, but I didn't even cry at Dad's funeral." She said, "Amy, that doesn't mean you love him any less. Sometimes, it takes people different amounts of time to sink in." She told me I handled it pretty well. She said most kids when someone passes away, go into severe depression, and I stayed positive. I was always a positive person; just in case, she contacted a social worker, and I did some counseling to make sure I'd be okay. Another social worker came in once a week and did activities with me and got me to talk about him and remember some things about him. She told me about a weekend summer camp. It's a grievance camp, and all the kids there have lost someone. That was helpful. It gets your mind off the serious stuff. I talked to my mom about how much I missed him. After he passed away, I slept in her room for a while.

My mom made sure she kept a lot of his belongings to keep the memories for me and my brother, like his fishing pole, his running shoes, and his running trophies. He ran cross-country. That's how my brother got into running; they would do races together.

It sounds cliché, but my mom was my rock during that time. I tell her even now how much she helped me. If I hadn't had her love and support, I probably would have reflected on it differently and had more denial.

I use that experience as a learning opportunity. I'm a firm believer that things happen for a reason. I tell my mom there is a reason why dad died at such a young age and that he had cancer. It's hard for us to see the purpose now, but down the road I will know. Maybe that's why I was meant to go into social work. His death was my first interaction with a social worker, and I knew I wanted to help people so they wouldn't have to go through things alone. I am getting my Master's in Social Work. My brother became a doctor. So, it has impacted his life, too.

I love Tom, my stepdad. I miss my dad every day, but I'm happy Tom is in my life. If his marriage to my mom had not happened, I wouldn't be the same person today. Tom has brought out my sense of outdoor adventure and traveling; we go the national parks and go hiking.

I remember one time whispering to my mom in church, "Are you ever gonna get married again?" It was not that long after my dad died. That may sound strange. But I think it's important, especially when you're young, to have a father — even if it's not your biological father.

The story goes, and Tom told me this, that his friend said, "Have you talked to Holly recently? Her husband passed away, and it would be a nice thing if you reached out to her to let her know you're still friends and ask her if she needs anything." Tom and Holly had dated back when they were in high school. At first, Tom was standoffish because he didn't want Holly to think he was hitting on her or being insensitive. Then, they met for breakfast. That was them getting back in touch for the first time.

Had my mom and Tom not broken up when they dated several years before, my brother and I would not be here. That's another example where things happen for a reason. But I think it's cool that they found each other again.

Do you have any spiritual or religious practices that helped you with your grief?

I always prayed in silence. But when I was alone, I would talk to my dad because I felt like he was there. I know he is my guardian angel. When a loved one dies, you just know they are watching over you.

I was born and raised Catholic, even though there are some Catholic beliefs I don't necessarily agree with. After my dad passed away, they offered prayer requests. I wanted one to be in memory of my father, Dennis Walker, and they said that in church after he passed away. The church was like another family outside my biological family. I remember people came up to us, and they brought us food. They were saying if you need anything, we're here to help. So, church is very helpful.

Is there anything else that has been helpful?

It sounds simple, but just talking to someone helps me. I talk to my mom or my best friend. They understand.

My dad liked birds, especially purple martins. He would put out those white birdhouses for purple martins, and he hated those black birds that would try to chase the purple martins out. He also liked picking blueberries from our blueberry bush.

We live in the same house; we've never moved. After he passed away, my mom put together a memory table. It was a wooden table, and it had one of the birdhouses, his running shoes, these western boots, his watch, his wallet, his glasses, and his running trophies. It used to be downstairs in the family area of the basement. Within the past year, my mom and my stepdad have been fixing up the downstairs to make a guest room. One day, I saw the memory table was gone. I don't think my mom thought I would be as upset as I was. I was hysterical. Those are the only things of his that I had. I ran upstairs saying, "Mom, are you getting rid of this stuff? You could have at least warned me!" She said, "I'm sorry. I'm not getting rid of it. I'm just putting it in storage." It's in storage so when my brother and I move out, we can have his things if we want.

Do you have any suggestions for someone going through something similar?

Until something like this happens, you take your parents for granted. Ever since this happened, I have thought, "What would happen if I lost my mom?" That would be horrible. She was my support system when he passed away. My advice to kids would be to cherish your parents. Be their best friend. My mom is one of my best friends, even though we don't always get along — you're always going to have that. Definitely spend as much time with your parents as you can. At the end of the day, friends come and go, but your parents are there. They love you regardless if you make a stupid mistake. They love you no matter what.

For kids going through this I would say: I know a lot of times it makes you sad to even think about it. But try to remember as much as you can about the person. That's another coping mechanism that helped me: trying to remember all the memories because it made me smile to remember some of the precious moments we shared. I go through old pictures. My mom put them in albums. Now pictures are digital. I'm definitely more of a hands-on person. To have actual things in my hand is better than on the computer or cell phone. Just for a moment, when you look at certain pictures, you almost go back to that time.

My dad was a big UK (University of Kentucky) basketball fan. Oh, my gosh, he's probably looking down right now like, "If you left that out of the interview, I would be so mad at you!" (Laughs.) That's another memory of when I was little. Me, my brother, my mom, and my dad would all sit on the couch and watch UK basketball. I don't follow them like I did when my dad was alive. But sometimes I watch the games because I feel like it's another connection to my dad.

When I was little, he had gotten me this tabby cat. I told him I wanted my own kitty. It was a win-win because he got his little girl a kitty, and he got a barn cat to kill the mice. (Laughs.) The cat's name was Kasper. Kasper just passed away this year, during spring break. We knew it was going to happen soon because she was losing sight and only knew to come to me by my voice. I was so sad when Kasper died because that was the only living memory from my dad. I told my mom, "It almost feels like another part of him is leaving me." She said, "Amy, I know it feels that way. But you'll always have the memories. The cat is a material possession. The memories will never leave you."

⊶ ⊷

Rexene L. Lane (brother, car accident)

"There has been a lot of healing. It's all over the place, but it's there." — Born in Ohio, Rexene describes herself as a Buckeye and a preacher's daughter (Baptist Independent Fundamentalist). She is in her 50s. Wearing vibrant, bright colors, she announces that she recently has gone back to college for an advanced degree in Art Therapy. She lost her younger brother, Richard (Rick) Steven Lane, in a car accident.

I graduated college with a degree in music education. I majored in voice and minored in piano. I also had a cosmetology degree, and that's what I did after I finished college. In those days, I shared a trailer with my brother Rick. I don't have any other siblings.

Rick started out in banking. He was working as a loan officer in a private loan company. He had gone to Jerry Farwell's school and never finished the first semester. He had a full ride scholarship because of football. I think he just missed everything back home. He started dating someone, and she got pregnant. They ended up getting married. He thought the marriage would get him back in good graces with Mom and Dad after dropping out of college, but

Diana J. Ensign, JD

he got divorced about a year later. That's why his trailer was open. So, I moved in. He was 21, and I was 24.

We were kind of like party central. We hung out with his friends. I started smoking weed, drinking, and doing all the things other hairdressers were doing. That was 34 years ago! (Laughs.) I went from this girl who stayed a virgin until she was 24, to this woman with an insane life going on.

My relationships were a mess. I learned I needed to get into rehab. It was taking a lot to keep down my pain level. To be able to tell you these things shows a lot of healing and acceptance.

In 2001, I had to put one of my cats to sleep. Then, I had my gallbladder taken out. It was a hard year. My brother was in his third marriage and had five kids now. My brother and I had not talked very much that year. We had always been close.

After I had my gallbladder out, I hadn't been able to sleep. So, I went over to his place for a while to see him. That was the first time I'd talked with him in months. We talked, we laughed, and I hugged him. I told him I loved him. I told him I missed him. The next morning, Rick was killed. I felt like that night with him was a gift. It would have been much harder on me had we not spoken that night. I know how guilt, remorse, and regret work.

He was killed in an accident with a truck. It was a super foggy morning. A semi-truck had pulled across the highway. It was so foggy the truck driver couldn't see the on-coming traffic. Had the truck driver gone to the traffic light 300 yards down, the accident wouldn't have happened. It was a white semi-truck without a label or anything on it to make it visible. My brother was traveling down the highway and ran into the semi. A guy in a pickup truck behind my brother came to Rick's funeral. He said it was so foggy that if it hadn't been for the flash of Rick's pickup hitting that semi, he would have hit it. He felt like Rick saved his life. That information helped us as a family because there are all those questions: "Was Rick speeding?" and so on. That guy confirmed what happened.

What has helped with your grief?

The grief process was extremely painful. That first year was definitely the hardest. We felt sorry for the kids losing their dad like that. All of us had a lot contact with his kids, especially the first year. That was great for the family. I did a lot of visiting of the gravesite. There were all the typical feelings you go through with grief, but it felt like they all hit at once. I had a lot of anger. My anger came out toward the truck company.

I was very close to my brother so I missed him tremendously. Knowing we had that Friday night together was a major help. I had friends I could go and talk to about it. I also had a ring I wore. My brother had been really big into the whole Y2K thing, saving water and food in his basement. I just thought that was ridiculous. I used to tease him about it. I bought a gold ring that said "2000" forward and backwards — the 2's came together to make a heart in the middle. So, I wore that ring.

At first, Rick kind of took on the hero image. Later, we realized he had a lot of issues and brought some of the issues on himself. Not the being killed, but the other things that we had to deal with when he died: stuff that had to do with his children, his wife, or ex-wives and ex-girlfriends. Of course, some of my family think Rick's life was taken because of how he was living. That is their Christian belief system. I don't believe that. I believe when it's your time to go, it is just your time.

Anniversaries are hard. His birthday is hard. On Facebook, I'll change my photo around his anniversary. I'll start feeling it around August, definitely by September. By then, I become very aware that I'm about to lose him. Not like when it first hit. But every year, I go through those steps. With the passing of time, I'm able to return to normal life in a shorter amount of time and not carry that along. Time was a big help.

One of the hardest things is seeing someone with a similar body shape or hair. It just sends you through … (Trails off.) It takes your breath away.

Do you have a favorite memory of your brother?

I have lots of memories, starting with when he was born and my mom came home from the hospital. I was yelling to everybody, "Come and see my baby brother!" I hadn't even seen him myself yet! I was just a little over 3 years old.

I remember going to King's Island and Cedar Point with our parents and riding all the amusement park rides together, especially the roller coasters — and loving every minute of it. After I got my driver's license, we drove around and jammed to the radio, singing at the top of our lungs. He was always game for whatever craziness I came up with.

I have great memories of singing with him and my dad in church and learning to play the guitar together. He had me sing at two of his weddings — the exact same song. (Laughs).

We always loved each other. We rarely fought or even disagreed. We had each other's back. We shared many similar talents and interests. He was truly my best friend. Whether I had great news or terrible news, he is the person I wanted to share it with first.

Do you have any spiritual or religious practices that help with your grief?

I've been working on my own recovery since Rick's death. In my 12-step program, I heard for the first time people giving permission to develop your own concept of God. For my entire life, if I got a flat tire my belief was that I was bad and God was swatting me down. If I got sick, it was because I had done something bad and God was swatting me down. I didn't realize it, but I guess my concept of God was Him up there with a great big fly swatter, just waiting for me to do something wrong. In recovery, I was able to realize that was not the God I want to believe in. I became much more open minded.

I also love myself. I have not perfected that, but I've come a long way, baby. (Laughs). A big step for me is letting go of the Christian things I don't believe. I went through a stage of being very angry. Now, I allow people to believe what they believe without judgment, and that's pretty much the case for how I feel about all religions.

Those are issues I work on. There has been a lot of healing. It's all over the place, but it's there.

Anything else you found helpful?

I recently enrolled in a graduate degree program in Art Therapy. I had to turn in the application and letters of recommendation and portfolio, and I had an oral interview. There were 25 entries and only 10 admitted into program. I hadn't heard anything. I said to myself, "It's meant to be whether I get in or not." That is growth for me because it's easy for me to go to shame, or I'm not good enough. Then, two and a half weeks later, I got a congratulations letter. I had been accepted! The program is through the school of Art & Design, for Art Therapy.

I feel amazed and terrified. I'm terrified that I can't do it, or I'm not smart enough not pretty enough, not thin enough. I have been saying that all my life. Now I say, 'Trust this is my journey." Or I say, "Until a door closes, I'm gonna keep walking."

I feel my brother has left a lot of pennies around. He's with us in some way or another. It has been a process of accepting his life and what it was. It was far from perfect. He had his imperfections. I took him off the pedestal, but I still love him, always.

Paul J. Brown (parents, heart disease)

"I put myself to my daily task realizing, at age 12, I was the man of the family now." — Born and raised in Cleveland, Ohio, Paul is a former math and science high school teacher. He says, with a laugh, "I retired after 41 years of teaching and lived to tell about it." In his spare time, he works on house projects and tutors high school students. Paul lost his father when he was 12 and his mother when he was 42. He has one surviving sibling, Margot, and one deceased sibling, Martha. Married to Mary Ann Verkamp, they have two adult children, Sarah and Jeremy, and five grandchildren.

I was 12 when my father died. He was 50 years old.

My father had a few jobs. He worked at a local drugstore chain, where he was a buyer/purchaser. My mother was a schoolteacher, which was pretty unusual at the time. She was the second youngest of five children and had four brothers. She had gone to college, which was rare for a woman in her time, but my father had not. One of her brothers helped finance her college.

Dad had been sick and pretty much bedridden for four years before his death. He didn't take care of himself. He got sick when I was about 8. Most of my memories of him are as a sick man. It was not easy. We always hoped that someday he would get better. There weren't any actual things that supported the belief, but we had hope because that's what you did. You hoped, and you prayed.

Both of my parents were chain smokers and possibly alcoholics. They weren't abusive, but they both drank quite a bit. Dad built up arterial sclerosis (hardening of the arteries) and diabetes (diabetic neuropathy), where you lose feeling in your limbs — to the point where he couldn't walk. He was such a social creature that he couldn't stay in his bedroom upstairs. We lived in a three-story, historic old home and had one bathroom on the second floor. After a while, when he was sick, dad moved his bed to the living room so that he could be part of the action.

Mom taught at the Catholic elementary school where we went, and that is what we consider one of the miracles in our life. She had stayed home after having kids. Then, after Dad got sick, the local Catholic school called her up and asked her if she wanted a job. We felt like this was God intervening in our lives.

Dad tried working from home. He did cold calling for a juice delivery company, the Home Juice Company. This was at the time when milk got delivered to your door and sometimes eggs. This company delivered gallons of juice to your front door, as well. I don't know that he made much of a go with that, but it gave him a feeling that he was contributing and doing what he could to bring in some income.

How did your father die?

He died a hundred yards from home. On the day that he was obviously deteriorating, as often happens with people near death, he couldn't get enough oxygen. He was just breathing and gulping for breath. They called the ambulance and put him on a stretcher. I watched him go by from the front porch as they loaded him up. He was gasping and trying to say something to me. Then, when the ambulance was about a hundred yards away, the siren went on. They left my sister Martha and me home alone while Mom went with Dad to the hospital. We're pretty sure he died about the time the siren went on.

My mother and her sister-in-law came home from the hospital, and we could tell from the looks on their faces that he had indeed died. Mom said, "Dad's gone." And we had a nice long cry session. We talked about making funeral arrangements; the funeral home was just up around the corner from where we lived. Other family members went to arrange that. I really don't remember much about the funeral itself, except that we rode in a limousine to the cemetery, and it was a chilly day. My sister was on one side, and I was on the other, and my memory is that we played with the switches on the power windows because we rarely spent time in a car with power windows. We were making the windows go up and down.

When Dad died, my sister Martha was about 14, and my sister Margot was 17. Margot had graduated from high school and had to take entrance exams for nursing school. It was either the day after he died or the day after the funeral; I don't remember which day. But it was the very next day, and she had to take public transportation because we lived way on the west side, and the exam was on the east side of town. She had to do this by herself, and she had never done it before. She made her way out to this exam and has talked about what a traumatic experience that was for her because she didn't know anyone else there. Other people had groups of friends who talked and giggled at the break, and her thought was, "Why are you happy? My father just died." Margot did pass her exam and became a nurse and made that her lifelong career.

What helped with your grieving?

Mostly, I put myself to my daily task realizing, at age 12, I was the man of the family now. There was a lot of responsibility there, and I did a lot of growing up in a big hurry.

The house was old, and we were very poor. There were things that needed to be done, and I realized that if I didn't do them, they wouldn't get done. There wasn't much money around. In our single bathroom in the house, the sink would routinely get clogged and would get bailed out into the toilet next to the sink. We went years washing in the sink and then bailing it out rather than having it drain. Sometime later, I tore up the floor and found the clog was in the cast-iron pipe below the floor. There were other maintenance things around the house that I had to learn to do. That's part of the reason why I still like to collect tools these days. (Chuckles.)

I also did electrical wiring. I had a high school friend who knew a bit about electricity. He eventually went on to become an electrician. He helped us run new lines into the kitchen that could accommodate the refrigerator and the dishwasher. There were places in the house where the plaster was cracked that were not drywall and pieces started coming out of the wall. I had to teach myself a bit of that. I got angry one day combing my hair because it wouldn't stay in place, and I just randomly threw my comb across the room. It went through a window shade and hit the glass and cracked the window. (Laughs.) So, I had to learn how to repair old wooden windows. It was the kind with the rope and the counterweight along the side, and I had to learn how those worked, as well.

We had a coal furnace, and we didn't always have coal. The home we lived in had been my mother's family home for generations. Her parents had lived there and her brothers when they were younger and some as adults. We had a full attic on the third floor where there was a collection of furniture and other items. Some of it would be old antique furniture these days, but there were times when we had to break it up and burn it in the furnace because we couldn't afford coal for the furnace.

One of the saddest moments of my life was watching my father calling different coal companies, asking for credit because he couldn't pay for it, and we were freezing. One particular time, I recall watching him hang up and break down and sob. That moment is burned into my memory.

Do you have a favorite memory of your dad?

A favorite early memory is when he took me to Detroit. I was young. We flew on a plane from Cleveland, and we stayed at a nice hotel.

I don't remember anything else we did but when we came into the hotel room there was a fruit basket waiting on the table for us, and that was just so exciting. Then, we took the train home: just him and me.

He also used to show me how to do different things with tools, even though he couldn't get around at that point. I would bring things to him, and he would show me how to use a handsaw or a drill correctly. One time he brought home a metal drawer set, which I now have in my garage. It has three sets of drawers, each with dividers. He was quite the organizer. He loved office supplies. Even when he didn't have money, he had a good relationship with the local office supply store. He loved to keep things in ledgers. After he died, I had a paper route. So, I got a ledger book. I still have that book and use it for recording significant events.

Dad was quite the jokester, as well. He was very organized about it. He kept a card file with jokes according to category. People would call him up for jokes. One fellow who was our insurance man, a blind fellow by the name of Mitchell Darling, would call Dad up and say, "I'm giving a talk to this here group, and I need a couple of jokes." Dad would reach over to his card file and say, "Try this one" or "This one might work." (Laughs.) That's where I get my sense of humor.

Did your religious or spiritual life play a role in your healing?

I'm sure it did, in terms of my maturing psychologically and spiritually. I had a semester of college in South Bend, Indiana, across from the Notre Dame campus. It was a junior college. Then, I joined the religious community, the Holy Cross Brothers. I was one of six kids from my high school class who joined that religious community. I went away for a year of spiritual study with the brothers and that was on a farm — what better place to learn about spirituality than on a farm! (Chuckles.)

That year away we had regular conferences, and many of them were very personal and reflective of your life and the challenges you faced. I'm sure a lot of healing took place. I was about 19. I had the good fortune of being able to attend Notre Dame, thanks to the Holy Cross Brothers. I was part of their community, and they paid for everything in those days.

After I got a Bachelor's degree in Chemistry, I went to teach at this place called Memorial High School in Evansville, Indiana, where I met all kinds of wonderful people. I met and fell in love with a nun. That's a whole other story. (Laughs.) We got married in 1978. We had our son Jeremy two years later and then our daughter Sarah two years after that. We have four grandchildren and another one on the way, a girl, due at Christmas.

Anything else you found helpful in dealing with your loss?

We were big into counting our blessings. There were many times when we may not have had money for this or that, but we were fortunate that my mother got the house that I grew up in and that she was born in.

Mom had adult onset diabetes, and her health got worse. She kept smoking her Camel no-filter cigarettes her whole adult life, a habit Martha picked up, as well. My sister Martha ended up dying at age 59.

Mom, like Dad, ended up with fluid building up in her legs to the point that it would weep. It was gradual congestive heart failure. With Mom's illness, it was always two steps forward and three steps back. Martha had lived with her for a while, and then Martha's daughter helped take care of her. Then, it got to the point where she had to have assisted living. Mom had just turned 80. She went to a local nursing home, and she died one week later.

We were on our way up to see her. It was spring break for us, so we had the kids with us. We drove up to find out she had died the previous morning. Fortunately for her, it happened suddenly. She was eating breakfast, lifted up her spoon, and died. I'm grateful she went quickly.

What helped you in grieving her passing?

I felt guilty afterward because one of my first emotions after she died was relief. I knew she had experienced such a hard time of it, in dealing with it, and the family had made great sacrifices. She was determined to stay on her own, and so someone had to be with her. One of my first emotions was relief that the family no longer had that burden on them. No one could afford to put her in a nursing home earlier. My sister's husband Pete was helping financially to support the move to a nursing home.

Mom had taught in the same elementary school for 20 years, and many of her former students still lived in the neighborhood. So, there was a huge turnout for her funeral. That was really comforting for us.

Lots of good memories with Mom, and with Dad also, but his time, with me in particular, was much shorter.

Do you have any other suggestions for someone going through loss, especially losing your dad so young?

For me, it's about keeping the memories of the good times. My parents were such generous people. A story that Margot and I remember is when a guy that worked at a factory where my dad worked had just gotten divorced. Well, Dad brought Eddie Sampson home for what was going to be just a little while, and it ended up being two years. We had nothing monetarily to share with this guy, but we shared our home with him. That's the kind of guy my father was. Eddie ended up falling in love with the girl next door, literally, and they got married and had several kids of their own. They were like family to us. That was something different back then. In those days, you really had good neighbors, and many of them were considered family.

Mom taught school, and I helped make out the report cards and that sort of thing. The whole process of teaching was something I was quite familiar with by the time I entered my first year teaching. I created this way of doing multiple-choice tests so I could hold it up to a hole-punch cardboard and see instantly if the answers were correct. People would say, "Wow, you're a first-year teacher?" I was very comfortable with that sort of thing by then.

One of mom's favorite lines, when she'd come home from school to the three of us kids who were excited to see her and jumping on her, she would say, "Get away. I'm going upstairs and taking off my girdle, and I'm going to sit and stare for 30 minutes." (Laughs.) In my first week of teaching, I called my mother and said, "You know how you used to say that? I understand perfectly. No girdles involved but the whole sit and stare thing I get." (Chuckles.) You need the deprogramming time.

I think of Mom when I teach and when I tutor, which I am still doing.

I mentioned earlier that Dad had brought home these sections of metal drawers. They are in my garage now and Dad, in his fashion, made little labels that slip in the slots in the front. Every now and then, I'll run into an old one that is in his writing, which is nice. I think of him every time I see those drawers.

Margot has a coffee table in her home that used to be a very tall table, but my father had given me instructions on how to cut the legs; he just decided one day it should be a coffee table. It is now in Margot's guest room, and I think of Dad when I see it. A lot of the house projects I do now I learned in the house I grew up in. I do all sorts of aspects of remodeling — plumbing, electrical, drywall, trim work, flooring, and mechanical. Having married this farm girl from southern Indiana and then moving to two acres, I also do lawnmower and tractor repair and engine rebuilding.

I always feel when I do these things that I'm honoring my father.

⊷⊶

Bonnie L. Bomer (baby, birth defects)

"I have gifts to offer. I have gifts to share. I have talents. I have blessings." — I met with Bonnie and her daughter Theresa at their apartment. They graciously treated me to chili. Both Bonnie and her daughter are visually impaired, and two adorable black lab guide dogs sit nearby. Bonnie lost her baby, Tommy, three days after his birth. We met on the anniversary month of her loss. She works as a disability advocate. Her daughter Theresa, who is in her 30s, joins us in this conversation. They both share an infectious sense of humor and are quick to laugh.

I was married for almost 35 years to Voldemort. (Laughs jokingly.) That's not his real name; it's a *Harry Potter* reference and comes from a friend who said, "He who shall not be named." (Laughing.) I'll keep his real name out of this.

My husband was still in college when I got pregnant. At that time, we were living in a university town, near Penn State. We got married in '75. Soon afterward, we were blessed with a baby boy.

We had no idea that this baby was going to have problems. Tommy was full-term, but he weighed only 2 pounds and some odd ounces when born. Very tiny. They had given me anesthetic and when I woke up, I asked, "Did I have a boy or a girl?" The doctor said, "You had a boy but he's not doing very well, and we don't think he'll make it." Then, he turned around and walked away! (Shakes her head). He came back in a little later and looked at me. I was sitting there crying, and he said, "If you don't eat, you'll never get better and get out of here." I thought, *Okay, your bedside manner sucks.* There's just no other way to put it.

Tommy was born with spina bifida, which is a birth-related problem that results in part of the spinal cord being exposed. They brought Tommy to me, but the doctors wouldn't let me touch him or hold him. They didn't want me to bond with him. It was a very cold and un-nurturing environment. I wasn't even allowed to touch this baby. Afterward, Tommy was sent, lifeline I guess, to the Pittsburg Children's Hospital. I couldn't travel to be with him because I was in the hospital. They did some corrective surgery on him and tried to cover the part of the spine that was exposed. He was also born with hydrocephalus, which is when fluid builds up and causes the brain to swell. Also, his brain was underdeveloped. So, the doctors said he was extremely disabled.

I didn't have any family or close friends living there. I remember this time as pretty much of a struggle.

Tommy was born on February 12. My parents drove from Ohio to Pennsylvania to see us. It might have been February 13 or 14. I was discharged from the hospital early because the doctors didn't want me to get attached to the other babies. There was no follow-up and no direction or counseling. I was just sent home to recover.

The next morning, the hospital called us and said, "Tommy did really well in the surgery. We think he may be able to go home in a few weeks." We were amazed, thinking, "Wow, that is awesome." We were wondering how we were going to take care of this baby. We had no idea.

On their return trip back home, my parents stopped in Pittsburg and saw the baby. My mom called me, and she didn't know how else to tell me. She was a nurse, and she said, "There's just not going to be a way for you to take care of this baby. He's going to be way too medically involved." And I'm like, "Well, we'll do what we can."

Then, the doctors called and said Tommy's condition had deteriorated. Tommy was in a neonatal hospital, and we were hundreds of miles away with no transportation. They told us he had a massive internal infection, and they thought he might not make it. I told my husband, "Don't go to work tomorrow." He said "Why?" I said, "Because I don't want to be home alone when they call." We sort of knew Tommy was not going to survive.

He died on February 15. He was three days old.

Is there anything that helped with your grief?

For many years I blamed myself. I thought I did something wrong during pregnancy. Maybe I drank or ate something I shouldn't have? One thing that didn't help was that my family was real religious. They told us Tommy should never have happened. One of those, "It was our fault because we weren't married when he was conceived." It was a guilt trip thing. I blamed myself for a long, long time. I'd go through a bad depression every February.

Three years later, Theresa was born. Her and Tommy both have the same initials. I have no idea how that happened because Theresa was originally going to be named Elizabeth. But she was Theresa when she arrived.

I am legally blind. I have enough vision to get me into trouble, and the dog has to get me out again. (Chuckles.) I was born with congenital blindness and my daughter Theresa has it. I knew congenital meant it was from birth, but I didn't realize I could pass it to my children. We found out when Theresa was two or three years old that she has the same eye condition I have. It's a form of retinal dystrophy. It's like tunnel vision. Both of my parents could see. We're not sure where the visual impairment came from.

THERESA: We also have a condition known as nystagmus, which means we can't control the eye movement, and the eyes sort of dance. I am also legally blind, and the nystagmus makes it a challenge to focus. To actually sit and read takes a lot more energy.

[*Bonnie continues*]: When my husband was younger, he always had this wicked sense of humor. He had this friend named Mike. Mike was pretty much into drugs. He was trying to get clean from them, but when he first met me, he went to my husband and whispers, "What's wrong with her eyes?" I had gone to the bathroom, and I heard him. My husband says, "What do you mean?" I heard Mike say, "Well, they move up and down and all around and back and forth. What's wrong with them?" My husband glanced over at his friend Tom and says, "Tom, you notice anything wrong with her eyes?" And Tom says, "No, I didn't notice anything." And then he says, "Hey Jim, you notice anything with her eyes?" Jim says, "No, I didn't notice anything." And he says, "Mike, what you been smoking?" (Laughs.) I came out, and I said, "Is there really something wrong with my eyes?" By that time, Mike is like, "Oh God! I'm going crazy!" I said, "Okay, I'll let you off the hook." (Laughing).

Are there any religious or spiritual practices that helped you with your healing?

When I was growing up and people learned I couldn't see as well as other people, they would say, "Your parents must have done something really bad for you to be born like that." They get judgmental. I kind of have fun with that, like, "Oh really? I just met you, that must be my punishment." (Laughs.) It's interesting because I remember my grandparents taking me to faith healers when I was a kid. They put me up on stage, and when I didn't get cured, they told me it's because I didn't have enough faith. I was 10 years old. I was devastated. It was terrible. I had no self-esteem. I kind of tried to blend into the woodwork and not stand out. Finally, when I was junior in high school, I remember thinking, "You know, everyone thinks I'm not going to be worth anything." My mom had a teacher tell her one time that I wasn't going to be worth shit when I grew up. I thought, "I'm going prove them wrong." I've had to prove it to myself at times.

I started realizing there's a purpose. Even back in high school, I said, "There's a reason I was born this way, I don't know what it is, but I'll figure it out as I go."

When I went to Unity Church as an adult, I was still doing the self-blame thing. It seemed like everything I turned to in Unity was speaking to me. It was very much along the lines of, "You are blessed. You are worthy. You are a child of God." All the affirmations resonated so much with me. I walked into a church and heard them say, "You are not a sinner. And you are not going to hell."

I believe God has been guiding my steps all along. These past few months particularly, because it's the anniversary of Tommy's birth and death, I realized that if I hadn't had Tommy, I wouldn't have done volunteer work for the March of Dimes. If I hadn't done that volunteer work, I wouldn't have gotten into disability services at all. There's no such thing as coincidence. I went to the County Board of Mental Retardation and Disability, and I said, "I need a job, and I have this disability." There was a program for people with mental disabilities, and I became a case manager. I had never been around people with disabilities. I had been around a few blind folks, but not with this clientele of people with a variety of disabilities. I got such an education working in that program that I went on and got my Master's degree in Public Administration. I was hooked. Disability advocacy is what I do, and it all started with my little baby.

Those three days that Tommy was on this earth changed my life.

[I ask Theresa if her brother's loss has affected her life.]

THERESA: It's hard to believe that someone who was born three years before I was born — someone I never physically saw — could have such a huge impact on my life. I went through a lot of my life wondering what it would have been like to have my brother. When I was around 15, I had this dream that I was walking along these white hallways. I ended up standing in front of this young man. He was wearing all white, and he was thin with red hair and blue eyes. He said, "Do you know who I am?" and I said, "I don't know." He said, "I'm your brother Tommy, and I just want to let you know that I love you. And I'm still your brother." I woke up and sat straight up in bed. Ever since then, I've known that he is one of my guides. I'm here as I am, and I'm here to show everybody it's okay. You can be whatever you are. That's something Tommy has been showing me throughout my life.

[*Bonnie joins in*]: Theresa told me, "I dreamed about Tommy." I described him to her. She said, "How did you know that's what he looked like?" And I said, "Because I've seen him, too." I know he has bright red hair and brilliant blue eyes. He's kind. He's gentle.

[*I return the conversation back to Bonnie.*]

Do you have thoughts on what might be helpful for someone dealing with loss?

When I lost my baby, there was no support. I hope it's different now. It would have helped if the doctor or hospital had linked me up with someone to talk to, counseling or a church, or given me some resources.

Unity Church has grief and loss groups. Those things would be helpful. People need to connect with each other or with others who have experiences handling grief. Also, people need to understand it's not something they did. It's not a punishment from God that you lost a baby. It's that your baby left. That understanding was a defining point in my life and led me to where I am today.

I work as a disability rights advocate. It's my optimal job because I can cause trouble and get paid for it. (Laughs). And I'm good at it. I'm blessed because I'm doing what I want to do. I'm helping people. The people I work with are on a journey. They're trying to get either financial stability or housing stability or job stability. Things that everybody else wants these folks want, but they have more barriers. The attitudinal barriers are the biggest ones we face. I tell people the only things we can't do are drive a truck or a plane and play tennis. We can pretty much do what everyone else can do, but we find different ways. There are adaptations for reading, and I can hire a driver. I like to say, "I have a car, but I can't drive it because the dog can't reach the pedals." (Laughs.) We have fun!

Sometimes you have to find another way to get the point across. I have a client who emailed me today and he said, "I don't know what to do?" So, I explained that it was time to file an appeal. I don't remember now what else I told him, but he said, "That's the first time I laughed all day. Thanks!"

It's weird because all these things that have happened in my life, I should be walking around sad and rejected. I can't because there's so much out there in this world that is beautiful. Some events are transformational. They challenge and change us. They push us into a new stage of life. When my son was born, I couldn't understand why he arrived and then left just three short days later. But I believe Tommy transformed my life. He came here to set me on my life's path as a woman, as a person who's legally blind, and as an advocate for people with disabilities. I carry Tommy's wisdom and love everywhere and always, in my heart.

I look at it as: Tommy was here to teach me something. I sincerely believe that all of our experiences here are meant to teach us something. The message I got was that regardless of who is around and what happens, I'm still loved and I am love. I have gifts to offer. I have gifts to share. I have talents. I have blessings.

Anything else you want to share?

I do have one last remark: Do you know why blind people don't go skydiving? (Pauses for dramatic effect.) It scares the crap out of the dogs. (She laughs, shaking her head and smiling happily.)

⊨⊣ ⊢⊨

CHAPTER 6

A DEEPER FAITH

*"Faith is the bird that feels the light and
sings when the dawn is still dark."*

— *RABINDRANATH TAGORE*

May we be healed ~

A Buddhist legend of the young man Siddhartha tells of a prince who is secluded by the castle walls from all forms of suffering. He does not witness illness, old age, or death. One day, the story goes, the prince ventures out of the castle and sees first-hand the suffering of people in his village. He sees people who are ill, people who are old, and people who have died. This encounter propels him on a lifelong quest to understand the causes of suffering. Along his journey, he learns the path of the middle way: neither an extreme denial of the body nor an all-encompassing passion for the flesh. Finally, while meditating under a Bodhi tree, Siddhartha becomes enlightened. This man, known as the Buddha, dedicated the remainder of his life to teaching awareness of the present moment through a meditation practice.

Like Siddhartha, the individuals in these narratives explore the causes of suffering and the meaning of life by embarking on a religious or spiritual journey. While the story of the young prince derives from the Buddhist tradition, numerous religions adhere to wisdom stories from spiritual teachers who proclaimed profound insights regarding the Source of life. Similarly, the individuals here share their unique passages to a fuller understanding of death and the purpose and meaning of life.

Vanessa (who lost her son) follows the Christian faith and teachings of Jesus. Loss brought her to a deeper recognition of Spirit, rather than flesh. Other people like David (who lost both parents), combine Christian beliefs with additional meditative and spiritual practices. Still others, like Haley (who grew up atheist) found that her boyfriend's death during college became a catalyst into the spiritual realm — a journey that does not fall into any particular religious category.

These individuals readily acknowledge that their faith quests — in the midst of intense grief — were not easy. Healing arrived after an extended period of what Vanessa refers to as her "wilderness time." Forgiveness is also a significant component in many of these stories — whether it involves forgiving others, forgiving the self, or making peace with God.

As Delynn (who lost her son) says, *"The journey is about loving and forgiving."*

⛬ ⛬

Seeking Solace

Rev. Vanessa A. Robinson (son, car accident)

"The light of knowing and believing, even after death, carried me through." — *Vanessa is married to Dea K. Robinson, whom she has known since grade school. She has two children from a prior marriage: Annjatica and Michael Dwayne Beasley Jr. (Mike Jr.)*

She lost her son, Mike Jr., when he was 20 years old. Recently, Vanessa has embarked on ministry studies and leadership at Wesleyan Seminary.

The car accident, well, that is how God works.

Mike Jr. had pretty good grades in high school. He was outgoing. He personally drew people to him. He could run with the geeks or run with the streets, though he wasn't part of the street gang. He had a cousin in the police force and a cousin in a gang. He and his sister were close. Annjatica would use him as a sounding board, and he was very protective of her. Everyone in the family loved him.

When Mike Jr. and his high school sweetheart were in college, she got pregnant. They were engaged to be married and had the baby. Mike Jr. got a job at the Westin Hotel and transferred to a local college. It's not easy for African American men, and Mike Jr. was trying to do the right thing. They named the baby DeVon Michael. At first, Mike Jr. wanted to name him Divine. I said, "He's already divine, but that's not his name." (Laughs.)

Mike Jr. was doing well at work and still attending college. The day before the accident, he had dropped me off at the beauty salon. He was late picking me up. Spirit said to me, "It's not important." Mike Jr. was very handsome. His nickname was *pretty* because he was this boy with big eyes, dark hair, dark eyebrows, thick lashes, and green eyes. The beauty salon women took notice when he picked me up. He was taller than me, and he had a habit of putting his chin on my head and asking, "You good, Mom? Sorry I'm late." I was upset, but I said, "Okay." It was a peaceful, beautiful day when he took me home. That day, he went to see people he normally didn't see. He stopped by to visit a cousin and his dad. Mike Jr. said, "Just stopping by to say hi." That was Friday.

On Saturday, I went to a baby shower. When I came home, I was not tired, but for some reason I laid down to rest. I got a phone call from the hospital. They asked, "Do you have a son named Michael Jr.?" I said, "Yes." They said, "He's been in an accident." I sat on the bed and thought, "*I need to put on clothes that match because Junior's a stickler for that.*" I put my clothes on and drove to the hospital. I was like two people. The flesh one wanted to panic and rush. The spirit one said, "It's okay. I got this." I drove calmly to the hospital. While I was waiting to see the doctor, I was thinking, "Who do I call?" I knew somehow that he had died. I called my daughter and Mike Jr.'s cousins and his dad. Then, I went in and saw my son. I was thankful that he looked asleep. He was on a ventilator, but there were no vital signs. His brain was dead. I became the one to keep everyone else calm. There were two chaplains and one said, "She's too calm. Give her some drugs." I could hear them. The other one said, "Why give her drugs? She's calm." The doctor said I was in shock.

I played music in the room and sat with my son. I said to myself, "This battle is not yours. It's the Lord's."

Other family members were in a different place. They were young and didn't understand death. Several family members didn't want Mike Jr. removed from life support. I prayed about it. I said, "Lord, he belongs to you. It's your will." That evening, the doctors removed the life support. It was a hard decision. No one wanted to let Mike Jr. go. But he was already gone.

Afterward, we found out the details of the accident. Mike Jr. had been driving and was going through an intersection. A guy in a truck ran a red light. Normally, Mike Jr. wore his seatbelt. But for some reason, he didn't have his seatbelt on. The impact of the truck threw him out the window on the driver's side. He landed on the parking lot, and his head hit a water grid, and the car ran into the building. The ambulance came. It was daytime. The truck driver had been drinking.

DeVon was 18 months old when his father died.

What helped you cope with your grief?

Forgiveness. The family wanted to sue the truck driver. But that man didn't wake up that morning saying, "I'm gonna kill somebody today." Put yourself in his place. He drinks because he's suffering. Him killing Mike Jr. is not his intention. He may have family or kids. He didn't intend to kill someone. And he's got to live with what he did. That's living hell for him.

You can't just *talk* God. When you get in that storm, it's a spiritual fight. You want to be pissed and blame somebody. But we are all born to die. Nobody gets to say when, where, or how. That helped me get through it. Be ready. Mike Jr. was ready. Even though we were divorced, I never shunned Mike Jr.'s dad. Mike Jr. understood. He said, "I want Dad to know who God is." Three months before Mike Jr. died, he walked with his dad at church when his dad gave his life to Christ. That's what Mike Jr. wanted to see. That was his purpose here.

After Mike Jr.'s death, I moved to Iowa, and Mike Jr.'s fiancé moved to Atlanta, Georgia, for her job. When I moved to Iowa, I took a detour for a while. I had to find out who I was without my son. I needed to get away from, "You should do this" or "You should do that." Iowa was my wilderness time. I was in Iowa for about two years.

Meanwhile, DeVon's mom met a great guy, and she called to ask if I wanted to come to Atlanta to see my grandson. It was the best reunion. Our purpose was for her and me to come together. She calls me Mom. She has two other kids now, and she is very blessed. At the time of my visit, DeVon was three years old. When he heard loud music in a car going by, he would run to door, saying, "Dadda!" He wanted to see his dad. I said, "You want to go to heaven where your dad is?" And, he said, "Yes." I said, "You know how much you miss your daddy?" He nodded. I said, "If you go, we'll miss you." He said, "I don't want my momma to miss me."

When DeVon was 12, he came to visit me, and I played a video of Mike Jr.'s high school graduation. DeVon hadn't heard his dad's voice since he was a year and a half. He was amazed. He said, "Can

I hear it again?" I gave him the video. Devon is in college now. He is an artist, and he sketches incredible cartoons.

Do you have any religious or spiritual practices that helped with your grief?

I didn't go to church for three months. I was in a battle with my-self, saying, "God took my baby and killed my baby." I had to get to a place of knowing that wasn't true. Mike Jr. didn't belong to me. I was a vessel for this person. You grow them up to love and to be, but when people hold on to loved ones, that's the flesh side of it. God did not take my son. My son belonged to God. I needed to let go and not stay in that dark spot. I had to focus on Spirit instead of flesh. I won that fight. God is good, blessing me.

It's a journey we all have to make. If you never let them go, you won't have any peace. The light of knowing and believing, even after death, carried me through.

What else has helped with your healing?

Endurance. Depression is a grieving process. It's energy. It needs to go through you; you can't try to bottle it. Exercise helps and be-ing positive. Release and move on. By releasing negative energy, you attract positive people.

While I was living in Iowa, in prayer time, I heard, "Go home, your husband is there. He will be familiar to you." I wasn't too crazy about that because I thought it meant my ex-husband. At that time, I was working and active and loved it. I said, "God, your will, if you want me to go, you prepare the way."

So, I moved back home. No job. Nowhere to stay. I ordered a rental truck, and the money from the church was just the right amount to pay for it. I went back and stayed with a friend. Then, I found a house with three bedrooms, but there were drug dealers nearby. I called the police, and I walked the streets with my head up. By the time I left, a year later, that drug house was boarded up. That devil is a lie. These are God's people.

Later, I moved again and attended a church on other side of town. I saw a man I knew at the front. He was a deacon. It was Dea's church. When God says something, believe it and walk it. Dea and I have been married now for over five years.

Since the beginning of all this, everything has come together.

Do you have any suggestions for someone going through something similar?

My daughter and I always talked about Mike Jr. People want to act as if someone didn't exist, like putting a cork in a bottle. You can't release negative energy when you do that. We celebrate his birthday by fixing his favorite foods. We want to remember and celebrate him.

We have to process through and allow Holy Spirit to do the healing.

The journey, I call it a pathway. It's like driving. We can determine where we go, as long as we don't look back. If you're looking back in the rearview mirror all the time, you're going to crash. Stay focused. Look forward.

⊷┼ ┼⊶

David W. Douglas (parents, cancer & heart failure)

"I was angry with God." — David is soft-spoken. He is married to Pamela (Pam) Haas and runs his own computer repair business. He is in his 70s. David is an only child, and he lost both parents in his 20s. His parents were Florence (Edna) and Floyd Douglas.

210

I lost both my parents when I was 25. Because I was an only child and had no siblings for support and no church attendance, I grieved for probably 10 years. I thought I had gotten over it.

More recently, my wife Pam and I moved to a new home. Of course, when you move you go through your collected items to see what you should keep or throw out. I found a wonderful scrapbook that my mother had kept when she was in high school. It was from when she and my father began courting. She included little love notes, letters, and pictures galore. I was really drawn into thinking this was a nice treasure book, until the last page. I turned the page and there was a long strand of her brunette hair. I was immediately plunged back into grief, wondering why she did not survive while this lock of hair had survived. When a feeling like that comes over me, I pray for my parents. A minister told me that maybe, at those times, they're praying for me as well. That was comforting.

My mother died of esophageal cancer. She was 54. Twelve years prior, she had been able to pray away metastasized breast cancer. She was a Christian Science practitioner and active in the church as an organist and soloist. At the time of her death, I was in an unhealthy marriage. I was 20 years old when I got married, and I heard through the grapevine how upset my mother was with my situation. When she got another form of cancer, I believe it might have been because I was in that marriage and couldn't see that I shouldn't be in it.

After my mother passed away, my dad was very lonely. He wasn't taking care of himself the way he should have been. Of course, back then everyone fried everything they ate. If my mother let him, he'd eat pork chops every night of the week, two or three of them. My father passed six months after my mom from heart failure. He died on his 58th birthday.

Both my father and my mother were the youngest of their siblings. Because I came along so late in their marriage, most of my aunts and uncles were well over the hill or already under the turf. All of these things can really contribute to a sense of loneliness and grief.

I dealt with my parents' deaths with anger. Actually, I was angry with God. I also thought that somehow it was my fault.

My first marriage lasted about 15 years, and then we got a divorce. I got married again, right after the first divorce. It was very good at first, but it went downhill. I just figured, "Here's another divorce." Sometimes when you haven't handled your misery, you find yourself in situations that have the potential to make you really miserable.

I was on the brink of despair.

What has helped with your healing?

I began attending a Methodist church. They had a singles organization and a good divorce recovery program. They also had different groups that would meet for specific healing processes. We had meditation and bible readings. Pam and I were in the choir together at church. One Sunday, the minister preached a sermon on suicide, among other things. Two weeks prior to that one of his friends, a man of cloth, had walked into Lake Michigan. I had been to the verge of suicide myself, and as we were putting our music away, I said, "Wasn't that a great sermon today?" And Pam broke down in tears. When she looked at me, she saw that I was crying, too. We didn't start dating until a couple of years after that, but I knew from that moment that she could love me. So, it really makes a difference if the person you are with is supportive. During my prior marriages, I was blocking the grief. Now, I have somebody in my life that loves me unconditionally and also is very spiritual.

I've come to realize that each of us is on our own path. We are responsible for our choices and experiences.

Do you have any religious or spiritual practices that helped with your grief?

I was originally raised Christian Scientist, which is metaphysical. I was resistant to spirituality before. My mother taught me all the precepts of metaphysics. When a parent tells you something the response is often, "Yeah, sure." One time I asked her, "If God loves us so much, why does he let all these bad things happen, like wars, storms, and mass plagues?" She gave me the same answer — back in the '50s — that I am hearing now in the Unity church. She was a very forward thinker. Her answer was that thought, stress, and any human emotion can express energy, electromagnetic. That energy can go out and come back in the form of storms and can agitate other people to precipitate wars, unrest, and riots.

Deepak Chopra proved this, too. For experiments, he would get thousands of people together to meditate, and the crime in the streets in that city would go down drastically during the time they were meditating. Being a medical doctor, he had to take urine samples from the people who were meditating. If you can imagine that! There's a chemical that is found in a person who meditates that isn't found when someone is not mediating. He also tested people out in the street who had no idea about the meditation going on in the building, and they had the same chemical in their urine. It's like the meditation creates a force field that goes out and makes everyone feel better, even though they don't know why. So, I have a daily meditation practice.

I believe my parents are in heaven, and I'll see them again. The big turning point for me was a book I read years ago, *Many Lives Many Masters*. It's like we take the same souls through reincarnation, those who are near and dear to us, more than one time around. Of course, Gary Renard, who is *A Course in Miracles* teacher, says once we have forgiven everything, we're all done with reincarnation. We all go home to God and become part of the whole.

When I found my mother's scrapbook, I was drawn down into a whirlpool of grief again. I just had to meditate my way out of it. There are wonderful guided meditations and also meditations with sounds of nature and chimes of singing bowls. Those meditations are really helpful.

Do you have any suggestions for others going through grief?

Get therapy from someone who is not just a clinical expert, but also a spiritual person. The sad thing about it is, we're not ready to hear a message until we decide we're ready to hear it. So, make yourself ready. Just try it. Everybody works on grief a different way. Find the way that works the best for you.

⚬⚬⚬

Hayley McGinley (boyfriend, car accident)

"So much of who I am today is because of Adam and our relationship, and how I've changed and evolved as a result of his passing." — Hayley is 28. She is cheerful and down to earth, wearing jeans, a colorful scarf over her shirt, and white moonstone earrings. She just started her own business, an artisan gluten-free bakery called Native Bread. Originally from a small town with a high school graduating class of 45 students, she lost her boyfriend, Adam Maletta, while in college.

Adam and I met in high school. I was in my freshman year, and Adam was a junior. I had the biggest crush on him. We had one class together, Home Economics, and he sat next to me, which I thought was awesome. (Laughs). We didn't have any classes the next year because he was a senior, and I was a sophomore. After he graduated, we reconnected over MySpace, back when MySpace social media was popular with everybody. Adam sent me a friend request on MySpace, and the day I got it, I freaked out.

Then, we started messaging each other back and forth. That's how our relationship began. At the time, I was visiting my grandparents for summer break. So, for about a month, we communicated over MySpace and made plans to hang out when I got back.

We started dating right before the first day of my high school senior year. He was taking classes at a college extension campus and living at home.

The first seven months of our relationship, I was crazy about him, like you are when you're 18 and young. At first, he was just playing it cool or whatever. I remember I never told him anything that upset me because I was afraid he'd never talk to me again. I would hide it and keep it inside. One night, I decided since we'd been dating seven months I should be able to tell him if he does something that upsets me. So, something happened that made me mad, and I told him about it. He said, "Oh, I'm so sorry," and he was really understanding.

But then my fear that he would never talk to me came true. He just dropped off the face of the earth. I didn't hear from him for a couple of months. Finally, I got the nerve to confront him about it. We got together at his house, and I was completely honest because, at that point, I didn't have anything left to lose. I said, "You know, you broke my heart. We dated for seven months, and you just really hurt me." He had no idea! He was like, "Oh, my God, I didn't realize." We had a very deep conversation. Looking back, we always said that was the night we fell in love.

When I graduated high school, I went away to college. I majored in Human Development and Family Studies, with minors in sociology, psychology, and human sexuality. While I was away at college, Adam and I fell into a rhythm. I would visit him one weekend, and then we would switch off and he would visit me. Every other weekend one of us was driving 3 hours. For two years, we did the long-distance thing. It didn't bother us. We were just so in love. We'd miss each other during the week, but we knew we'd see each other on the weekends.

The summer before my junior year of college, I started feeling like, "I'm going to be 21, and he is the only man I ever had a relationship with." I wanted freedom, and I wanted to experience college as a single young woman. I stayed on campus over the summer and ended things with him — over the phone, of all things to do. (Sighs).

He understood, but it was hard for him. I broke his heart. We sort of kept in touch for a couple of months, randomly. The last time I ever spoke to him was on the phone; he was making a last ditch effort to get me back. I held my ground. I said, "No, I need this space."

My 21st birthday was August 5. Adam had wanted to come visit me for my birthday. Only, I didn't invite him. So, he wasn't there. Two days later, on August 7, I got a phone call from his dad. I missed the call, and his dad left a voicemail. He said, "I'm calling to let you know Adam was in a car accident last night, and he's not doing well. He is in the hospital." I was in the kitchen in my apartment when I got the message. I just collapsed on the ground. I lost it. I knew from the message how serious it was. Maybe my subconscious knew at that moment that he was going to die.

Two of my girlfriends drove me to the hospital so I could see him. He survived the initial accident. At the time of the accident, he was by himself, driving down the road, less than a mile from his house. He was going home. Nobody knows what happened. He lost control going around this really sharp corner and slammed into a telephone pole. A woman who lived nearby heard the crash. She went out and found him in his car. He had fallen over and had hit his head, hard. I don't know whether he hit his head on the steering wheel or on the side of the window. But this woman found him, and he was bleeding. He was unconscious, but still breathing, gasping. This women held him and spoke to him, and said, "I'm here, keep breathing, you're okay." She was just an angel. She came out to rescue him and called 911.

Adam was in that hospital for a couple of days. When I saw him, he was hooked up to all this equipment. I could barely recognize him. His whole face was bruised and swollen, and he had tubes everywhere. He was unconscious and on a breathing tube and all that. Essentially, what happened is that his brain suffered severe swelling and there was immense pressure on his brain. The hospital drilled a hole into his skull to relieve the pressure, and then there was this tube sticking out of his head.

At first, there was hope that he was going to be okay. The way they test the pressure on your brain is that there is a number, like a 0 to 60 scale. We should always be at 0. But if it gets to 60, then that's the point of no return because the brain has suffered such enormous pressure that even if you survive, you will be a vegetable for the rest of your life. Adam's brain pressure was around 50 and then was slowly going down. So, the doctors were saying it looked promising, and he might pull through. Then, they airlifted him to a hospital in Chicago because he was not getting any better.

My mom drove me to Chicago. The last thing I had heard from his family was that the pressure was going down and things were looking better, and he might wake up in the next few days. I was excited and so full of hope. I was thinking, "I'm going to be by his bed, and he's going to wake up and see me." I had all these visions of things going back immediately to the way they were with us, and I'd be his girlfriend again, and we'd get married.

When I got to Chicago with my mom, I saw all his family in the front foyer. I saw his mom standing between two women, and they were literally holding her up. His grandpa was the first one to walk up and give me a hug, and all he said was, "It's not looking good." I said, "What do you mean it's not looking good?" But I knew. I guess the first night in Chicago, Adam's brain pressure skyrocketed to over 60. The doctors said the other hospital did it wrong because if the tube was removed, Adam would instantly die. It would be like pulling a plug on a drain. I said, "Where is he? I want to see him."

We walked to his room and as soon as I saw him, it hit me. All my hope just flew out the window. I had to get out and go somewhere private because I knew I would lose it. I was only in the room a second, and I said, "Where's the bathroom?" My mom took me, and I fell on the ground and was just screaming and wailing. It was an animalistic thing. I had never experienced all those feelings and physical reactions: the way I sounded, the way my body responded, the way I was behaving, was just so raw. My mom was holding me and rocking me back and forth. That moment is engraved in my memory.

Adam was in the Chicago hospital for four nights. After my mom scooped me up off the bathroom floor, I spent the rest of the time lying in his bed. The nurses were so sweet. They scooted his body over so I could put my head on his chest. Even though it was a machine-induced heartbeat, I kept my head on his heart and listened to it. I told Adam all the things I wanted him to know: How much I loved him, how sorry I was for breaking up with him, and how much I regretted it. I was bargaining, saying essentially, "If you come back to life, then I will marry you." I knew it wasn't going to happen, but I still experienced those things.

Knowing his brain was already dead, his parents had to make the incredibly hard decision to take him off life support. Adam was a full donor. We had that conversation when he renewed his driver's license. I remember, he asked about being a donor, and I said, "Yes, of course. You could help so many people if something happens."

That last night, his mom came in and gave me a hug goodbye. There was nothing more anyone could do. The accident was on August 7, and seven days later they took him off life support.

What helped you cope with your grief?

Fall semester classes started soon after he passed. That was really awful. When we were dating, we spoke on the phone multiple times a day, and at night we would talk on the phone for hours. We were together three years. So, when I started classes my junior year, it was hard not to have that communication. I was in the habit of checking my phone while walking between classes. I went to my classes. But I couldn't stay focused and absorb what I was learning. My mind was consumed by the grief. I just couldn't believe he had died.

I started forgetting things. I was in the apartment I shared with my sister Kelly. I had used the oven to bake something and had forgotten to turn the oven off. Kelly is my older sister. Normally, if I had done something like that, my sister would get pissed and yell at me. But she was so gentle and sweet. I would just forget these little important things because my mind was on Adam and all the "what if" questions.

Honestly, I just felt very alone with my grief. I was at college. So, I wasn't near my parents. I had my friends and my sister, but I felt like if I opened up about my sadness, even to my sister, I would be placing a burden on them. I never wanted anyone to feel obligated to sit and listen. I always internalized things anyway. I just pushed all the pain and sadness down inside.

So much of my identity was wrapped up in our relationship. When he passed, I didn't know who I was anymore. I was walking around like a zombie with this dark heaviness on me. I realized I needed an outlet or someone to talk to. I looked into grief counseling but decided against it.

The things I did do to cope? I cried a lot but always alone in my room. I would cry myself to sleep every night for a long time. I didn't discover anything helpful until a year after he died.

One day, I was at the bookstore. I was just walking around the aisles, with all the different labeled sections, and I saw a section on grief and loss. I was like, "Oh my God, why didn't I think of this before?" It never occurred to me that I could reach out to books as a modality to help me cope. It wasn't until my senior year of college that I got a book on loss. I flipped right to the section on losing a significant other. That helped me some.

Do you have any religious or spiritual practices that helped?

My whole life I had identified as an atheist. I wasn't raised with going to church, and my parents aren't religious. After Adam died, I still felt his presence and energy all around me. I was confused because I had always thought that when you die, that's it. You are put in the ground or cremated and you're gone. But I felt him, and I had a strong desire to talk to him.

I got on the computer and searched: "How to talk to dead people." I discovered this practice called astral projection, which is a fancy word for soul travel. That piqued my interest. It was all about how your soul can leave your body and meet up with people who have died. I thought, "I need to learn how to do this." I went back to the bookstore, and I found a book called, *The Beginners Guide to Astral Projection*. I always thought the word "spirituality" was just hocus-pocus. That book was my first step into that realm. It was a catalyst for my journey into my spirituality.

After I graduated from college, I discovered Eckhart Tolle's book, *The Power of Now*, which completely transformed and shifted my perspectives. A year later, I traveled to Thailand to teach English. I was meditating every day and had a lot of time to read. I read Neale Donald Walsch's books, *Conversations with God* and *Home with God: In a Life that Never Ends*. It breaks down what happens when you die. Reading these books was like remembering. Those books helped me cope the most.

I had a remarkable experience while I was in Thailand. I had gone to sleep, but I was woken up because my bed was vibrating, from head to toe, vertically, really quickly. I thought it was an earthquake. I was lying on my stomach with my head turned to the side. I opened my eyes, and I am freaking out with my heart racing. And then, in that same moment, I saw a gray shadow, vibrating back and forth with my bed. I felt terror coursing through my veins because I thought there was a ghost in my room. Then, I heard Adam's voice. In that instant, all my fear went away. I don't know how I did it. All I can say is that I moved into the experience and stopped resisting it. I stopped being afraid. I opened up and allowed myself to receive. When I did that, Adam was in my bed, underneath me. He was there. It was the most real experience, just like we're sitting here now having this conversation. The first thing he said to me was, "This is never going to happen again." I said, "I don't care. You're here. I love you." We kissed. I held his face in my hands. I asked him if he was okay and he said, "Yes." I asked him if I was going to see him again when I die, and he said, "Yes, of course." We talked. Mainly we just held each other. I got afraid and said, "Are you going to leave me now?" He said. "No." I laid my head back down on his chest. And when I opened my eyes back up, he was gone.

I believe I was able to have that experience because my mind and my spirit were so open. I was able to receive anything the universe wanted to send my way. I only recently shared this story. Prior to that, I had not shared it other than to a few select people. Even my parents don't know this story. I didn't want people to think I was crazy.

Adam was definitely a soul mate of mine. That was another thing that was hard after he passed. I always believed we have a single soul mate. My definition of soul mate was that there is only one person we are meant to be with and for me it was Adam. That was a huge battle in my grief. I was asking, "Well, what's the point of me living if my soul mate is dead? What's the point of going on if there's nobody else in the world for me?" I struggled with that until my beliefs started to shift through the books I was reading. I believe now that we can have more than one soul mate.

Is there anything else you found helpful?

I was grieving and experiencing significant grief for years. I would say I didn't really feel like myself again for six or seven years.

A huge part of my healing came from the place where I started working, a new age boutique store, and meeting the owner, Vicki. Being in that space, I felt like she cradled me. It was a healing space. Vicki gave me healing energy, wisdom, love, and support. She saw my light, *always*, even when I was still very depressed. For the first time in my life, I also took some time to rest and pamper myself. I was easy on myself, and felt like I was stepping back into myself. My confidence, my self-esteem, and my essence were returning. It was a long journey.

Do you have a favorite memory of Adam?

We would sit outside at night, under the stars, and just talk. I had this connection with him that I have never experienced with anybody else. I felt so much like myself when I was in his presence.

Another experience I treasure is when we were dating, and his family invited me to join them on their vacation to this house on a lake in Wisconsin. It was a big group with his brothers and their girlfriends and his whole family. We would wake up early with the sunrise. We'd fish all day and then come back and clean the fish, fry it, and eat fish for lunch. In the afternoon, we'd go out on the speedboat and go tubing. I learned how to waterski on that trip. It took me three days, but on the third day, I finally stayed up. Then, we'd go back out at night and fish again. That was just a beautiful week with his family.

That's another big loss for me: the loss of his family. I keep in touch with his mom. I just adore his family, and it was hard for me to know she would never be my mother-in-law, and his brother would never be my brother-in-law, and I would not marry into the family. That loss in itself was extremely difficult.

My fondest memories are just the conversations Adam and I shared. Even at night, on the phone, we would fall asleep together. We would set our phones next to our faces when we were finished talking, just to hear each other breathe. Oh, my God! (Laughs).

Do you have any suggestions for someone reading this book?

Don't be afraid to open up to people. I might have released the grief sooner had I been more vocal and open about what I was feeling. Find a support group or a counselor or somebody you can talk to on a regular basis that you feel comfortable sharing your experiences with. When I did finally open up to people, I felt so much better.

I love talking about Adam. It keeps the memory of him alive. So much of who I am today is because of Adam and our relationship and how I've changed and evolved as a result of his passing.

It feels good to share the story now, without so much heaviness.

⊷┼ ┼⊷

Delynn Curtis (son, cancer)

"The message is to trust Spirit." — *Delynn has intense green eyes, pale skin, and flaxen hair. She is a spiritual teacher and a body movement instructor. Delynn has three children: Vanessa, Rod and Jerry. (Vanessa Hughes' story is in the PROLOGUE). Delynn lost her son Rodman (Rod) to cancer. He was 26 years old.*

Rod was meant to be here, and I am honored that I got to be his mother. All three of my children are amazing.

What happened with Rod is that he came home a couple of days before Thanksgiving. We were planning this glorious Thanksgiving dinner because all my kids and their partners would be there. Rod told me he had been sick the week before and was throwing up. I could sense something was going on. I said, "We have to get to the hospital. This isn't right."

The doctors did a MRI and a biopsy and told us it was cancer. It was a rare cancer called leiomyosarcoma. It is extremely aggressive. To show the aggressiveness, he was diagnosed in November and passed away in April. The tumors were in his stomach, over his liver, and grew so fast that it blocked his artery in his leg. One leg was the size of three because of the swelling. He tried to go through radiation. He had horrific pain. Of course, with a 26-year-old, no one wants to say it's hopeless right out the gate. But that is how this cancer is. One day they are fine and then … (Trails off.)

I tried to find alternative medicine doctors. But Rod was incredibly sick. We couldn't drive him 10 minutes down the road because he was in so much pain and throwing up.

The doctors at the hospital were greatly impacted by my son, and everybody was trying everything they could. They put him through some kind of chemotherapy that was unbelievable. I heard my son screaming from down the hall. It was unbelievable. (Crying.)

The doctors thought if Rod got through the chemo, they could attempt surgery. But they didn't know because it was over his liver. At one point, the doctor thought the tumors had shrunk a little. My son's spirits were lifted. He had all these amazing plans for his life ahead of him. He and my other son were planning to open a business together, and they were inseparable. We were feeling like, "Wow, we have a chance here."

That night my nephew picked me up so I could get some rest. Later that same night, I got a call telling me that Rod had been taken down to ICU. Apparently, they had given him some liquids, and he aspirated. I came and the hospital staff wanted to know who had the power of attorney. I said, "What? He doesn't have one." The woman went into my son's room, and I heard her ask him if he wanted to be put on a respirator, life support. He screamed, "Momma, am I dying?" I came running down the hall. (Crying.) I said, "No Rod, I don't believe you're dying. You're just transitioning." Then, I said, "The doctors want to put you on a respirator. What do you want?" He said, "Momma, I just want to be me. I want to go home."

I lived in this beautiful house on 25 acres of wooded property with lots of windows. Rod felt like it was paradise, close to nature and peaceful. So, I told the doctor I wanted to get my son home. The doctor said Rod wouldn't survive the 3-hour ride to get him there. I took the doctor's hand and very passionately said, "My son says he wants to go home." I rode in the ambulance with Rod and put my hands over his head because he was struggling all the way home. I signed a Do Not Resuscitate because I didn't want to go back to the hospital and have them do more things. We got him home, and in three days he passed.

Rod handled the end with peace. His calm. His presence. Unbelievable. Rod's last words to us were to remember what I had taught him: love every day, forgive everyone, and start over in the moment.

When he passed, I went outside to feel the early morning sun and to help my heart. Butterflies appeared from nowhere, dancing and fluttering around and on me. My son was free. (She wipes her eyes, crying.)

We decided the best way to honor Rod's story, which is just beginning, is to be happy. To live in trust of God. No matter what is going on in this world, it's not as it seems. Joy is what we're supposed to experience. That seems really crazy amidst this story, but if you would have seen my son smile and felt his presence. Rod could walk into a room and the whole room would soften. He had over 500 friends at his service.

What has helped you cope with your grief?

Spirit has taken me to wonderful people. My children, Jerry and Vanessa, gave me the gift of a retreat in Utah. I continued my exploration of *A Course in Miracles* and went to a yoga class nearby. The point wasn't the retreat or the yoga class, it was to meet certain people. I can sit back and watch how Spirit is bringing me to a place of trust. I don't know how this will all unfold. But what Rod and God want me to do is to listen and be led.

I briefly attended a grief support group. Support groups may help other people, but I can't get out of it that way. Dancing gets me out of it.

A woman I met helped me understand that with Rod's death there's a purpose. That affirmation has given me comfort. She also gave me permission to cry as hard as I wanted to. Truly, every moment I'm being led. I'm just listening, following, and doing as I'm asked. And here I am today, with you.

Do you have any religious or spiritual practices that helped?

I have a calling and spiritual connection to dance movement. That's my life's work. At age 11, I auditioned for the New York City Ballet, and got accepted to study there. I chose not to attend. I was aware, even at that young age, of the competitive world of dance. Instead, I pursued my life, got into theater, and learned choreography. I trained as a dancer my whole life and never stopped taking classes.

More recently, I was told I am going to be a spiritual teacher. I thought, "Well, that's goofy. I'm a dancer." But my spiritual teachings are just another way of connecting with people, which is what

I do with dance. All spiritual paths show people how to go within and listen for internal guidance and direction. Peace and joy come when you realize your oneness with that Source.

Do you have a favorite memory of Rod?

I remember Rod at my parents' 50th wedding anniversary. Rod was two or three years old. He loved to dance, too. He was like this ball of light with so much joy and energy. After his transition, I was teaching a movement class and this woman stopped. She said, "Rod is standing behind you, laughing and dancing, and putting his arms around you." He's my dance partner now.

The journey is about loving and forgiving. No matter what this world is throwing at you, this Source of life is giving you continuous opportunity to start anew, to be alive, to live in joy and happiness.

Do you have any suggestions for someone experiencing grief?

The story seems so dramatic, and it is. There are days I don't how I'm going to do it, especially if I sit and dwell on it. But the message I got is to trust Spirit.

For the first few months after Rod passed, I thought it was my fault because we had gone through some bad times when the kids were young. We were homeless for a while. All my counselors said Rod had a purpose and nothing was going to change his time to leave.

Rod still appears to me. One person, during a Reiki session, said she saw him, and he told her, "Just so you know, I'm not here for you. I'm here for my momma." (Laughs.) That's Rod, very to the point and practical. Rod is definitely here. He is not going to leave me. He will keep helping me.

I also saw him after he passed. It was a year later, on Thanksgiving. My son Jerry was coming down the hall, and we were leaving to go to my daughter's because she was having Thanksgiving dinner. I heard Jerry's footsteps, and I heard another set of footsteps. I had been putting on my makeup. I know this sounds bizarre, but when I turned around, I saw Rod standing right next to my son Jerry. I saw him in physical form, smiling, with long gorgeous hair. It was only about 30 seconds. He was letting me know that he hasn't gone anywhere.

Death is not real. That's how I get through it. I recognize that the physical form changes. It's the same with me. I had a serious car accident as a teen and then later had back surgery. But I'm a dancer inside, *always*.

⊷ ⊶

CHAPTER 7

CREATING A LIVING LEGACY

*"When you are sorrowful look again in your
heart, and you shall see that in truth
you are weeping for that which has been your delight."*

— *KHALIL GIBRAN*

May we be a source of healing in the world ~

In the well-known *Parable of the Long Spoons*, the people in hell are seated around a large banquet table filled with scrumptious food in the center. They are able to reach the food with their long spoons. Yet, they are starving because their arms do not bend, and they cannot bring the long wooden spoons to their mouths. In this parable, the people in heaven are joyous and well-fed even though they face the same circumstances with arms that do not bend and long spoons that do not reach their mouths. In heaven, people have learned to feed each other.

Regardless of whether our belief system includes a concept of heaven and hell, this parable reminds us that we accomplish more — and serve the greater good — when we are willing to work together and help one another. Our families, neighborhoods, and communities greatly benefit from small or large actions motivated by love. As a famous Bible verse states, "By their fruits ye shall know them." For those who are not religious, a similar idea is expressed in the quote, "Actions speak louder than words."

Being a source of healing in the world can take many forms. The individuals and couples in this section have made a decision to put their grief to positive use in a variety of ways, such as setting up scholarships to help students with financial need and establishing nonprofits to serve the community with drug overdose awareness, violent sexual assault prevention, or support for basic human needs in underprivileged areas.

We all experience periods in our life when we need people we can lean on. Similarly, there are times when we feel called to serve, which can also be a path of healing.

Jeanine (who lost her son) says, *"Getting involved with the nonprofit helped with the grieving process."* Don (who lost his son) further explains, *"Braden's loss put life, and our whole purpose for being here, in a different perspective. It increased my motivation to do something worthwhile, something that improves the life of others."*

Assisting our communities (whether in our neighborhoods or across the globe) is one way to honor the memory of those who have passed. Ned (who lost his daughter) states in his interview that the memory of their daughter Laura will not be forgotten. Her legacy will live on in the work done by the Laura Kate Winterbottom Memorial Fund to end sexual assault.

As Mother Teresa aptly observes, *"Not all of us can do great things. But we can do small things with great love."*

Making a Difference

Jeanine Motsay (son, overdose)

"I found little niches where it's okay to be broken, and that has helped me to heal." — Jeanine is finishing up an advanced degree in counseling at Christian Theological Seminary (CTS). She is 49. She lost her son Samuel (Sam). He was 16. Jeanine formed the non-profit, Sam's Watch, and set up a scholarship at his high school. Sam has one younger brother, Nick. At the time of our interview, it is coming up on the two-year anniversary of Sam's death. He died on Mother's Day.

I married Frank Motsay when I was 30 and got pregnant with Sam on our honeymoon. I had Nick shortly afterward. The boys are 17 months apart, one grade difference in school. I was married to their biological father for seven years. Frank is now in Grand Rapids, Michigan.

I later married Ed Ocho. Sam walked me down the aisle, and Nick was Ed's best man. We were married 10 years. Everybody grieves differently. In our particular situation, in the marriage, it just kind of tore us apart.

I spent many years in business operations types of positions. As my kids were getting into high school, I wanted to be around for them more. I took a position working from home that made it possible for me to be there when the boys left and when they got home without all the traveling.

Sam was a sophomore at Center Grove High School. He was your typical teenager. He had a GPA of 4.0 or above. You could ask him on any given day his GPA, and he knew it. He also was involved in sports. His sport of choice was basketball, and he played on the school basketball team. He was old enough to have his driver's license, but he could get where he needed to go without a license. He had lots of people to drive him places, which was very different from when I was his age and lived in a rural community. He also had a moped that he could drive to school for practices, and he was in no hurry to get a license. To me, that seemed to indicate he was not seeking a lot of independence.

My boys spent holiday breaks, spring break, fall break, and much of their summer break with their father. Their father was engaged in their lives; he still is with Nick.

That's the whole thing. There wasn't any advance warning. They talk about the importance of being involved with your kids. So, we were involved. In fact, that weekend, I drove Sam to his basketball games. In the afternoon, he helped unload the groceries. Then, I took him to evening games, and it was on the way home that he mentioned he wanted to hang out with his friend. Sam went to elementary, middle school, and high school with this friend. They played basketball together, and he lives in our neighborhood. We know his parents, and we know his family. I said it was it okay if Sam stayed over. My only caveat with the plan was that the next day was Mother's Day, so I told him I needed him to be home early because we had plans. Of course, he was okay with that.

Around 9 o'clock the next morning, there was a ring at the doorbell. My anticipation was that it was Sam coming home. They had just gone through this doorbell-ditching thing, where you ring the doorbell and then hide. I thought, "Okay, he's trying to be funny. So, I'm just going to ignore that." (Laughs.) Then, the doorbell rang again. Ed answered the door. It was the Johnson County sheriff and someone from the coroner's office who walked into our house. We didn't know who they were at the time because they were in plain clothes. It was Sunday morning.

They began to tell us that a young male was found deceased at such and such address. The address isn't really registering anything to me. I'm thinking, "Okay, Sam and his friends got involved in something, and somebody got hurt, and now I'm going to spend this day talking to Sam about it and being a parent." But then, as the sheriff was talking, he pulled out a wallet. As soon as I saw the wallet, I knew that it was Sam because I had bought the wallet for him, and he had picked it out. Without any further words, it was just the realization that my life had changed forever.

The police weren't sure at that point what had happened to Sam. What we learned later is that his friend and another boy — who were basketball players as Sam was — were subject to random drug testing at the school. Somebody who goes out and drinks or smokes marijuana is caught on those random drug tests. So, if you wanted to do any experimentation and avoid getting caught, that would not be the way to go. They talked to peers and from those conversations arrived at the idea of doing something like acid or LSD, which goes quickly through your system in 8 to 10 hours. If you go to school on Monday and get pulled in for random drug testing, it's not in your system anymore.

The boys reached out to an older teen they knew through classmates, somebody they trusted. That person I found out had trouble with drugs early on and was addicted to benzos (Benzodiazepines, commonly called Valium or Xanax), which is an anxiety prescription drug. To have the money to pay for his high, he agreed to get these boys what they were looking for. But he didn't know where to get the drugs. So, he reached out to somebody who was a little bit older, in his mid-20s. That individual knew somebody they could get the drugs from, and that person was also in his mid-20s. They purchased what they thought was LSD and sold it to Sam and his friends.

In fact, what that dealer sold them was not LSD. Instead, it was a synthetic hallucinogenic drug made with research chemicals. He had purchased the powder form of that synthetic over the internet, received it in the mail from overseas, and mixed it with 150-proof alcohol. He mixed it with that to dilute it and then sprayed or mixed it onto blotting paper to make acid-looking tabs. What happens with the synthetic hallucinogens is that just a granule, the size of the end of a pencil, is lethal. Depending on the concentration and how it has been diluted, it can be a dose that is lethal or not. All three of the boys took the same thing. Afterward, Sam was tired from all of his activities and said he just wanted to lie down. He went into another room and went to sleep. The other two boys played Xbox or video games. It wasn't until the next morning that they checked on Sam. At that point, he was dead.

On Tuesday, the police raided this dealer's home. They found not only the substance that killed Sam but also cocaine and other drugs. There were several felony counts. He was under house arrest at that time for another charge, and so he automatically went to jail over that violation, and then the additional charges became pending for court trial. I spent a lot of time last summer in both Johnson County and Marion County courts. The 19-year-old boy who was trying to fund his addiction is currently in jail. The second individual died from a drug overdose. The dealer eventually had his sentencing and got 25 years in prison.

Because I worked from home, after Sam died every morning became such a burden. I would walk by his room and realize what's not there. It was terribly, terribly painful to go through Sam's room. I did it in stages. First, I did one closet, then, I did another closet. Then, it was his desk. My mom and a lifelong friend that I met in first grade have always been there with me. (Crying.) They spent a lot of time with me over the past two years. There were days I would not have gotten out of bed had it not been for them. So, they helped me with that. When I think about Sam now, it's not so heavy.

What helped with your healing journey?

Initially, we were privately processing what was happening. But it became fairly public. We had reporters show up at our house and the court hearings. As I was learning what had happened, it seemed to me that if I had known more, I could have had a conversation with Sam that hopefully would have led to a different outcome. Even law enforcement wasn't familiar with the drug Sam had been given. When he died, there were still two tabs, and they had those analyzed by a Purdue chemist, David Nichols, who has worked with this particular hallucinogenic drug in his medical research. That is how they quickly arrived at what killed Sam. Many times police don't find out what it is or where it came from. In our case, it went full circle, and we were allowed to have answers that other families don't always have.

Because law enforcement didn't know about this drug, the Johnson County sheriff put on a forum in August, just before school started. They invited state police, community members, and other law enforcement people. The sheriff asked if our family would participate. I didn't even think about it and said yes. Then I thought, "What am I going to share?" Then, "Am I the only one who has anything to say?" So, I talked to Sam's two friends from that night, and the three of us wrote letters to Sam about what we knew at that point and what we wished they had known. (Crying.) There were about 300 people at the forum. It was very cathartic for the boys because they got to say what they wanted to say and how sorry they were. That was a huge part of the grieving process for all of us. Nick stood up there with me when I spoke with his arm around me. (Crying.) It really helped.

There wasn't a lot of information out there about synthetic drugs. Six months before his death, the drug that killed Sam was not illegal. It was available for purchase on the Internet. That gives mixed messages to teens. One day it's okay, and the next day it's not.

We started a nonprofit called Sam's Watch, so teens, parents, and communities know about the dangers of synthetic drugs. Unlike other drugs where you can have an addiction that goes on for some time, with signs along the way — such as changes in behavior, in friends, in hygiene, and in grades — with synthetic drugs the first time you try something, you don't know what you're getting, and it can kill you. It can happen with initial experimentation. That's the danger we want to share.

We held another forum in Hamilton County. From there, I started speaking in schools. I believe if Sam had better information, he could have made an educated decision. I also learned about brain development. Because the brain isn't fully developed until age 25, teens cannot always judge situations and understand the consequences, nor can they necessarily curb their curiosity.

The first year, we had 43 schools that participated in the Sam's Watch program and 32,000 students. This past year, we reached out again. We had we had over 33,000 students.

Getting involved with the nonprofit helped with the grieving process. I started writing blogs, sharing about grief as I was experiencing it. All of this is a real stretch for me because I am a very private person.

Is there anything else you found helpful?

When Sam died, we went as a family to Brooke's Place, which is a grief-counseling center for children and families. Everybody grieves differently, and Nick decided he didn't want to go anymore. The counselor was fine with that. Nick is a great help with Sam's Watch.

I'm not who I was before this happened. I had a very nice executive position. The focus on revenue, budget, forecasting, selling and client development, all of those things have a different meaning when you lose someone. I went back to my roots from my bachelor's degree in Psychology. I wanted to help people because I felt like I needed so much help. I'm working on a clinical mental health counseling degree.

Another saving grace was that I got involved in two different support groups. One is a group of mothers who have lost children.

You can be who you are with these people. If you see something and you think, "Oh, that reminds me of Sam," you can say that. (Crying.) You have someone who understands what you're saying. That group was lifesaving. The other support group is for parents who have kids who died from drugs. Those two support groups really helped me process what was happening.

Do you have any religious or spiritual practices that helped?

Very much so. When we first learned that Sam died, I called the pastor. He didn't answer the phone because church was going on. A law enforcement officer went by the church. The junior pastor was giving the sermon, and so our senior pastor called me. I told him what had happened, and he said he would be right there. When he arrived, he told me that as he was leaving the church, he heard through the speakers in the hallway, the junior pastor reading Psalm 23: *Though I walk through the valley of the shadow of death, I will fear no evil for thou art with me,* (crying), which was comforting to me.

The other thing the pastor said that I still cling to is: "All is well with Sam." And because all is well with Sam, I will be well, too.

Sam chose a confirmation verse a year and a half before he died. His verse was John 14:2. It says that Our Father is building a house for us, and if that were not true, then he would tell us so. We all have a room in heaven. That is what Sam believed. On the liturgical calendar, a week after Sam died, that was the verse: John 14:2. In his service, the senior pastor said he never had anybody choose that verse in all of his years, but that was just like Sam.

Then, I went on to try to understand, "What is heaven?" I read about parents who lost kids, with the idea that you don't feel so alone when you read about other people, and those readings resonated with my ideas about heaven. I also talked to my pastor and came to a place where I was comforted by what I had come to believe.

Nick is a junior in high school. He is 17. He is an age that Sam never got to, which is kind of hard. This is also the year that Sam would have been a senior. A lot of the friends he had all these years are graduating, and you see what colleges they're going to and all those things. Sam had plans.

Sam had always been a fan of Michigan State. Michigan is where his dad is from and where we lived when he was very young. I thought for sure when we started talking about colleges that Michigan State would be at the top of his list. Then, just a couple of weeks before he passed, I asked him, "Where is it you think you'd like to go?" I was waiting to hear Michigan State, and he said, "I think I want to go to IU." I said, "Why is that?" He said, "I want to go there because it's close to home." (Crying.) So, he had plans. We're seeing these other kids going on to their futures and seeing how different our life is now.

We have a scholarship that we are going give to one of those students at Sam's high school. Donations were made in Sam's memory for that scholarship. There is a whole selection process, and we will be giving that scholarship out at the end of the school year.

Three Whiteland High School (which is near Center Grove) seniors reached out to me, and they put together a documentary about Sam, called "The Power of Choice." It was voted the most popular video by the students. It has Sam's coach in it and Nick in it and myself and pictures of Sam. When they showed it in the theater, a little boy sitting behind us said toward the end of the film, "I don't want that boy to be dead!" So, it is powerful.

Do you have any suggestions for someone going through something similar or for the family member of someone who is experiencing grief?

It's different for everybody. But one thing is, you can't avoid it, you can't run from it, and you can't hide because it will always be there waiting for you. (Crying.) So, you might as well face it and feel it. At the end of the day, it means you loved somebody.

[As we stand up to leave the restaurant where this interview took place, a woman at the table behind us comes up and introduces herself to Jeanine. The woman tells Jeanine that she overheard our conversation, and she just lost her baby two months ago to cancer. Jeanine gives the woman her contact information in case she wants to get in touch. They are both teary. The woman thanks Jeanine for sharing her story.]

⊨⊹⊹⊱

Edmund (Ned) & JoAnn Winterbottom (daughter, violent sexual assault)

"We need to give something back to this community." — Ned and JoAnn live in New York and are in their 60s. They lost their daughter, Laura Kate Winterbottom, to a violent sexual assault. Understandably, they declined to discuss those details or focus on that aspect of their daughter's story. Instead, they have turned their personal suffering into a legacy of honoring Laura's memory through The Laura Kate Winterbottom Memorial Fund.

JOANN: We have an older daughter, Leigh. Our middle daughter, Laura Kate, was born on September 12. Our son Aran is our youngest child.

NED: The Laura Kate Winterbottom Memorial Foundation was set up as a corporation, and the website logo, LKW, is the logo Laura used for herself when she was doing freelance graphic design.

JOANN: Art and teaching art were her areas of interest. When she was killed, she had just finished applying for a full-time job teaching art for children. At the time, she was teaching art in an after-school program and living in Burlington, Vermont.

NED: The Foundation has a dual mission. One is to do something about the sexual violence that took Laura's life. So, we raise money to support organizations dedicated to ending sexual violence and also those organizations that are helping victims or survivors of sexual violence. The other part is to honor who Laura was in life. She was a very compassionate person and very active physically. She liked the outdoors, the environment, and nature. She hiked and rode a mountain bike and did things like that, and she was an artist. We try to help art or environment programs for underprivileged kids.

JOANN: Activities such as sending kids to outdoor camps in Vermont.

NED: We just came back from a ceremony in Vermont for the opening of a building called the King Street Youth Center. There are a lot of immigrant and underprivileged kids who use the center, and we raised money to have an art room and a full-time art program in that building. It's called Laura's Art Room.

Every September we run a 5K walk/run in Burlington. It's called Laura's March to End Sexual Violence.

JOANN: Basically, we raise money for programs of other organizations, where the programs are either not funded at all or are underfunded. That's where we come in and help.

NED: We've given away around $130,000 to approximately 40 different organizations.

JOANN: At Laura's March last year, we raised money for programs such as the Sexual Assault Nurse Examiner's program. Those are specially trained nurses in sexual assault at the hospital, the

University Vermont Medical Center in Burlington. Also, we raised money for Hope Works, which used to be a Women's Crisis Center, but now also serves men and children.

Tell me a bit about your healing journey.

NED: When we first experienced this, the victim advocates in Burlington were terrific. They set us up with a grief counselor, and she was very helpful and gave us insight into what we would go through. We've been in therapy. That's something that has been helpful. And we work on the Fund. That's a focus of our family life, and we all work on it. It's a big job. We have some time off, but we work at it pretty much fulltime.

JOANN: You never get over the loss, but what you learn to do is to live with it. In our case, we try to be as engaged and productive as we possibly can be. We found things to engage us, distract us, and occupy our time usefully. The Fund is one of those things.

NED: A police chief who was involved when Laura was killed said to us that when something like this happens to people, they could do one of two things. They can become obsessed with the perpetrator of the crime. Or they can focus on something else and try to do something useful about the thing that caused the death.

JOANN: Ned and I are in complete agreement on that. The perpetrator is a nonentity to us.

Do you have any religious or faith practices that help?

JOANN: I'm open to that, but so far it hasn't worked for me.

NED: She has read every book on spirituality and loss you can think of. (They both laugh.) I go to church occasionally. Let me put it this way. I'm not on good terms with God. There's a poet called Edward Hirsh who wrote a poem about the death of his son, Gabrielle, and he said, "I'll forgive God when he gives me my son back." I'm not quite there, but organized religion and conventional ways of thinking about things don't provide much help with grief.

JOANN: Yoga and meditation helped me. I've been doing yoga for over 20 years now. It helped to keep me balanced and more focused — both physically and mentally. About a year after Laura was killed, I joined a meditation group. That has helped me, too. Guided meditation has been a blessing because it helped me realize the past is over, and it can't be changed. The future is totally unknown and hasn't unfolded yet. So, I try to practice living in the present, as mindfully and productively as I possibly can. Not a single day goes by when I don't think of Laura. I have to admit that I still struggle with thinking about the "what if's" and how things might be for her now and for us as a family if she hadn't been killed. The other thing I struggle with is refraining from thinking about the details of what happened to her. How she was ravaged. That takes energy, and I have to make a concerted effort to stay out of those dark places. So far, I've succeeded, and I can't ask for more than that at this point.

NED: The two of us dealt with it completely different in the beginning. JoAnn wanted to know all the details, and I didn't want to know any. When they would talk to JoAnn about what happened, I would leave the room. I still don't know many of the details. I've discovered a few along the way, but I don't want to know them.

JOANN: I went to all the hearings. It took two years for the case to be concluded. He wound up pleading guilty. As a result, we were spared having to go to trial. (She pauses and then continues.) Another thing that has helped us, I don't think a single day goes by that we don't talk about Laura. It's not a forced conversation; it just comes naturally. Something will have been said, or something occurs that reminds us of her. She remains a very vivid presence in our family. On holidays, we set a place for her at the table, and I take her ashes with me everywhere I travel. I don't think I'm being delusional or in denial. It's just that my memories are all I have left and whatever rituals I do to keep Laura close to me are very important and comforting to me.

Do you have a favorite memory of Laura?

NED: Here's my favorite Laura story: Laura was about 10 years old, and we were going on vacation. Suddenly, Laura starts yelling at me, "Dad, pull over." I'm like, "Why do I have to pull over?" And she says, "Dad, there's a caterpillar on the front window of the car! You have to pull over!" So, I pull over, and Laura gets out of the car and picks up the caterpillar and puts it down by the side of road. The caterpillar starts crawling back out toward the road. Laura is standing there yelling at the caterpillar: "Go back! Go back! You'll be killed." Finally, she picks up the caterpillar and carries it down through a drainage ditch, to the other side of the ditch, and off into a field about a hundred feet away. Then, she gets back in the car, so we can continue our drive. That's the way Laura was.

JOANN: She was a very compassionate person. She did a lot of volunteering.

NED: The other story I have of Laura is when she was in high school. She was on the track team and did the shot put, disc, and ran. I remember watching her and then turning to JoAnn and saying, "Isn't she the most beautiful thing you ever saw in your whole life?" (Crying.) And she was.

What has helped you with your grief?

NED: We learned from the grief counselor that there is a barrier that goes up in your mind to protect you from the shock you have gone through, and that it will come down when it's ready to come down. For me, I would say that some of it is still up, even after all this time. It may always be up. I don't know. You just have to learn to accept whatever your method of dealing with this is. Your interior journey is your own interior journey.

JOANN: In the beginning, the pain of the loss was extremely sharp; I felt it in every cell and fiber of my entire being. Over the years, the pain, it never goes away, but it dulls considerably, so much so that you can tolerate it. It impacted our daughter Leigh pretty badly. She was with Laura the night she was killed. In fact, she had walked Laura over to her car and said goodnight and then continued on home. I don't know how to describe the impact. Leigh is a very private person.

NED: I did learn from the grief counselor that the loss of a sibling is a really horrible thing. It's that person who will know you longest in your entire life, longer than your parents or your children. Losing a sibling is almost as hard as losing a child.

JOANN: For Leigh and Aran, Laura is a very large presence in their lives. They may not talk about their feelings or talk about her as often as Ned and I do, but she's with them. That's exemplified by all the hard work and constant work they do for Laura's Fund.

Have you felt her presence in other ways since she passed?

JOANN: That's one of my regrets. That hasn't happened. My daughter Leigh has and so has Aran. It was very comforting for Leigh.

NED: I've had several dreams about Laura that were more than dreams — or at least more vivid than my regular dream life. I felt like she was there. It was comforting, but bittersweet. I was really glad to see her, and, at the same time, after the experience was over, she wasn't with me physically. I'm glad I experienced that, but in some ways it hurts.

JOANN: There was an article in the *New York Times* science section called "Sick with Grief." The last paragraph of the article says, in effect, people "reinvent their lives by revising goals and making plans that do not include their lost loved ones." That is what Ned and I have done. We are continuing on with our lives, and we have been forced to reinvent it and change our goals.

NED: One thing that helped us get through all of this is the support we got from the Burlington community — especially beginning with the law enforcement people involved in Laura's case. They have excellent victim advocates, and the prosecutor is a friend of ours to this day. The police chief is on our advisory board, and there are people there that we met through this process who are friends of ours now.

JOANN: The guy who killed Laura wasn't caught for 10 days, and the detective in charge of the investigation would call us every single day, not only to give us an update but also to find out how we were doing. One of the reasons why we decided to establish Laura's Fund in Burlington is because of the community there. Laura's friends got together and had a memorial service for her, and it was just a tremendous outpouring of support for us. We were walking away from that ceremony, and our son turned to us and said, "We need to give something back to this community." So, it was a combination of all the support we got from the professionals and all the support we got from the community that made us feel that we had to establish something in Laura's memory and do good works for the community.

NED: The Mayor of Burlington, two years ago, proclaimed September 12 to be Laura Kate Winterbottom Day. That's her birthday.

JOANN: The day that she was killed, March 8, is International Women's Day, and the Mayor decided to have Burlington's Women's Day on March 8. I was asked to speak at the Women's Day event and have been asked to speak again this year. We usually spend that day together privately, as a family. But I accepted last year. I figured I'd do this in memory of Laura and as a way to mitigate the whole sadness and horror of the day. I accepted again this year. Some might say coincidence or others might say serendipity, but I was going through Laura's books and a page fell out. The page had her goals for this year. I'll be reading it because what she wrote is very inspirational. We keep Laura alive that way.

NED: The most important thing is to focus on the positive and keep negative thoughts out of your mind. At first, I would have easily wanted to kill the person. I'm a civilized person, so, I wouldn't do it. But the anger and desire for vengeance that I experienced were overwhelming. I said to my therapist, "It's a good thing the State gets to decide this, and I don't." That's how I felt at that time. But once he was sentenced, it was non-important to me anymore. I tried to not think about that, and I don't allow myself to go to that place.

JOANN: A national consultant on sexual violence — who was Chief of Security at the University of Vermont — was the keynote speaker at Laura's March last year. His wife is a professor who teaches criminal justice. She keeps a poem Ned has written, "A Loss for Words," and uses that poem to help her students understand the nature of the loss, to help them understand that people survive it, and to help them understand that every statistic is a person.

⊱ ⊰

Cathy A. Burton (husband, car accident)

"Our son started a scholarship in Don's name, and I contributed to it. Don is every bit a part of our continuing story." — Cathy was married 34 years to her husband, Donald (Don) Bruce Fisher. Don died at age 56 from burn complications after a car accident. With Cathy's support, their son Burton established a scholarship at Ball State University to honor Don's memory. Burton, a sophomore at the college at that time, is the school's youngest donor ever. (He declined to be interviewed). My interview with Cathy took place at a restaurant seven months after Don's death.

On our first real date, Don flew me around the San Fernando Valley. Don was a pilot and had learned how to fly while in high school. It was wonderful! He literally swept me off my feet. We fell in love immediately. After a few months, we were engaged. But my parents always brought me up that I needed to finish college before anything else. I went to Cal State Northridge and majored in art history. We married two weeks after I graduated. For my graduate degree, I went to Cal State Chico, where I got my master's in Cultural Anthropology.

Don never finished his degree. He was very interested in outdoor recreation, mountaineering, backpacking, and wilderness survival. Then, his interests went deeper into aboriginal living skills. One thing about Don, he knew a lot of things other people didn't know. The Cal State system hired him to teach short courses at their Desert Studies Center. He was able to teach college courses even without a degree.

I had promised Don that once I had my master's we would start looking for a place for him because he had allergies. He got a fungal infection called "valley fever." People die from it. He was in the hospital about 10 days.

While he was in the hospital, I looked through the classifieds and found a job listed at the Indianapolis Children's Museum. I went to his hospital room, and he raised his little puny head and said, "That's not in one of the nine western states." (Laughing.) This is a guy who was teaching mountaineering in the Sierra Nevada. He came to Indiana with me for the second interview. He looked down from the plane and said, "It's awfully flat out there." I began working at the Children's Museum, and our son Burton was born while we were in Indiana. Later, I worked at the Eiteljorg Museum of American Indians and Western Art for 18 years.

The car accident was this past June. Don was in the hospital for almost three weeks before he died. We had our 34th wedding anniversary while he was in the hospital. He had just turned 56 in May.

The day of the accident, Don had an appointment with a doctor. He was driving our old van. We were having financial troubles and just limping along with the one vehicle. That morning, we had forgotten Don needed the van for his doctor's appointment. He called me after I'd dropped him off. I drove back to IUPUI (Indiana University-Purdue University, Indianapolis), where Don worked, and then he brought me back. It was great that, when we got out of the car to switch places, we hugged and kissed each other. That was the last time I was able to talk to Don.

He went on to his doctor appointment. While driving back from his appointment, Don was on a section of highway that had concrete barrier walls on both sides. The tire blew. Apparently, Don tried to get over to the side of the freeway but hit the right wall. The crash caused a spark to ignite some recycling that we had in the back of the van. There was an empty fuel canister like you'd use for a camp stove, and the fumes ignited. The fire happened immediately. Don then veered over to the opposite side, where he was trapped against the left wall. His door was against the concrete barrier. He quickly got out of the van on the passenger side, but he got burned over one-third of his body.

When he arrived in the emergency room, the doctor said to Don, "You have severe burns, and we think the best thing to do is sedate you and then start working on you." According to the doctor, Don said, "I think that's a good idea." (Laughs.) I had an event at the time and wasn't near my phone. Eventually, someone got ahold of me and said, "You need to call the emergency room. It's serious." I didn't get over there until about 2 hours after the accident, and they were still trying to work with Don in the emergency room.

Good friends were around me immediately. I called Burton; he was home for the summer. A friend went to get him after taking me to the hospital. That friend lent us a car for a couple of days. Friends came over that evening and asked if there was anything they could do, and friends brought food. My workplace was great during it all. They took good care of us.

What happened with Don, the reason he died, had to do with complications from putting in a second, smaller trachea tube. He died because the tube became dislodged.

Burton had answered the phone. I was in the shower and had a towel wrapped around me. We were huddled in the hallway at our house and heard that Don had died. We got over there as fast as we could. All his medical team was so upset. The doctor had been there for another patient, next door to Don, when he heard the alarm on the breathing apparatus. He tried CPR and tried to revive Don and couldn't. Don had a lot of inhalation injuries. The doctor said either Don dislodged the tube, or it came out on its own. They let us have as much time as we wanted alone with Don in his room.

What, if anything, has helped with your grief process?

Earlier, when I met with the nurse social worker, she had said, "He's really ill." She's the first person who said it. I knew he'd have to be in a rehab facility, and I was worried about him losing his hands the way he was burned. She was the first person who said, "Hey, he's *really* sick."

I understood I might lose the house, and I had to start thinking about how to get things together. While Don was in the hospital, Burton had to leave Ball State University. The hospital room alone is at least $5,000 a day. An amazing person at work set up a GoFundMe site to help with the hospital care bills. Thirteen thousand dollars came in to help us. I had financial concerns, but I didn't care because Don had lived. He got out of the van. Whatever else was going on, this man who was typing for a living, hadn't lost his fingers. Also, no one said, "We need you to pay us right now." One of our Eiteljorg board members donated $5,000. They knew Don, and they knew our son Burton. I just would not have made it without that kind of support.

Don left us a wonderful gift. IUPUI has opportunities here and there for employees to get great insurance. Don had signed up for life insurance through IUPUI. With the life insurance, I was able to buy a car. Burton was able to go back to Ball State University. I paid off two mortgages. Of course, I would sell the house in a minute to get Don back. Love is stronger than any material possession we had. I loved him very much. (Crying.)

What are your favorite memories of Don?

Don had numerous creative interests. In that way, he was like a Renaissance person. He could design labyrinths, and he made The Man in the Maze labyrinth, from the Tohono O'odham Nation (a Native American tribe), on the front lawn at the Eiteljorg. It's not a Chartres labyrinth where he could just copy it. He had to measure it out. He was also doing quillwork and demonstrating that skill down in Brownsburg. While Burton and I were moving things around to get ready for Don's Celebration of Life ceremony, we found boxes and boxes of quill paper.

He belonged to an origami group, and he had a made a thousand cranes for a person on the IUPUI campus. The people there made a thousand cranes for him and gave them to us when we had the Celebration of Life ceremony. He made jewelry from paper. He was always doing creative things. He loved astronomy and, at one point, thought about doing a business for projecting starscapes on ceilings. He did that for us at the museum. He painted the summer sky in our theater ceiling; we could dim the lights and talk about the night sky. He read and read. He enjoyed *Star Trek* and Tolkien and read both fiction and nonfiction.

Shortly after Don died, my boss came over to the house to tell me that the museum was willing to give us any space we wanted for Don's Celebration of Life ceremony. But we knew that while Don was a volunteer there, the museum was really my spot. Our backyard joins the community. So, we decided to have the celebration there. It was in July. We were able to gather people from various groups. We got the word out to all the people on campus. People I had forgotten came. People from the Children's Museum that he'd met and people we'd lost of track of over the years showed up. Don was more internal and didn't feel like he had a friendship base. But all those people, if Don had only known how much they cared about him. It was a big party. That's what Don would have enjoyed.

Don had started Monarch butterfly tagging and Monarch releases with a group in town. The only formal thing we did was we said a few words when we gathered people up and released the Monarchs.

Several months before Don died, he told Burton and me that if anything happened to him, he had left a letter for each of us.

When Don was in the hospital, I realized he had just changed the passwords on all the bills. Burton went to the room to figure it out, and there were two flash drives. One had the passwords, and the other one wasn't labeled. It had the letters. We didn't open them until he died. One of the things Don said in my letter was, "You never know, if a butterfly lands on your shoulder, maybe it's me." He knew a lot about the Monarchs. One butterfly did land on my shoulder during the release. Butterflies have always been significant to us. For many, there is the belief that butterflies carry the souls of the dead. One of the Pueblo artists I talked to said the butterflies came to her at granddaughter's graduation; her parents had passed away.

Do you have any spiritual or religious practices that helped?

Don wasn't affiliated with a church. He explored various faiths and spiritual beliefs. I consider myself a secular humanist. I was comfortable, even before this all happened, that I haven't had to reach out to a higher power kind of thing. I had people say they were praying for me. I thought that was great. I could use any help I can get, and I wasn't going to judge them or define how people should speak who were trying to comfort me. That is the way they share their condolences with someone who has just lost a loved one.

To accept help is one of the biggest lessons I've learned when faced with a crisis. Burton and I had the great gift of the loan of our friend French Eason's car. Not only were we offered the car, but people offered other things as well.

I was also able to say no. If people wanted to start a food parade, I could say, "There are only two of us. Thank you, but we can't keep eating."

Then, like now, I try to respond and give. Now, I can certainly afford to be a generous person. I made myself extremely happy this fall. We had an art show going up, and I went through the show with my good friend who was blown away by one print. Later that day, even though we hadn't opened the show yet, I went to the curator, swore her to secrecy, and asked if I could buy the print for my friend. I was so happy to be able to buy a present for this woman who has been amazing with my son and me. Such a good friend.

Tell me about the scholarship your son set up.

Burton knew how much Don regretted not having a bachelor's degree. A lot of doors were shut to Don when he needed to progress financially. Burton went to the assistant dean at Ball State University and said, "I want to create a scholarship so no one else feels like I did," meaning a financial reason where they couldn't continue in their chosen program. Our son started a scholarship in Don's name, and I contributed to it. Don is every bit a part of our continuing story.

We haven't given enough to create an endowment, but the school assures us that what we're giving is enough to make a difference. The school has it set up for need, and the grade point can be as low as it is allowed to be by the school for a need-based scholarship. There's a tremendous need out there. College is expensive.

The woman I'm working with at Ball State said, "Your son is my rock star." She said to him the other day, "Burton, we want you to say something when we announce the scholarship, and I want to take your picture. You are the youngest person to ever set up a scholarship like this." Burton doesn't want the spotlight. But I explained to him why it's important. I understand because I work for a nonprofit.

Burton and I hadn't been back to California in 10 years. There were people I hadn't seen since before I left. It was my home. I wanted my son to know about it. We went up to the Sierra Nevadas and had Christmas with my sister and her husband. We left Don's ashes in the Sierras. It was a beautiful spot. There was a waterfall. The Sierras were above. There was a bridge and granite rocks. The pines and red willows. It was the environment he had loved. We were sad together, and we were glad that Don's remains were in a place he loved.

⊷ ⊶

Roberta (Bert) & Donald (Don) Miller (son, suicide)

> *"Braden's loss put life, and our whole purpose for being here, in a different perspective. It increased our motivation to do something worthwhile, something that improves the life of others." — Bert and Don are retired and live in Colorado near their daughter Adrianne, her husband, and their two granddaughters. Their son Braden passed away at age 21. They co-founded the nonprofit Friends of Belle-Rivière (FBR), which provides support to the residents of Belle-Rivière, Haiti, by meeting basic human needs for food, clean water, health, education, and sustainable commerce.*

BERT: Braden had been attending Grinnell University in Iowa and had gone his junior year to live in Bogota, Columbia.

When he came back to the States, he was physically very weak. He had several bouts of different illnesses while in Columbia: Anemia and dengue fever (a debilitating mosquito-borne disease in tropical areas, also known as Breakbone Fever). We just thought it was physical — that he was physically drained — rather than a mental or emotional issue. But once he took his life, we figured out it was more. When we look back on it, on some of the things he said, such as when we were going past a mental health place and he asked, "How much do you think it costs to go in there?" Afterward, you look back and think of all the things that should have given us a hint. At the time, that wasn't even in our minds.

We never thought he had any problems before Columbia. He was well-liked. In high school he had been into drama, major roles in plays, music, and was a great piano player.

DON: The semester Braden was in Colombia, Bert was diagnosed with breast cancer and went through a huge process of attempting to heal from that disease. Then, I was officially retired — or released from my job — and trying to find a new orientation. After that my dad was officially diagnosed with Alzheimer's. We moved my parents into assisted living. I say all this simply to put into context the collective disorientation of the period, which climaxed with Braden's mysterious situation and ultimate death. That pretty much left us in what I refer to as oblivion. After his death, the world was a different place.

Braden went to Columbia for a one-semester program and decided to stay beyond that program once the semester ended. He was out on his own, and we didn't have good contact. This was pre-email and cell phones. We occasionally talked to him on the telephone, but not often.

He seemed to have gotten sick early in his stay, but we didn't know much about that. We know he was in the hospital. His illness got more complicated because it wasn't just one illness. He didn't want to return, but he reached a point where he was not able to negotiate on his own any longer. He came home reluctantly. We could see immediately on his arrival that he had changed deeply. He was not well. His mental state was bad or even worse than his physical state, but it was not easy to evaluate even by physicians because his physical symptoms were mysterious and his mental condition even more so. We were struggling to understand what was going on.

BERT: At one point, Braden said he wanted to stay down there another semester on his own to see if he could live on what he earned, just like the Columbians. There was so much poverty and many of his slides were of all the destitute people: young kids on the streets and overturned buses. He thought he could prove that if you earned some money, you could get out of that poverty. What he discovered was that there's no way. You can't do it. He was very disappointed, and then he gave up and just traveled there for a while.

When he came home, Braden did go to work for a friend of ours. He talked about changing schools because all the students he had been with in Columbia were from Earlham College. Later, he said he didn't want to go back to school. But then his girlfriend from Grinnell came to visit. After she left, Braden said he was going back to Grinnell. He was so mixed up. Right after that, he went missing. He was supposed to have gone to work, and he didn't come home. When I called our friend to see where Braden was, he said Braden never showed up for work. He was missing almost one week. We had called the police and put out a missing person's report.

Then, we got the phone call from a ranger in the Badlands. He said our son had suicided at a trailhead, and he was in his car. That happened on a Wednesday, and it was Friday when we got the call. Braden had telephoned us Tuesday evening and told us he was coming home. He told us where he was and that he had a gun, and he had thought about suicide. I just remember telling him to throw that gun away. He asked to talk to Adrianne (his sister), but she had been in bed for an hour or so. I said, "Well, she has to get up early to go to work." I just figured, well, he's coming home. He will see her then. We called the police again after he called us. We told them he had a gun, and he was in South Dakota. But when we spoke to the ranger, he said there was no police record out there that they were looking for anybody. We don't know how that all went.

What helped you during this process?

BERT: The support we got from family and friends was the most helpful. We were at St. Thomas Aquinas church at the time. We had a lot of support from those people. They kind of took over. We also had nieces in town that helped.

We went to a meditation retreat where Don and I both talked with one of the Buddhist nuns, and we told our story. All I remember her saying was that things happen for a reason but just live in the moment. And I remember thinking, '"Well, that's ridiculous." (Laughs.) It didn't seem helpful at the time. But the retreat itself was, and once we understood what she was talking about, it seemed to soak in.

Do you have any religious or spiritual practices that helped?

BERT: We went to New York for a Thich Nhat Hanh (Vietnamese Buddhist monk) retreat. The following year, he was in San Diego, so we decided to go again. Adrianne was in San Francisco at the time working, and she wanted to go, too. After the retreat, she went back and quit her job. Then, she went to the Thich Nhat Hanh center in Plum Village, which is in France, and she was there for three months. She wanted us to come over to experience what she experienced, and so we went and spent a week in Plum Village.

Shortly after that is when Don looked online for a meditation sangha because —after two retreats and the week at Plum Village — we felt like we needed community. The church wasn't working for us anymore. For one thing, it was painful to go back. All I did was cry anytime I went to church. So, we stopped going. But we still needed community. Eventually, Don found the Friends of Awakening Sangha. It was just a small group, 12 people at the most.

What was helpful about the meditation retreat?

DON: It was more of a focus on awareness of the internal approach rather than external religion's approach. Both of us had been in a strong Catholic context for a long time, and somehow all the things in church at that time seemed useless.

With Braden's loss, when we finally heard Thich Nhat Hanh's words and saw his manner and that of the other practitioners, it seemed like the first thing that seemed true, if you will. The whole church thing was full of external activity, and the sangha was much more interior. It was accompanied by the simple heart-to-heart talk that each member of the group, at different times, would offer — spontaneous, no ritual, no framework. Just people being who they are. Somehow, that made more sense.

BERT: At the first retreat, Thich Nhat Hanh talked about how we change forms. He talked about how if you take a piece of paper, it was once a tree, and if you light the paper it goes to ashes, and then it's smoke, and the smoke goes into the air — it keeps changing forms. That's how we are, too. That helped me with the whole process. It was a tangible thing I could hold onto: that Braden's spirit is still around. He has just changed forms.

Don and a friend had gone to the Badlands where Braden's car was taken, and they were getting the car to bring it back home. I went to a psychic fair, and the psychic immediately told me my husband was gone somewhere, and it was a sad occasion. She said Braden was looking at his life and trying to figure things out, and he was in nature. That was totally Braden. He loved nature. So, it seemed she did know and could communicate with that level. I never told her anything, and she picked all that up.

DON: I saw a psychic in New York, George Anderson. I had read his books and was intrigued by his ability to communicate with the dead. He talked in a fair amount of detail about our relationship, Braden and mine. Just offering details that no one could possibly know in any other way. He clearly was connected. Then, he explained Braden's attitude and mental state at the time and his confusion. Braden didn't mean to pull the trigger. He was playing with the gun, and it went off. He was contemplating suicide, but he hadn't actually fully intended to pull the trigger. But the gun went off. That was surprising and somewhat confirming. That was helpful to at least hear Braden's explanation from that place in time.

BERT: I also went to Chesterfield, a psychic community. A gardener was working on the grounds. He said hi, and we started talking. He said a couple of weeks ago, someone from the other side came in, and it was a young man who had suicided, and the young man was very sorry that his parents and sister had to live without him. I said, "I had a son just like that." And the gardener said, "I know."

It was like we were searching in any direction and finding all these psychics to help us. And they really did. They made us believe that Braden's spirit is still around, and people can connect to it, and we also can connect with the person. We just have to be aware and in tune. These are the things we were searching for.

What are your favorite memories of Braden?

BERT: Some of the stories that were shared at his service told how he took people to the prom that might not otherwise have gone. Instead of picking the girls he hung out with a lot, he picked the wallflower. When those people spoke at his service, we saw a part of him we never knew.

DON: I like to think of Braden when he had his final piano recital in high school. It was a culmination of years of practice. It wasn't part of a school program, but he performed in a small auditorium and invited friends and relatives. It was a major accomplishment for him to be able to do that. What I remember was his style, more than the music — the way he handled himself — and how he was not at all pompous about his performance.

He also had a wry sense of humor. Often you couldn't tell if he was joking or serious. He liked to play tricks, and he liked to do the unexpected. Frankly, that was part of the mysteriousness of his disappearance and the whole mystery that surrounded his illness. He was tremendously accomplished and balanced. That's why it was so difficult for us to imagine there was a serious mental issue involved here. He was extremely normal in so many ways.

Is there anything else that helped with your grief?

DON: Nothing fixes it. Not even time. Maybe time makes it somewhat better. I don't know. But nothing fixes it. To a great degree, it remains as mysterious today as the day he disappeared.

What is the connection between Braden and your nonprofit work in Haiti?

DON: It took a long time for me to get back on my feet after Braden's death and to come up with a sense of purpose or value. I had been to Haiti on two occasions prior to Braden's death. The first two visits were with a friend from our church. Later, I went back to Haiti on my own to learn more. Then, Takuya Sato from the Friends of Awakening Sangha went to Haiti with me. We started what became the Friends of Belle-Rivière project. Braden's loss put life — and our whole purpose for being here — in a different perspective. It increased our motivation to do something worthwhile, something that improves the life of others.

BERT: Braden was so interested in trying to see if he could live in a country that was impoverished. And he could not. There was not good medical assistance and so forth. Don is carrying on something Braden was passionate about also.

How has the loss affected your daughter?

DON: The Thich Nhat Hanh retreat in San Diego and the retreat in Plum Village led her to a psychotherapy program at Naropa University. Naropa was a place where she could enhance her meditation practice and be with other people doing the same thing. She met her eventual husband there. He had been to Plum Village for several months and had been strongly influenced by Thich Nhat Hanh. It's safe to say that her life was changed by all of this.

Somehow Braden's passing influenced us toward the whole idea of a meditation practice. Braden's death has impacted our lives tremendously.

Do you have any suggestions for someone going through something similar?

DON: I'm not sure anybody can offer advice. There are no solutions for overcoming the death of a child. You experience it. Maybe the hardest part is learning not to blame or take on a sense of guilt through all of this. You just can't help second-guessing the circumstances and wondering what you could have done to prevent the ultimate outcome. Obviously, it doesn't change anything. It goes on forever.

BERT: I read a lot of books about death and what happens afterward. That helped me grasp it. I read Thich Nhat Hanh's books. Everybody has to choose what suits him or her on how to handle it. It took us two years before we figured out that we needed to go on the retreat. There was a lot of tension between Don and me because we both felt guilty, and we didn't know how to handle that guilt. It was a hard time. Everybody who goes through it will have some of those feelings.

DON: I would say it took us two or three years just to find a sense of direction. The value of the Buddhist orientation was that it gave us the motivation to go inside for the search, as opposed to going outside for help to some external source. I didn't find going to a counselor or a church helpful. Despite our very long Catholic tradition, all of that fell away — crumbled like dust. When the chips were down, it made no sense. It was only when we went inside for our search that we started to sense direction.

(He pauses momentarily and then continues.) You'll have quite a job trying to make sense of all this.

[I reply]: *Luckily, I'm not trying to make sense of it. I'm just offering it up.*

⊱ ⊰

EPILOGUE

"In one of the stars I shall be living.
In one of them I shall be laughing. ...
You, only you, will have stars that can laugh!"

— ANTOINE DE SAINT-EXUPERY,
THE LITTLE PRINCE

May our hearts remain open ~

The death of my father took me on a healing journey not unlike the people in this book. That journey introduced me to meditation, along with numerous other spiritual practices discussed in my previous book, *Traveling Spirit: Daily Tools for Your Life's Journey*. I ended that book with the true story below:

> When my children were young, I watched them playing a game at the nearby neighborhood park with some other children. They were taking turns jumping down from the jungle gym. One child climbed back up whenever another child had jumped down. I asked my daughter what they

were doing. She said, "People come down from the stars, and when one jumps down to help those on Earth, the other one goes up to help from the stars."

A few years back, a friend gave me the book, *The Little Prince*, by Antoine de Saint-Exupery, which I had not read until after my interview with Justin. She brought *The Little Prince* quote to my attention.

Many cultures believe the very young and the elderly are closer to Spirit because the veil between this world and the Spirit realm is thinner for them. During intense grief, we might also find ourselves somewhere between the world we recognize as our practical or material reality (jobs, education, possessions, and so on) and the less familiar world — of dreams, memories, mystery, and symbolism — we inhabit after loss. Being *in* the world but not *of* the world is a living paradox not only in grief but also in the essence of our very existence here. We are human, and we are more than human. As scientist Carl Sagan so aptly said, "The cosmos is within us. We are made of star-stuff."

If any wisdom can be found as we face the physical passing of people we love, perhaps it is from those courageous souls who remember the stories that bring healing . . . and who re-tell those stories, again and again.

⊫⊣ ⊢⊨

Justin Phillips (a year later)

> *"It's helpful to have a purpose. It allows for some meaning behind the loss."* — *At the two-year anniversary of her son's death, I met with Justin a second time to discuss her outreach work in the area of the heroin overdose. Justin is the founder of Overdose Lifeline, and she worked to get Aaron's Law passed.*

After Aaron died, I learned about naloxone, which is the heroin overdose reversal drug. The police department had a pilot project where officers could carry naloxone kits. I decided to raise money because getting those kits was not in their budget. To do so, I started the nonprofit called Overdose Lifeline.

In addition to raising money, I wanted to address the stigma around addiction and be more public about it. If we talk about it more, maybe we can save lives because people will be able to ask for help. When you lose someone to drugs, there is a lot of shame. It's a unique kind of loss. For instance, when you lose a child from cancer, everyone rallies around you. But if it's drugs — heroin especially — people act like it might be catching.

The nonprofit's next step was to make the naloxone kits available to anyone, which is what Aaron's Law does. It allows for a third party prescription. I can go to the doctor and explain I need a prescription for naloxone, and the doctor can write the prescription. The law also allows entities to register with the State Department of Health to be distribution sites for naloxone. For example, Overdose Lifeline can distribute naloxone without a prescription to families or individuals who need it because we are a registered entity.

The nonprofit also serves as a resource. Our website is: Overdose-Lifeline.org. We have a prevention education program we developed primarily for eighth and ninth graders, but it can be adapted for any audience. There is a 12-minute video. It is intended to get the message across that this is not a class of drugs that you can experiment with during normal adolescent experimentation. It's too dangerous. We also have an Overdose Awareness Day.

Right now, pharmacies aren't stocking the reversal drug, and doctors don't understand about writing the prescription. Last week, I testified before the governor's taskforce. I explained that this is one thing they can do if they really want to address the drug crisis and help make Aaron's Law more effective. The governor's task force is working on these issues now.

I never pictured this to be my life. (Laughs.) But here we are.

In the year since we last spoke has anything else transpired in your grief and healing process?

Year Two is almost harder than Year One. I hadn't gone through that experience of a full year of firsts. The longer it goes, the more aware you are of how permanent the loss is. It really isn't a dream or a nightmare. There's no possible way to change it. You can't understand it if you haven't had that experience because you can't understand it even when *you have* the experience. Maybe some of the numbness is wearing off. There is a high degree of shock that carries you through that first year.

What have you found helpful in your healing?

The nonprofit work has been important. It's helpful to have a purpose. It allows for some meaning behind the loss, and it puts the loss in some sort of context. The nonprofit has an eight-member board. They are amazing people, and I know I can count on every single one of them. We have accomplished a lot in a year and a half.

My daughter is doing well, and my oldest son worked on the video for the nonprofit. He also got married in a very private ceremony that honored Aaron.

I have someone making a quilt with Aaron's clothes and incorporating symbolism and art into the quilt. It will have a feather out of clothes. On the day that Aaron passed away, my cousin was walking a labyrinth in California and a feather came down. She told me the story and shared that feather with me.

I have two tattoos, one is Aaron's tag and one is a blue heron. I'm going to have a feather and a star constellation incorporated into the tattoos.

I've also been listening to an on-line mindfulness summit and believe it will bring me some peace.

I'm talking to you because that is doing something and having a purpose. I'm still very aware of that moment when we were standing at the grave, with that big open hole, how desperately I wanted to get in that hole with Aaron. It's painful. It's better to be here with you talking. That helps. It does. I hope five years from now or ten years from now, I won't feel like I want to talk about it all the time. I want to find that balance. It's definitely not happening in year two. (Laughs.) But people say it takes four or five years.

I continue to find ways to keep Aaron present.

I named a star for him. It's close to the Leo constellation, which is his horoscope constellation. A woman designed a logo for me using the constellation and Aaron's star. I'm getting stationary with the logo and the Little Prince quote. I'm paraphrasing, but it basically says, *"In one of the stars I shall be living. In one of them I shall be laughing. And so it will be as if all the stars were laughing when you look at the sky at night,"* by Antoine de Saint-Exupery. No one has to know what the quote and logo on the stationary mean. I know.

That's how I keep Aaron alive and close to me.

⚊⊹⊹⚊

ACKNOWLEDGMENTS

I have enormous gratitude to everyone who shared such intimate stories of loss. It takes courage to speak honestly from the heart. Thank you!

I also want to thank the following people who helped make this book so beautiful:

Book Cover: Painting by Colleen Murphy.

The book cover image, *Birth of an Angel,* is an oil painting by artist Colleen Murphy. She believes angels surround us always, and she works with them in her art and in life. *Birth of an Angel* reflects her awe of the Universe and her appreciation of the spiritual side of life, especially with angels. She has lost people she loved and has communicated with them on the other side of this realm. Colleen@ColleenMurphyFineArt.com.

Book Cover Graphic design: JD Bills, www.jdbills.com

Editing: Donna Mosher, Segue Communications, Inc., Donna@Segue-Communications.com

Proofreading: Zach Dunkin, Slam Dunk Communications.

Author Photo: Emily Schwank, Raincliffs Photography, http://raincliffsphotography.com/

Author Website: Marg Herder, CircleWebWorks, http://www.circlewebworks.com

To order additional book copies (discounts available for non-profits and bulk orders) or to request a speaking appearance contact the author at her website: www.dianaensign.com

ABOUT THE AUTHOR

Diana J. Ensign, JD, is a contemporary author in the field of spirituality. Her book, *Traveling Spirit: Daily Tools for Your Life's Journey*, provides spiritual guidance for dealing with life's challenges. The journey to wholeness begins within. *Traveling Spirit* explores the link between practicing our daily spiritual routines and building a more loving world community. Signed copies of her books are available on the Author website. www.dianaensign.com. Her books are also available on Amazon.

Diana's background includes Buddhist meditation, Al-Anon, Unitarian Universalism, Native American ceremonies, Goddess rituals, Science of Mind, Shamanism, and religious readings across a diverse spectrum of beliefs and practices. She is certified in Reiki III and has benefited from yoga, tai chi, and qigong. Her favorite source of spiritual insight is nature.

Born in Florida and raised in Michigan, Diana holds a Juris Doctor from Wayne State University Law School in Detroit and a Bachelor degree in English from the University of Michigan in Ann Arbor. She is married and has two grown daughters.

Diana also writes the *Spirituality for Daily Living* blog found on her website: **www.dianaensign.com**

CPSIA information can be obtained
at www.ICGtesting.com
Printed in the USA
LVOW03s1944281217
561100LV00002B/193/P